GREAT SECRETS of HISTORY

GREAT

IN CAMERA A session of the Yalta Conference, held behind closed doors at the Livadia Palace in February 1945. As the Second World War drew to a close, Joseph Stalin (far left), Franklin D. Roosevelt (centre) and Winston Churchill (far right) sat down to determine the shape of the postwar world. Deals and concessions were made that affected the lives of millions, but – as so often in history – the full facts did not emerge until later.

SECRETS *of* HISTORY

Gripping stories of truth and lies, deception and discovery

Reader's
Digest

CONTENTS

1 CONSPIRACIES AND LIES

2 INFORMATION IS POWER

3 POLITICS AND WAR

4 CRIME AND CORRUPTION

5 DARK SCIENCE, HIDDEN ARTS

6 BURIED TREASURE, HIDDEN TRUTH

THE SECRETS OF THE PAST

Our knowledge of the past is fragmentary and incomplete. It is a patchwork of evidence, a collage of facts and artefacts that can be ordered and assembled in any number of different ways. The resulting picture of events can be misleading – or downright false.

This is something that historians constantly have to contend with: we know less about the past than we would like, far less than many people think. Sometimes the historical record is skewed or incomplete because important moments went unrecorded, or were forgotten as the years and centuries rolled by, or were obscured by conflicting accounts and unreliable testimonies. Sometimes the truth is buried – literally or metaphorically – by guilty people who want to cover up their deeds forever. And sometimes the real story is hidden away for the best possible reason: to keep it safe until a time when the world is ready to hear.

Great Secrets of History is a book that aims to tell the truth about significant moments of the past. Its six chapters range across every period and every continent. Some of the stories deal with the big historical issues: world-shaking revolutions and conflicts, state crimes and acts of genocide, episodes of empire-building and international diplomacy. Others will lead you down some less well-travelled but equally fascinating byways of history: the one-man tricks and hoaxes, the unlikely fates and curious incidents, the acts of unsung heroism or of downright criminality. You will find that every tale contains an element of secrecy and concealment – and, often, a corresponding moment of revelation and discovery.

Several of the stories in this book take place during wartime, because in war secrecy is a powerful weapon. Armies and governments routinely employ subterfuge and espionage to gain an advantage over the enemy. Secrecy and lies were also woven into the fabric of existence for those who lived in the totalitarian dictatorships of the last century. And for that reason, you will find a number of stories in this book that are set within the borders of Soviet Russia or its communist satellites, and also inside the shorter-lived despotism of the Nazi era.

Historically, libels and half-truths have been used to attack the standing of figures as diverse as Genghis Khan, Leon Trotsky and the French playwright Molière. The same insidious techniques have been deployed at times to undermine the status of entire groups within society: England's Roman Catholics in the 16th century, Europe's Jews in the 19th and 20th, South America's freethinkers and dissidents in the 1970s and 1980s. On occasion, those same oppressed peoples have used cunning and deception (and, incidentally, incredible courage) to fight back or protect themselves.

So secrecy is a thread that runs through all of the stories in this book – but so is humanity. Each tale in *Great Secrets of History* casts a light on human nature, at its worst and at its best. As you read the book, you will be variously astonished, appalled, perplexed and moved by the things that individuals, organisations and nations have done – for good or ill, for themselves and for others. Knowing these secret histories, understanding the motives and the ends of the people involved, is an act of homage that we rightly pay to the past.

KKK

"if your heart's true
it calls to you"

Chapter 1

CONSPIRACIES AND LIES

Throughout history, deception and cover-ups have been a core human activity. Individuals, organisations and governments have constantly strived to mislead, outwit and besmirch each other.

The red policeman

Russian revolutionary Yevno Azef was the head of a terrorist organisation plotting to assassinate the chief of the tsarist secret police, while at the same time being the star informant of that secret police. In these dual roles, his contradictory duty was to tell his boss that he was trying to kill him.

For a few weeks in February 1909, Yevno Azef was the world's most notorious man. He had just been exposed as a double agent by a Russian revolutionary 'court of honour', conducted in Paris. Azef's Russian comrades were pondering how to shoot him without attracting the unwelcome attention of the French authorities when he managed to slip out of the country.

Azef's disappearance was a global sensation. 'POLICE AND REDS BOTH HUNT AZEF' screamed a headline in the *New York Times*. 'Where is Azef?' asked the article. 'Who will get to him first? Who will be his executioner, the Russian police or the revolutionists?' Some papers inside Russia claimed that he had already been found and the sentence carried out. Other publications reported reliable sightings of him in Uruguay, in Vienna, in Simferopol and in Nice. Britain's *Evening News* claimed to have interviewed him in a London hotel: 'I have not lost my principles because I never had any. As a revolutionary and as a spy I had magnificent accomplishments …'

That interview was fictitious, but the feats ascribed to Azef were real enough. Until his career came to an abrupt end in Paris, he was by far the most successful stool-pigeon ever to have worked for a police organisation. In Russia, most informers were good for two or three years at most. Azef had played each side against the other for 15 years, and at the time of his downfall was receiving a generous monthly stipend of 1,000 roubles.

FIRST RADICAL STEPS

Yevno Azef was born in 1869, the son of a poor Jewish tailor. As a boy (and, come to that, as a man) he was quite startlingly unattractive, and this perhaps contributed to the formation of his introverted, suspicious nature. In his teens Azef, like many young Russian Jews, became involved in anti-government politics and joined a group in which dissident literature was discussed. That circle was broken up by the police, and some of its members were arrested. Azef took fright, stole 800 roubles and fled to Karlsruhe in Germany.

It was in Germany, in 1892, that Azef began his double life. There were many Russian revolutionaries living as political exiles in this part of Europe, and there were plenty of operatives of the *Okhrana*, the Russian secret police, keeping a beady

eye on them. The young radical Azef, by now penniless and hungry, offered to sell information on the many revolutionaries that he encountered. The police saw Azef's potential and agreed to take him on as a paid informer. In 1899, at the behest of the *Okhrana*, Azef returned to Russia charged with the task of infiltrating revolutionary groups in Moscow. He quickly became a confidant of Andrei Argunov, leader of the Northern Union of Social Revolutionaries, and used this acquaintance to gather names of members of the organisation. The police arrested dozens of subversives.

As a direct result of this depletion of the Northern Union's ranks, Argunov

decided to appoint Azef head of his foreign network. Azef was now perfectly placed to supply intelligence on the revolutionary movement, and his police pay rose from 50 to 500 roubles a month. His work brought him to the attention of Vyacheslav Plehve, the minister of the interior.

By 1906 Azef was a member of a different revolutionary group, the Socialist Revolutionaries, who were committed to terrorism and assassination as a political weapon. Their military arm, the Combat Organisation, carried out attacks. An SR fighter had killed Plehve's predecessor by the simple method of donning a respectable military uniform, walking up to him on the pretext of handing him a letter and shooting him at point-blank range. The minister died with the letter in his hand; it was notification of the death sentence that had been passed on him by the terrorists.

THE DEATH OF PLEHVE

Plehve thought himself safe from the SR Combat Organisation – not least because Azef, his prize asset, had recently been appointed its commander. 'My security is impeccable,' Plehve told a French newspaper. But the SRs were already planning his murder, and this put Azef in an awkward position – not just because of the obvious conflict of interests but also because his leadership role, and the degree of insider knowledge it brought, was making it hard for him to pass untraceable information to his handlers.

Azef distanced himself from the plan by delegating practical matters to others. He made sure he remained uninformed of the details. At the same time, he supplied the police with general and vague information, telling them that an important terrorist attack was in the offing and giving them descriptions – but no names – of the foot soldiers selected to carry it out. The police were forced to do some of the spadework (following suspects in the streets, for example), so when the conspirators were arrested it always looked like the result of competent police surveillance, never as if their men had been betrayed by a mole. To add another layer of obfuscation, Azef repeatedly gave orders for the attack on Plehve to be postponed, or allowed misinformation about Plehve's movements to be fed to his comrades.

In all this, his main motive was to protect himself. Azef worked to keep Plehve from harm not because he was devoted to the regime but because it

helped keep Azef himself safe. But he could not prevent the inevitable. In July 1904, while Azef was conveniently absent in Warsaw, one of his operatives tossed a bomb into Plehve's carriage as it passed through St Petersburg. The bomb blew the carriage apart, killing not only Plehve but also the driver and the horses. This successful assassination was an immense coup for the SRs, whose prestige in revolutionary circles soared.

The death of Azef's protector turned out to be a blessing for Azef personally, as it cemented his reputation as a scourge of the regime. When, all of a sudden, rumours began to circulate concerning his contacts with the police, they were always dismissed in revolutionary circles with the words 'But what about Plehve?' Yet not everyone was convinced by Azef's record. A dogged journalist named Vladimir Burtsev used his contacts to gather evidence on Azef's activities. That evidence – primarily the testimony of his handlers in the interior ministry – proved to be overwhelming. But still Azef's comrades in the Socialist Revolutionary Party refused to believe it. They even accused Burtsev of being part of a police plot to discredit him.

But there was enough material in Burtsev's dossier to require a rebuttal from Azef himself. A revolutionary committee was appointed to interview him in Paris. Azef agreed to this trial – for that was what it was – but made a bad fist of answering the accusations against him. The members of the tribunal – all of them long-standing comrades of Azef – realised to their horror that it was true: Azef was indeed a traitor to their cause. Yet somehow he persuaded them to allow him to go and fetch documents that would prove his innocence. He said he would present them the next day. That same night

Inside the mind of a double agent

Yevno Azef was neither a brilliant spy nor a master of deception – so how did he manage to carry off his double life for so long?

Azef's very mediocrity protected him. He was a born plodder who got results for both the police and the revolutionaries. These small repetitive successes created a fog of goodwill towards him from both sides. He never made a bomb or fired a gun. He was too cowardly to do the dirty work of terrorism. Politically he was indifferent – neither interested in revolution, nor devoted to the tsarist regime. He wanted to do well in both spheres, but was shallow enough to be untroubled by the ideological contradictions and apparently felt no pangs of conscience. His tangled allegiances bothered him only when his own safety was endangered. The revolutionary Leon Trotsky came closest to describing Azef's mindset when he wrote: 'Cleverness and subtlety are not always an advantage. If Azef had tried to weave a delicate psychological web, he would certainly have slipped up. Instead he let everyone see what an ugly mug he was – both physically and spiritually. They all thought of him: what a perfect lout of a man. And that's what saved him.'

he boarded a train and, as it pulled away, told his weeping wife he would write from Vienna. He carried a false passport, previously issued to him by the Russian authorities, and was not short of cash (he'd been salting away his salary for years – perhaps knowing that a day like this would come).

MAN ON THE RUN

Azef was not headed for Vienna. He went to Friedrichsdorf, the home village of his German mistress (he was as duplicitous in his love life as in his political work). Her name was Hedy de Hero, and she was a cabaret singer who had made her name in the *cafés chantants* of St Petersburg.

Once the newspaper furore died down, Azef and Hedy embarked on a tour of Europe, a kind of secret honeymoon. Azef bought Hedy jewels, and discovered a love of gambling. At every fine hotel they came to, Azef checked the guest lists for Russian names, always fearful that the SRs might have caught up with him. He also wrote to his wife, claiming that his services to the revolution far outweighed those to the police and that, on balance, he had served the cause well. He hoped this explanation would reach the party and produce an amnesty. After their long holiday, Azef and Hedy settled in Berlin, where they lived as Mr and Mrs Neumayer. They were more than comfortable until the First World War broke out in 1914. All Azef's money was in Russian bonds, which suddenly became worthless in Germany. The couple moved to more modest accommodation, and had to make money. Hedy sewed corsets, which Azef sold in a small shop.

In 1915 the German authorities arrested Azef as a dangerous enemy alien. In his damp prison cell, he contracted kidney disease, and was released in 1917 on the grounds of ill health. He died soon after, and was buried in an unmarked grave. Only Hedy knew of his demise, and by this time only she cared. It was the spring of 1918 – not long after the success of the Russian Revolution that Azef had fought to bring about, and simultaneously struggled to prevent.

The doppelgangers

Look-alikes or body doubles have been used by public figures for centuries, essentially to convince the people, or in some cases an enemy, that they are in one place when they are, in fact, in another. There are many reasons that they might want to do this: perhaps to avoid assassination, to create a diversion – or simply to escape the tedium of official functions.

Did the Iraqi president Saddam Hussein die of cancer in 1999 – seven years before his supposed execution? That was a rumour that circulated in Iraq, fuelled by the suspicion that he was in the habit of using look-alikes. His younger son Qusay was said to be running the country, while the role of Saddam was played by a doppelganger – a German word that translates as 'walking double'.

It seems Saddam Hussein did indeed use doppelgangers in his lifetime. The BBC foreign affairs correspondent John Simpson was able to verify this with the help of a German forensic scientist, Dr Dieter Buhmann, who subjected films and photographs of Saddam to detailed and precise measurements. It turns out that numerous propaganda photographs of Saddam were not him at all. When the controversial Austrian right-wing politician Jörg Haider thought he was being granted an interview by Saddam in 2003, on the eve of the Iraq War, he was, it seems, in fact in the presence of a double – a suggestion that delighted Haider's detractors.

STALIN'S STAND-IN
Felix Dadaev (on the left) worked as a double for Stalin (right) through the war years. He was almost 40 years younger than Stalin, so had to be carefully made up. He also had to put on 11kg (24lb) in weight. He studied hours of newsreel of Stalin to prepare for his secret role but met the Soviet leader just once.

Serving as Saddam's son

Latif Yahia (below left) spent four terrifying years serving as the double for Saddam Hussein's murderous son Uday (above left). This was not his choice. Yahia and Uday had been school friends, and at this early age they bore a clear physical resemblance. Later, when Uday asked Yahia to act as his double, Yahia declined. He was imprisoned in a tiny torture cell and his family threatened until he accepted.

To perform his role to Uday's satisfaction, Yahia had to undergo plastic surgery and dentistry. His role was to stand in for Uday at ceremonies and meetings, to serve in the army in place of Uday during the Iran–Iraq war, and to provide a morale-boosting presence to troops during the Iraqi invasion of Kuwait.

It was a task that was fraught with hazard. Uday abused his position with flagrant lawlessness, including extortion, torture, rape and murder; he made countless enemies and was constantly under threat of assassination. This meant, of course, that Yahia lived in fear of his life, and he survived several assassination attempts. Yahia fled Iraq in 1992, and in 1998 published a memoir called *I was Saddam's Son*.

John Simpson, who had met the real Saddam, gradually became adept at spotting the doubles and noted the tiny details that set them apart from the man himself: 'The general appearance of the face is somehow subtly different. The pebble-hard, obsidian eyes are less piercing. The lines of the face a little softer, a little more self-indulgent.' A military uniform, the trademark moustache and a pair of sunglasses were all that were needed to patch over these deficiencies.

DANGERS OF THE DOUBLE ACT

Being the spitting image of a public figure is more likely to be a curse than a stroke of good fortune. Soviet leader Joseph Stalin was so pleased with the performance of an actor named Mikheil Gelovani, a fellow Georgian who portrayed him in propaganda films in the 1930s and 1940s, that he demanded exclusive rights. No other actor was permitted to play Stalin, and that was the only role that Gelovani was allowed to perform. His career as an actor had been hijacked. Vanity also played its part: Gelovani was bigger and better-looking than Stalin, and Stalin was happy to use Gelovani's image to promote his own personality cult. Gelovani was not forced to live his life as Stalin, but others were. Felix Dadaev, a former circus performer, has claimed that he had been one of four doubles who were deployed as Stalin decoys. Their role was to appear at public functions and parades and to serve as 'bullet-catchers' when there was a risk of assassination.

Gustav Weler bore a close resemblance to Hitler, a misfortune that cost him his life in the final days of the Second World War. He had come to the attention of the Nazi leadership when he was arrested in the 1930s, apparently for using his resemblance to the Führer to mock him. It was thought a double might come in handy, but Hitler would have nothing to do with him. Martin Bormann, Hitler's secretary, found a use for him all the same. He had Weler shot in the head and left in the garden of the Reich Chancellery in April 1945 as the Red Army closed in on Berlin. The corpse did indeed fool the Soviet troops, who found him and delightedly photographed the body. It was only later that the real Hitler's remains were identified.

> *Mistaken identity was precisely the intention.*

It is possible that mistaken identity caused the death of the British film actor Leslie Howard in 1943, shot down by the German Luftwaffe as he returned to the UK from neutral Portugal in a civilian aircraft. With him on the aeroplane was Alfred Chenhalls, an accountant to the stars, who bore a resemblance to Winston Churchill. As for Howard, he happened to look a little like Churchill's bodyguard. While Howard and Chenhalls were in Portugal, Churchill was in North Africa attending meetings with US General Dwight Eisenhower. The prime minister could indeed have been returning home via Lisbon. Had German agents in Lisbon identified Chenhalls as Churchill? Or could the Germans have thought that, even if this was just a possibility, it was an opportunity too good to miss? Churchill himself later suggested, with regret, that his travel plans may well have contributed to Howard's

death. Whether or not British intelligence services were involved in some kind of deliberate deception remains hotly disputed.

DIVERSIONARY TACTICS

In one of the most famous uses of a double for a military leader, mistaken identity was precisely the intention. Weeks before the Allied D-Day landings in northern France in June 1944, a British officer spotted a startling photograph in a newspaper report from Leicester. It showed an Australian-born actor, Meyrick Edward Clifton James, playing the part of Field Marshal Bernard Montgomery in a morale-boosting show performed by the Royal Army Pay Corps Drama and Variety Group. Clifton James bore an uncanny resemblance to the real Montgomery. The film star David Niven, then working for the Army Film Unit, was despatched to recruit Clifton James, and the top-secret Operation Copperhead was set in motion. Clifton James was to impersonate 'Monty' – known by the Germans to be commander of Allied land forces – on a tour of the Mediterranean. The hope was that the Germans would be duped into thinking that the Allies would initiate their invasion of France from the south and that any invasion was not imminent.

Clifton James was first brought to London, where he shadowed Monty in order to perfect the impersonation of his voice, facial expressions and comportment. This he succeeded in doing admirably – although he struggled to emulate Monty's abstinence from tobacco and alcohol. Every detail of his appearance was fine-tuned, down to a prosthetic finger that was made for Clifton James's right hand, to replace one he had lost during the First World War.

On May 25, Churchill's private aeroplane took off for Gibraltar with the bogus Monty on board. The governor-

general of Gibraltar, duly primed, laid on a carefully choreographed reception party at his residence. A Spanish spy, known by the British to be working for the Germans, had also been invited under a separate pretext; he dutifully relayed what he had witnessed to Berlin. Bletchley Park, the British wartime decoding centre, picked up his message. Clifton James flew on to Algiers for a well-publicised meeting with General Henry Maitland Wilson, Allied commander of the Mediterranean and the Middle East. Then he flew in secret to Cairo while the landings took place in Normandy, returning to the UK five weeks after the invasion.

It is questionable whether this elaborate hoax had any real strategic effect, but the adventure required considerable courage and professionalism to carry off: Clifton James could easily have been targeted. However, he never received any official recognition for this service, something that he came to resent. He later recalled this episode in a memoir published in 1954 called *I Was Monty's Double*. The book was subsequently made into a film starring Clifton James both as himself and, of course, as Monty.

Field Marshal Montgomery, in fact, had two doppelgangers. The second one was Keith Demer 'Tex' Banwell, who toured North Africa in this guise, but he was much taller than Monty, so was not allowed to get out of his car in public view.

PRESENT-DAY DOPPELGANGERS

Modern photography and communications make the use of doubles more hazardous than it once was. In our image-saturated world, there is a high risk that any ruse will be rapidly exposed. But doppelgangers are not yet a thing of the past. Even a blurry telephoto snap – the kind of image that spreads on the internet – can still be an effective piece of misinformation. The success of a double depends on the public belief that people are who they claim to be, or who reliable sources say they are, and this leaves plenty of room for deception. When Osama bin Laden, leader of Al Qaeda, was killed in Pakistan in 2011, there were instant rumours that the man who died was someone else. DNA samples and facial measurements were taken specifically to establish that the targeted man was indeed bin Laden, not just someone who looked like him.

HYPNOTIC PRESENCE *Almost everyone who met Rasputin commented on his eyes. To some, his gaze was spiritual or strongly erotic; for others, it was repellent and terrifying. One way or another, his eyes held a power that bewitched the royal house of Romanov.*

The patriotic assassins

On a winter morning late in 1916, the imperial Russian police fished the body of Grigory Rasputin out of the icy river Neva. Even as his frozen corpse lay on the ice, it was common knowledge who had killed the tsar's favourite. But almost everything else about the circumstances of Rasputin's death remains as impenetrable as a night fog in Petrograd.

In some ways, the death of Grigory Rasputin was an open-and-shut case. Concerns about his influence on Tsar Nikolai II had been growing, and rumours had been circulating in Petrograd that an attempt was to be made on his life. Every foreign journalist in the city had heard about it – some of them from the lips of the would-be assassins themselves.

On December 16, the day of the murder, several of Rasputin's friends and admirers begged him not go out that evening. But Rasputin would not listen. It is impossible to say whether he was acting out of a kind of fatalism or a misguided sense of his own invulnerability. Perhaps the former, as he spent the day praying, moving sums of money to the accounts of his daughter, burning papers and letters – before dressing in his finest silk smock and waiting for what the night would bring.

There were four main conspirators. First, Prince Felix Yusupov, an Oxford-educated aristocrat of ancient line, foppish, decadent and fabulously rich. The murder was to take place in his palace on the Moika canal in Petrograd. Then there

was 25-year-old Grand Duke Dmitry Pavlovich, a beloved nephew of the tsar, and – in some people's eyes – the perfect person to succeed to the throne should Nikolai abdicate. Third came Vladimir Purishkevich, a right-wing monarchist and a member of the Duma, the toothless Russian parliament. He was invited to join the conspiracy after he made a speech in which he said 'the tsar's ministers have been turned into marionettes … whose strings are in the hands of Rasputin'. The fourth conspirator was a friend of Purishkevich, a Dr Stanislaus Lazovert; his job on the night was to handle the poison and drive the car.

CAKES AND CYANIDE
The murder plan was straightforward enough. Yusupov would invite Rasputin to his sumptuous palace for a late supper. Rasputin was sure to be keen. He had met Yusupov before (according to some accounts, the prince had asked the holy man to 'cure' him of homosexual tendencies), and Yusupov knew that Rasputin was attracted to his beautiful young wife Irina. He promised that she

would be there. (In fact, she was well out of the way, at the Yusupov estate in the Crimea, but Rasputin had no way of knowing that.) In advance of the murder, Yusupov prepared a cosy sitting room in the cellar of his palace. It was a vaulted space with a fireplace, and Yusupov had the room freshly decorated in the old-Russian style with red and brown frescos, wall hangings and a polar-bear rug. On the day, little cakes were prepared – pink ones and chocolate ones to match the décor. When the assassins gathered at the Yusupov Palace on the fatal evening, Dr Lazovert crushed some cyanide crystals and sprinkled them inside the chocolate ones only, so that Yusupov could safely eat the pink ones as he sat with Rasputin. More cyanide was dissolved in two glasses of sweet madeira, Rasputin's favourite tipple.

> 'Play something merry, my friend. I like it when you sing.'

At about a quarter to 12, Yusupov went in his car to collect Rasputin from his apartment. He waited until this late hour because Rasputin's building was guarded by police – but they were always dismissed at midnight. While Yusupov was away on this errand, the other conspirators remained in the drawing room above the basement snug. Their function for now was to create the impression that there were unexpected guests in the palace, that Irina was entertaining them, but would come down to the cellar shortly. This is what Yusupov told Rasputin when he

arrived back at the palace and ushered his victim down a back staircase to the basement room. Both men could hear voices upstairs, and the sound of 'Yankee Doodle' being played on the gramophone.

Most of the mystery surrounding the murder concerns what happened in the next two hours, while Rasputin and Yusupov were alone in the basement. In his memoir, Yusupov said that he persuaded Rasputin to eat some cakes and drink some wine, but, mysteriously, the huge quantity of poison seemed to have little or no effect. (Rasputin's daughter later claimed that her father never ate sweet things; it may be that Yusupov fabricated Rasputin's immunity to cyanide to make the man seem all the more demonic, and himself all the more heroic.) Rasputin asked Yusupov to take up the guitar that stood in the corner. 'Play something merry, my friend,' he said. 'I like it when you sing.'

WAITING TO STRIKE
At no point, apparently, did Rasputin ask when he could meet Irina, though Yusupov's story that his wife was upstairs bidding farewell to her visitors must surely have begun to wear thin as time passed. One historian has made the prurient suggestion that Yusupov himself, not his wife, was the real bait in the trap, and that a sexual encounter took place between the two men in that basement room – hence the long period of apparent inactivity. And all the while the other conspirators were upstairs, almost sick with tension, playing 'Yankee Doodle' over and over again, and waiting to hear that Rasputin had succumbed to the poison.

At about half past two, Yusupov came upstairs in a panic and told the others that Rasputin was still alive. Time was running short: they had to dispose of the body before morning. The four men made the impulsive decision to shoot Rasputin. Someone had thought to bring a pistol; it lay on the desk. Grand Duke Dmitry now handed it to Yusupov. The prince went downstairs with the gun behind his back. Rasputin was inspecting a decorative cabinet. 'You'd do better to look at the cross,' said Yusupov, referring to an ornate crystal crucifix on the mantelpiece. Then he shot Rasputin in the back. The other conspirators came rushing downstairs when they heard the crack of the pistol and found Rasputin on the floor bleeding and twitching. They watched him until he became motionless, then moved the body so that his blood did not stain the pristine polar-bear rug. After that, they all went upstairs for a drink – to calm their nerves and to celebrate the successful murder.

HE'S GETTING AWAY...

A short while later, Yusupov felt compelled to go back downstairs and inspect his handiwork. He checked the body for a pulse; there was none. He grabbed it by the shoulders and shook it, and it fell back to the floor. Then he noticed a slight flicker of the left eyelid – and before he knew it Rasputin had leaped to his

GOLDEN COUPLE
Felix Yusupov, prime mover in the killing of Rasputin, with his wife Irina, whom he used as bait to lure Rasputin to his palace. The murder failed in its aim of saving the Romanov dynasty: the old order collapsed just weeks later. The Yusupovs fled Russia and lived out their lives in France. Their palace on the Moika became a workers' social club.

feet. With an anguished roar, he rushed at Yusupov, shouting, 'Felix, Felix'. He clawed at Yusupov's clothes and tore the epaulette off his military uniform. Yusupov squirmed away and bolted up the stairs. Purishkevich saw him coming. 'He was literally faceless,' said Purishkevich. 'His beautiful blue eyes seemed huge and were bulging.' Yusupov let out 'an inhuman cry' and called to Purishkevich as he bolted up the stairs, 'Shoot him – he's getting away.'

Rasputin had staggered out into the courtyard of the palace. Purishkevich pursued him, carrying the pistol that Yusupov had already used once. Dmitry Pavlovich may have followed too. Four shots were fired, possibly from two separate guns. Purishkevich always maintained that he alone fired the shots, but that may have been a deliberate lie, told to protect Dmitry Pavlovich. The Grand Duke had come with a gun of his own, and was certainly the better shot, but there could be no question of him taking the throne if he was shown to have committed so sordid a murder with his own royal hand.

THE CORPSE IN THE ICE

One of the bullets fired had entered Rasputin's head. He was dead beyond doubt, but Purishkevich kicked Rasputin hard to make sure there was no spark of life left in him. The body was dragged back inside the palace. Yusupov, still beside himself with fear and rage, was waiting with a leaden dumbbell handle. He belaboured the corpse with it, screaming his own name, 'Felix, Felix' – Rasputin's last words to him – with every blow. He continued until he was exhausted and spattered with the dead man's blood.

The four conspirators now wrapped the body in a carpet and tied it with ropes like a great parcel. They loaded it into the back of a car – an anonymous military ambulance, not Yusupov's expensive vehicle – and drove to the Great Petrovsky Bridge on the edge of Petrograd. They heaved the body over the parapet of the bridge, intending that it would sink and never be discovered. But in their haste they forgot to weight it down. Moreover, one

> *He belaboured the corpse until he was exhausted and spattered with the dead man's blood.*

of Rasputin's boots came off and landed on a column of the bridge. It was this boot that caught the attention of a police officer three days later and quickly led to the recovery of Rasputin's frozen body.

By that time, the secret was out. Tsar Nikolai personally handed down punishments – remarkably lenient ones – to the two aristocratic plotters. Yusupov was confined to his country estate, while Dmitry Pavlovich was sent into exile in Persia. Purishkevich had left for the front on a hospital train the day after the murder and was, for now, beyond the tsar's reach.

The assassins had every reason to be pleased. Rasputin was gone for good. But for the rest of that cold December, devotees came to the Petrovsky Bridge with ropes and buckets – to draw water sanctified by the battered, bullet-riddled corpse of Grigory Rasputin.

Who wanted Rasputin dead?

For years, Rasputin had been playing a dangerous game. He had the protection and goodwill of the imperial family – but in almost every other section of Russian society there were people who despised him and would have been glad to see him removed from the tsar's entourage.

The ostensible motive of Rasputin's assassins was to change the political order in Russia. Tsar Nikolai's position as absolute ruler was becoming increasingly fragile, and they hoped that, once Rasputin was gone, Tsarina Alexandra would succumb to a nervous breakdown ('Her mental balance depends entirely on Rasputin,' Yusupov had said). The tsar would come to his senses and, like a man freed from a spell, see that a constitutional monarchy was the only way to save the Russian state.

Monarchists and courtiers hated Rasputin for bringing the Romanov dynasty into disrepute: what was this unwashed, dissolute, illiterate peasant doing so close to the Russian throne? In government circles, Rasputin was loathed for the power he held over affairs of state. At a time when the tsar was constantly dismissing ministers and appointing new ones, no politician could hope to gain high office without Rasputin's say-so. And no one could expect to remain in office for long unless they pandered to the man that the tsarina called 'our friend'.

Rasputin was not just a Russian problem. British diplomats in the Russian capital deplored Rasputin's meddling in the war against Germany. They suspected that he was advising the tsar and tsarina to make a separate peace with the Kaiser – a move that would have allowed Germany to transfer large numbers of troops and deploy them against Britain on the Western Front. According to one theory, British agents were closely involved in his murder.

Among the masses, Rasputin was seen as a mere *strannik*, a wandering pilgrim of a type that was common in rural Russia. Ordinary people resented him because he seemed to have become greedy as a result of his high connections. So when word spread that Rasputin had been killed, almost everyone apart from the imperial family was glad to hear it. 'A dog's death for a dog,' they said.

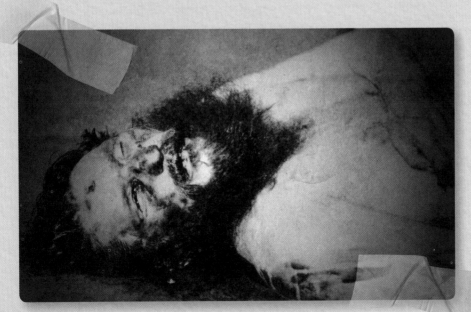

BODY OF EVIDENCE
It is widely believed that Rasputin was still alive when he was dumped in the Neva, that he fought to get out of his bonds and out of the river. The evidence for this is that water was found on his lungs at the autopsy, but this is not necessarily proof of drowning. The bullet to his head was almost certainly fatal.

The king of sleuth-hounds

Wilhelm Stieber rattled the seedy criminal world of 19th-century Berlin before turning his analytical skills to political and military intelligence. He became the mastermind of the first large-scale systematic spy network and is hailed as the father of modern espionage.

They were called 'the Kaiser's Second Army'. At the start of the First World War, the Allies knew and feared the regiments of German spies in their midst. 'On the eve of the war,' declared *The Evening Post* in faraway New Zealand, '30,000 spies, drawing incomes in that capacity from Government, were resident in France. German espionage in France has interested itself in everything and everybody.' The newspaper went on to express its distaste for this underhand conduct. 'Nobody has cared to believe that for 40 years a foremost Power among us has been living with its eye at the keyhole of Europe.'

To *The Evening Post*, as to the general public in the British Empire at large, spying was by its nature a disreputable activity, a form of cheating that tarnished the otherwise honourable game of war. And when *The Evening Post* said that this underhand business had been going on for 40 years, it had one man in mind: Wilhelm Stieber. He was the godfather of modern espionage, the template and trailblazer for intelligence-gathering organisations that include Scotland Yard, the FBI, MI5 and MI6, the CIA and the FSB.

Espionage was not a German invention, of course, or indeed a 19th-century one. What set Wilhelm Stieber apart and made him an innovator was his methodical approach, which evolved from his early career in the police. Born in 1818, Stieber was brought up in Berlin. His father was a minor government official who became a Lutheran minister; his mother, Daisy Cromwell, was English and a descendant of Oliver Cromwell. This background gave Stieber a moral sense of justice that steered him throughout his career. He was supposedly destined for the Church, but while studying theology something happened to persuade him that his real vocation was the law. A Swedish student was wrongly accused of burglary. Stieber, by researching the case and applying what would now be termed 'psychological profiling', managed to prove the Swede's innocence and achieve his acquittal. Stieber's switch to law incurred the displeasure of his father, who cut off his funds. He now earned his keep by working as secretary for the criminal courts and the police. In 1844 he qualified as a barrister but decided to join the Berlin police.

According to his memoirs, Stieber was soon personally involved in cracking a number of high-profile cases, often using disguise to wheedle out vital information or to infiltrate criminal gangs. In one career-boosting investigation, he unmasked a tailor who had swindled a life-insurance company by faking his own death in Berlin. Stieber knew the court system well and was always careful to collect sufficient evidence to secure convictions: he never sprung a trap until he was sure it was escape-proof. Careful observation, intercepting mail, undercover operations, impersonation and disguise and the interrogation of witnesses – all these techniques played a role.

TRACKING KARL MARX

Early in his career, Stieber found himself contending with subversive groups that wanted to overthrow the political system. He infiltrated one such ring by disguising himself as a portrait painter (he had a talent for art). He also persuaded a locksmith to talk his way into the home of a ringleader and retrieve incriminating papers from a locked desk. News of these methods caused a stir. Citizens felt that their liberties were being undermined by a 'secret police' – which they were.

But Stieber the policeman was utterly convinced that society needed protection from political extremism – all the more so after the series of mini-revolutions that swept Europe in 1848. That year, King Friedrich Wilhelm IV of Prussia ill-advisedly decided to show his solidarity with the concerns of his people by riding alone through Berlin sporting republican colours. This confusing gesture sparked a riot. Stieber, who was on hand, personally intervened to rush the shaken king to the security of his palace. As it turned out, the

THIEF TAKER *Wilhelm Stieber in about 1860, at the age of 42. He was then at the pivotal point of his career, poised between being chief crime-fighter in Berlin and becoming Chancellor Bismarck's spy supremo.*

man Stieber saved was not Friedrich at all, but an actor employed as his double. Nonetheless, Stieber's loyalty and bravery brought him to the attention of the real king, who was grateful to Stieber for sparing him the humiliation that would have ensued if his cowardly ruse had been exposed. Stieber was rewarded with promotion to head of the Berlin force. In this new role, he continued his war on revolutionaries. A particularly strong threat was emanating from German exiles in London, and in 1850 Stieber personally went to investigate. He knew that the key figures in England were an impoverished editor named Karl Marx and the wealthy son of a factory-owner called Friedrich Engels. Stieber took on the persona of a radical editor of a medical journal. This pretence made it a simple matter to gain access to the easygoing Marx, who turned out to be surprisingly talkative.

As a result of his acquaintance with Marx, Stieber managed to get hold of a list of all his revolutionary contacts in Germany and France. Hundreds of arrests followed. This was a triumph for Stieber, but also a wake-up call: he now realised the scale of the anti-government network. He stepped up the counter-revolutionary activities of the police, recruiting informers and closely monitoring suspects. In 1853, Stieber became director of the 'Security Division' of the Berlin police.

NETWORKING FOR BISMARCK

King Friedrich Wilhelm IV died in 1861, and his son Wilhelm became the new king of Prussia. His succession to the throne also ushered in a new prime minister, Otto von Bismarck, who was determined to unite the patchwork of German states into a single country led by Prussia. Bismarck's first aim was to undermine ties with the dominant regional power, Austria. At this time, Stieber earned Bismarck's admiration by unearthing a plot to assassinate him in his carriage. The prime minister, who called Stieber 'king of sleuth-hounds', now commissioned him to create a network of spies inside Austria.

Stieber applied new methods to the task. He was the first to see that it was more secure to use hundreds of operatives, each garnering snippets of information, than to rely on a few star spies working in depth. Using a news agency as cover, Stieber developed a broad network of spies in Austria. They observed and recorded every logistical, geographical and political detail, and all their information was centrally analysed and coordinated. By the time war broke out with Austria in 1866,

Prussia had a complete picture of the enemy's military and political vulnerability, and won a decisive victory at Königgrätz. Bismarck's next target was France, then under the unpopular rule of Napoleon III. Stieber knew that the disaffection of the people made them ripe for recruitment, and by this time he had an almost scientific approach to assessing the potential of spies – knowing who was susceptible, who was reliable, what they would ask for in reward. This was often money, and Prussia was willing to pay: spying was seen as a route to cost-efficient war. 'Working out of my headquarters in Berlin,' Stieber said, 'I formed all types of people – officers, scientists, engineers and manufacturers, not to mention their wives, mistresses, relatives and friends, as well as secretaries, couriers, servants, coachmen, gardeners and houseboys, who only appeared to be insignificant, even the kitchen personnel – into a secret, unbroken network of spies spread across all of France.'

When the Franco-Prussian war broke out in 1870, Prussia was able to move its armies swiftly into France. Stieber travelled with Bismarck and King Wilhelm, surrounding them with armed plain-clothes security police very much like those that accompany every modern politician on the move. By January 1871 the king was installed at Versailles, where Bismarck oversaw his coronation as emperor (Kaiser) of a new united Germany. Bismarck had succeeded in his grand project, and this was a crowning moment for his king of sleuth-hounds too. But Stieber's true legacy is not national or geo-political. It lies in his methodology: the game-changing approach to secrecy and subterfuge that Germany's enemies so deplored, and that all the world's intelligence-gathering organisations have so enthusiastically embraced.

Monsieur Charles in the service of Napoleon

When Napoleon defeated the Austrian Empire at Ulm in 1805, he acknowledged the role played by one man, a spy named Karl Schulmeister. 'All praise to him,' said Napoleon. 'He's worth 40,000 men to me.'

Trickery came naturally to Karl Schulmeister, known as 'Monsieur Charles' to his patron Napoleon Bonaparte. Born in Alsace, the German-speaking borderland of northeast France, he first earned a living as a merchant trading with Germany. During the turmoil that followed the French Revolution, he effortlessly turned his hand to smuggling.

When Napoleon came to power and took France to war, espionage and subterfuge were a key part of his strategy. Some time before 1804, Schulmeister was recruited as a spy. He took part in the kidnap of the Duc d'Enghien, last of the Bourbon dukes of Condé. Falsely accused of being involved in a plot against Napoleon, the duke was lured from Germany, tried on trumped-up charges and executed. This episode persuaded France's enemies that Napoleon was a bloodthirsty tyrant, and hardened their resolve to oppose him.

In 1805 Napoleon was at war with the Austrian Empire. He marched an army south to engage an Austrian army in Bavaria. Schulmeister established that the Austrians were concentrated in the city of Ulm, awaiting reinforcements. Napoleon wanted to encircle Ulm before these reinforcements arrived, but he needed to ensure that the Austrians did not break away. Posing as a Hungarian count with a grudge against France, Schulmeister approached Baron Mack, commander of the Austrian army, and offered his services as a spy. He was of course a double agent, using the classic ploy of feeding snippets of intelligence to gain confidence. Baron Mack even appointed Schulmeister to his own staff as head of intelligence. Schulmeister now planted a terrific lie: he told Baron Mack that a coup against Napoleon was imminent in Paris and that the British had landed in northern France – hence Napoleon's army did not pose an immediate threat. Mack was not convinced until Schulmeister slipped back to the French lines and produced a fake edition of a French newspaper that confirmed his information. The Austrian troops duly remained in Ulm, Napoleon's forces encircled them, and they were forced into a humiliating capitulation.

Schulmeister afterwards served as commissioner of police in occupied Vienna and as director of the French secret service. As for the Austrians, they never forgave him and destroyed his estate after the defeat of Napoleon in 1815. But by that time Karl Schulmeister had melted into retirement. The one-time master spy settled in Strasbourg and returned to his mercantile beginnings. He ran a tobacconist's shop until his death in 1853.

Behind the mask of iron

The existence of the man in the iron mask is historical fact – not just a figment of a storyteller's imagination. The question of his identity was much discussed in his lifetime, but no name was ever put to the man. In the 300 years since his anonymous death, dozens of theories have been advanced about who he was and why he was subjected to such a cruel fate.

In 1789, shortly after a Paris mob stormed the Bastille, a gruesome discovery was made in the dark bowels of the prison. Behind a basement door was a sunless cell, at the back of which, chained to the floor, lay a human skeleton. The bones were clothed in a few rat-bitten rags, and the bare skull was enclosed in a kind of helmet made of iron. There was nothing to indicate the name of the prisoner – but these, surely, were the remains of the mysterious poor soul known as the 'man in the iron mask'?

They weren't. In fact, no bones were found at all. The story, printed on scandal sheets and distributed on the streets of Paris, was revolutionary propaganda, a way of compensating for the disappointing fact that the Bastille contained no political prisoners when its doors were forced open on July 14. But that is not to say that the man in the iron mask was himself a fabrication. He was a real person – and he did indeed die in the Bastille, in 1703, after many long years of anonymous captivity. Throughout his incarceration, people wondered who he might be and

what crime he had committed to merit such a brutish and unusual punishment. In the centuries since his death, hundreds of investigators and theorists have claimed to have discovered the identity of the man in the mask. All but one of the theories is wrong, of course.

HINTS AND ALLUSIONS

One of the first serious attempts to put a name to the hidden face was made by the great French thinker Voltaire. Writing in the decades after the man in the mask had died, Voltaire had the opportunity to speak to government officials who had been involved with the incarceration of the 'Mask'. Voltaire states that the man was first condemned to imprisonment in 1661 and offers this description of the prisoner's appearance and predicament: 'In great secrecy there was sent to the castle on the island of Sainte-Marguerite an unknown prisoner, above ordinary height, young and most handsome and noble to behold. En route this prisoner wore a mask with a chin piece that had steel springs so as to allow him to eat with the mask on his face.

A FACE TO HIDE *The despair of the masked man is palpable in this romanticised vision. The knight's helmet is perhaps closer to the truth than the artist realised. While there is no evidence that a mask was specially made for the prisoner, he was once seen in such headgear while being moved to a new jail.*

The order was that he be killed if he took it off. He stayed on the island until 1690, when a trusted officer named Saint-Mars, governor of [the prison of] Pignerol, was made governor of the Bastille and took him to the Bastille still wearing the mask. Here the unknown man was lodged as well as was possible in that castle. He was refused nothing that he wanted, and his main wish was for extraordinarily fine linen and lace. He played the guitar. He had the finest fare, and the governor rarely sat down in his presence. His skin was a little brown.'

> *Perhaps he was the older twin of Louis XIV, and as such the rightful king.*

Voltaire ended his long account with a crashing hint as to the identity of the man in the iron mask: 'When he was sent to Sainte-Marguerite,' he wrote, 'no man of consequence in Europe disappeared.' That is to say, despite his apparently high social status, his existence had been a secret all his life. It would have been politically risky to spell it out, but Voltaire was implying that the man in the mask was a sibling or more likely a twin of the reigning monarch, Louis XIV. Perhaps he was the older twin, and as such the rightful king, but had been passed over for some reason. This is what made it necessary to hide him from the world and force him to wear a mask: a mere glimpse of his face would reveal the king's guilty secret. At the same time, fraternal feeling prevented Louis from having his unfortunate brother quietly assassinated.

Voltaire's implied theory deals with the two central questions of the iron mask story: first, why did the man's face need to be covered; second, if he was so dangerous, why was he not simply killed and disposed of? Every subsequent version has addressed these two issues – and not always convincingly.

A REGAL RESEMBLANCE

Once the monarchy was toppled in the French Revolution, it was no longer necessary for anyone to be as coy as Voltaire had been about the royal family. Lesser writers added colourful detail, apparently gleaned from documents and sources close to the House of Bourbon. The older twin was born weaker, so for the sake of the dynasty it was decided to spirit him away and have him raised by a noble family near Dijon. But when he was 21 he happened upon a portrait of the king (he had never been allowed to see one) and realised at once who he was. He resolved to go to the court of King Louis and confront his brother. But the young prince's adoptive father loyally sent word to the king that the secret was out. Louis had no hesitation in having both the nobleman and his own royal brother arrested, and at the same time he instructed a blacksmith to fashion the dreadful mask.

This version reads like a fairytale, and that is exactly what it is. Louis XIV did not have a twin or secret sibling, but nevertheless there are many versions of this 'prince in the mask' scenario, each with its own ingenious way of marshalling the evidence. In many versions the man in the iron mask is an illegitimate half-brother of

Louis XIV, the result of an indiscretion or else an amorous power-play on the part of his mother, Anne of Austria.

There is an interesting variant which says that the royal brother was in fact a sister, and so the man in the iron mask was actually the woman in the iron mask. The idea in this instance is that Queen Anne, after many childless years, finally bore a daughter. The baby girl was replaced with an infant boy – the future Louis XIV – to guarantee a male heir and the royal line.

Another theory makes use of Voltaire's detail about the prisoner's brownish skin to suggest that he was born of an affair between Queen Anne and an African servant – and was made to wear the mask to hide the dark face that was proof of the queen's adultery.

Or was the man in the iron mask actually the woman in the iron mask?

An interesting codicil to the rightful-heir line of inquiry came in 1823, in a book written by a man who had been Napoleon's secretary during his last exile in St Helena. Emmanuel de Las Cases records a discussion he had with Napoleon in 1816. Apparently a story had emerged that while the royal 'Mask' – the true king of France – was in jail, the daughter of the commandant befriended him and eventually became his lover. She bore him a son, whom she took away to Corsica and to whom she gave her mother's maiden name: de Bonpart. A descendant of that boy, through the unbroken male line,

was Napoleon Bonaparte himself – the implication being that when Napoleon proclaimed himself Emperor of France in 1804, he was reclaiming the throne that was his Bourbon birthright. Napoleon himself did not believe the story for a moment, though he said it would have been very easy to convince the gullible French public of it.

THE ENGLISH CANDIDATES

In 1768 a French playwright named Poullain de Saint-Foix claimed to have spoken to a surgeon who, in his apprentice days, was taken to the Bastille to help bleed the mysterious prisoner whose face was never seen. The surgeon, by now an old man, told Saint-Foix that the man's face was covered with a napkin (not an iron mask), and that he spoke with a marked English accent.

This unreliable testimony produced a raft of English candidates for the man in the mask. Even as the prisoner languished in the Bastille, it was rumoured that he might be Richard Cromwell, son of Oliver Cromwell. But how could that be?

It is true that Richard Cromwell went to France after his brief, unhappy spell as Lord Protector (between the death of his father and the restoration of Charles II). The story that he was the man in the mask makes use of this slim biographical fact, claiming that Cromwell was kidnapped on arrival in France by agents of the French king, and subjected to the lifelong torment of the mask as punishment for the regicidal sin of his father. In fact, Richard Cromwell lived openly and unmolested in France, later returning to England where he lived in obscurity to a ripe old age. Only the fact that he disappeared from public life can have given rise to the idea that he was the man in the iron mask.

A more high-profile English pretender to the Mask is James Scott, first Duke of Monmouth. He was the first and favourite illegitimate son of Charles II, and he was feckless and foolhardy to the point of high treason. In 1683 he was implicated in a plot to assassinate his father and also his uncle, the future James II. But such was Charles's love for Monmouth that, when the plot was foiled, he merely exiled his son to Holland for a while, as he had done after previous misdemeanours. When Charles died, Monmouth mounted a much more serious coup attempt against the new king, James II. He raised an army, but his bid for power ended disastrously for the rebels at the Battle of Sedgemoor in 1685. Monmouth fled the field, leaving his supporters to their fate. But he was soon captured and taken to London, where in tears and abject terror he begged his uncle for his life. James declined to show mercy, and Monmouth was publicly beheaded as a traitor on Tower Hill.

> *The fact is that there is really only one credible candidate for the Mask.*

Or was he? It was noted by some contemporaries that Monmouth's demeanour at his execution was more calm and courageous than in the days beforehand. So was it really him on the scaffold? The theory goes that James had promised his dying brother that, when he became king, he would do Monmouth no harm. But the uprising could not go unpunished. After Monmouth's capture, one of his close friends nobly offered to impersonate him and go to the gallows in his stead. The real Monmouth, meanwhile, was spirited out of England and taken to France. He was put in a secure place – Pignerol prison – where he could never again threaten his uncle's throne. And of course he wore the mask so that the subterfuge could never come to light. It is an ingenious tale, but once more, it is quite untrue. Monmouth was definitely beheaded, and if he managed to summon up some courage to face his punishment, then that is to his credit.

THE FACE OF TRUTH

The fact is that there is really only one credible candidate for the Mask, and he was neither a king nor a king's son. His name was Eustache Danger (or D'Angers, or Dauger), and he was a common valet. In 1669 (not 1661, as Voltaire claimed) he was arrested – possibly in connection with clandestine negotiations between England and France concerning an alliance against Holland. One theory is that he was a courier, carrying messages across the Channel. By accident or design he saw the content of some secret letter and was incarcerated in the state prison of Pignerol to prevent his knowledge coming out and causing a scandal.

In this, Danger's first prison, special measures were taken to prevent his secret leaking out – but they did not include an iron mask. Nevertheless, the only person permitted to enter Danger's cell was the governor of the prison, an ambitious former musketeer by the name of Saint-Mars. In 1687, when Saint-Mars was made governor of a different jail, he was ordered to take his mysterious prisoner along with him.

Was Molière the Mask?

One surprising candidate for the man in the iron mask is the French playwright Molière. Though he enjoyed the favour of King Louis XIV, Molière enraged the church authorities with plays such as *Tartuffe*, a satire directed against pious hypocrites. When religious interests failed to get the play banned, they smeared Molière's name, claiming that his wife Armande was also his daughter. This seemed plausible, as Armande was the much younger sister of an actress, Madeleine Béjart, who had once been Molière's mistress. Incest was punishable by death at the stake. The story goes that Molière's death in 1673 was faked, with the connivance of the king, so as to save him from execution. The imprisonment and the mask were sad necessities: he was too well known as an actor for his face to be seen again.

Saint-Mars knew that by this time the identity of his prisoner was a matter of interest. He realised that his own status, as guardian of the secret, would be enhanced if he could feed that curiosity. During the transfer he had his prisoner wear a visored helmet, a cast-off from some old suit of armour. This was the only occasion on which the man wore anything resembling an iron mask, and it was nothing more than a deliberate publicity stunt on the part of Saint-Mars, a ploy designed to keep Saint-Mars' own name in circulation, while disguising the fact that his prisoner was, to be blunt, a complete nobody.

Years later, in 1698, Saint-Mars was made governor of the Bastille in Paris, and again he took his prisoner with him. But by this time the authorities had entirely forgotten about Danger and his dangerous secret. Saint-Mars again made the man hide his identity, but with either a so-called 'loo-mask' that covers only the eyes, or with a hood made of black velvet. Danger disappeared inside the Bastille and died there in 1703, having been a prisoner of the state for 34 long years.

Danger's fate was sad and unjust. But an occasional velvet hood is not nearly as good a story as a permanent metal helmet, and herein lies a deeper truth that is more important than the identity of its wearer: the mask is a perfect metaphor for tyranny. Voltaire, as a radical writer and a champion of liberty, instinctively understood this – hence his keen interest in the tale, and hence its revival by the revolutionaries of Paris.

A man in an iron mask is someone whose mind is literally imprisoned. That physical restriction, together with the diktat that the wearer be killed if he utter a word, makes a terrifying political metaphor, an image of the suppression of free speech. But it is also a fine premise for an adventure story. Voltaire told it as history; a century later, his compatriot Alexandre Dumas recast it in his musketeer romances as fiction. The tale has since been told time and again by Hollywood. The iron mask is, in a word, a great story. But it is worth remembering that behind the mask, there was a real and very unfortunate human being.

The charcoal-burners

Secret societies have abounded in Europe for more than 200 years. Some have been little more than philanthropic gentlemen's clubs; others have cherished radical political agendas. The Italian society known as the 'Carbonari' – the charcoal-burners – was one of the strangest and most notorious secret societies of them all, thanks to its bizarre practices.

In 1821, Pope Pius VII took the unusual step of excommunicating an entire organisation. The object of his ire was 'a multitude of wicked men, united against God and Christ, with the aim of attacking and destroying the Church, deceiving the faithful and leading them from the doctrine of the Church by means of a vain and wicked philosophy'. The papal brief went on to say that these men 'aim to give everyone the licence to create at will his own religion according to his own convictions, than which nothing more pernicious can be imagined. They plot to ruin the Apostolic See, against which they have a special hatred.'

This condemnation was directed not at a new heresy or a satanic conspiracy but at a political society to which thousands of respectable Italian men belonged. They were the *carbonari*, or 'charcoal-burners', and they flourished in the south of Italy.

According to its own myth, the Carbonari brotherhood was founded by men who had fled from tyrants during the Middle Ages to make a life in the forests of Scotland. Here they led a fraternal outdoor existence, rather like Robin Hood and his men. They eked out a living by making charcoal, hence their name. A band of Carbonari once showed hospitality to Francis I of France, who had got lost in the Scottish forest while out hunting. The king was impressed by the charcoal-burners' courtesy and comradeship, by their love of liberty and loyalty to each other, and he became in essence an honorary member. His patronage allowed the Carbonari to flourish even after they had left the forests behind. That, in any case, was one version of how the society was founded. Others claimed that the true founder of the order was Philip of Macedon, father of Alexander the Great; that the order started out as a trade guild in Germany; or that it began in the Jura mountains of France during the Hundred Years War.

RURAL FREEMASONS
Myths apart, the order probably arose some time after the French Revolution as a kind of rustic variant on urban Freemasonry. The movement grew, and by the end of the Napoleonic Wars the

FOREST BRETHREN *The Carbonari took their jargon and symbols from the craft with which they claimed a historical link. The place where they met was called a* baracca, *a forester's hut; the interior of the building was a* vendita – *Italian for a coal-trader's premises. The* vendita *contained a rough-hewn log that served as a throne for the grand master, who carried a hatchet as his mark of office.*

Carbonari had chapters in towns and villages throughout the Kingdom of Naples. Carbonarism attracted members from every walk of life: army officers and landowners, priests and intellectuals, noblemen and peasants. It was a large but diffuse organisation, with very little in the way of a hierarchy or a central governing body. As an inevitable consequence of its broad demographic base, the political aims of Carbonarism were varied and unfocused. But, generally speaking, the Carbonari were patriots and liberals who wanted a constitution for Naples and – in the long-term – a single pan-Italian regime.

But, if the society's aims were purely political, why did the Pope excommunicate all of its members as if they were dangerous heretics? The answer lies – partly – in the tangled, inconstant politics of Naples at the turn of the 19th century. Since 1759, Naples had been ruled by Ferdinand, a younger son of the Bourbon King Charles III of Spain. Ferdinand was married to a sister of Marie Antoinette. In 1799 a French revolutionary army invaded Naples and established a short-lived republic. Ferdinand was deposed and went abroad, but he returned the following year with a Bourbon army and reconquered his kingdom. A French army under Napoleon invaded Naples again in 1806, and Ferdinand fled once more. Napoleon installed his brother Joseph as King of Naples, replacing him in 1808 with his brother-in-law Joachim Murat. He was on the throne until the fall of Napoleon in 1815, after which Murat was executed by firing squad. This opened the way for Ferdinand, with the backing of the Austrian foreign minister Prince Metternich, to claim the Neapolitan crown for a third time.

THE CARBONARI UPRISING

The Carbonari remained underground during these troubled and turbulent years. Their numbers increased hugely, while the relentless political instability, the waves of repression, and the changing tides of foreign influence fed their vague hopes for a free, autonomous Italy. Ferdinand's style of kingship after 1815 was harsh and deeply conservative; his Austrian allies insisted on it, since they wanted above all to prevent Europe becoming embroiled in another war.

In January 1820, a revolution in Spain led to the adoption there of exactly the kind of constitution that the Italian Carbonari had long dreamed of. Inspired by the Spanish example, the Carbonari organised themselves into a fighting force – or at least into a marching force. In July, a large number of Carbonari, including many army officers, gathered at the town of Nola and advanced on Naples with the intention of demanding a constitution. The uprising was copied in the Kingdom of Piedmont in the north of Italy, and it began to look alarmingly like a civil war brewing. In Naples, King Ferdinand swiftly promised a constitution but had no intention of keeping his word. He

departed the city – yet again – and turned to Austria for help. Prince Metternich duly despatched an Austrian army, which defeated a much smaller army of Neapolitan insurgents at Rieti in March 1821. The Carbonarist uprising was over.

But for Prince Metternich, crushing the Carbonari militarily was not enough. In his eyes, they were a continuing danger to the post-Napoleonic European settlement. Their society, he said, 'still encourages the people to revolt from one end of Italy to the other; it maintains conspiratorial relations with all the revolutionaries of Europe. It has not renounced its aims, and will never do so until it is destroyed.'

The book was so shocking that the Pope had to act.

Even before the Austrian incursion was complete, Metternich wrote to Pope Pius VII with a request that any Carbonaro who declined to quit the organisation be excommunicated. The Pope agreed that the Carbonari were a menace, but he was unwilling to call the wrath of God down on their heads. He pointed out that there was no religious justification. So Metternich made it his goal to provide the Pope with that justification. He told the Austrian ambassador in Rome, Count Anton Apponyi, to seek out material that would compromise the Carbonari in the eyes of the Catholic Church. Apponyi searched long and hard – and in the end found something more than sufficient: a book containing a graphic and detailed description of the initiation ceremonies of the Carbonari. Nothing of this ritual was known to anyone outside the organisation, because those involved swore a dire oath to keep it secret. But this book exposed something so profoundly shocking to conventional religious sensibilities that the Pope could not fail to act.

THEIR RITES REVEALED

The initiation of a Carbonaro, it turned out, was a kind of blasphemous pastiche of the passion of Christ. A candidate Carbonaro, his eyes bound with a cloth and his hands tied, would be led by guards into the presence of an authoritative figure dressed as a priest, or perhaps a judge, in some secret spot and in the dead of night. There was in attendance a congregation of initiates, sitting in silence like a jury. The red-robed principal invoked a deity that he termed 'grand master of the universe', then turned to the frightened man in the blindfold. 'I am Pilate,' he announced. The bound man was made to drink from the 'cup of bitterness', then a guard would read the charges against him: he is 'a seducer of the people, wanting to become a despot and overthrow our religion, and to call himself the son of the living God'.

Pilate would say that the crimes were too serious for him to assess alone, then sent the accused to another judge, who called himself Caiaphas. This second judge passed the accused on to a third person – 'Herod' – who sent him back to Pilate. The assembly would now demand a crucifixion, and Pilate would consent, saying, 'I have done my duty. You wish his death, I give him to you. I wash my hands of the deed.' The accused, still blindfolded, was then handed over to the mob, who would strip him and force him to carry his cross to the place of execution. But at the last he was permitted to beg for mercy. Pilate would

remove his red robe and, revealing himself as the 'president', ask the reprieved man to take an oath of allegiance with his hand on a ceremonial hatchet. As a final act of initiation, the candidate would swear never to speak of what he had just endured.

There was more. The highest ranks of the organisation were told that the order went all the way back to Jesus Christ himself, and that Christ's disciples were the first initiates of the charcoal-burners' brotherhood. This foundation myth was as sacrilegious as any of the Carbonari's theatrical ceremonies. And there was a hint of the occult in some of their secret ways. A fallen Carbonaro was sometimes burned in effigy, or else a paper on which his name had been written was put to the flame. A member who committed a serious ethical breach – such as committing adultery – was expelled from the society and would have his name inscribed with charcoal in a 'black book'.

This was more than enough evidence for the Pope. He acquiesced to Metternich's demands and issued the papal bull of excommunication in September 1821. It had the required effect: the Carbonari movement was fatally weakened at its root, and gradually lost influence in its southern heartland. The more active leaders fled abroad; others were imprisoned. Some Carbonari drifted off in disillusion; a few joined hard-headed revolutionary groups or the more pragmatic nationalist movements that arose in the 1830s and 1840s. The strange idealistic, quasi-religious Order of the Carbonari faded away, but plenty of its former members lived long enough to see a unified Italian nation emerge in 1861. This was the event they had been hoping for when, as young men, they had played at crucifixion in the dark of a Neapolitan night.

The cross and the swastika

The practices of some secret societies have, historically, been deeply sinister. Fascistic organisations have had a tendency to spawn clubs where the elitist world view is dramatised and reinforced through clandestine rituals.

The Carbonari are not the only secret society to have attempted to alter the political direction of a country. A better-known and far more troubling case is represented by the Ku Klux Klan. Like the Carbonari, the KKK was born of political disappointment – in their case the defeat of the Confederate states in the American Civil War. And, like the Carbonari, the Klan based its hierarchy and its rites on those of the Freemasons. At its first

> ## The KKK, like the Carbonari, was born of political disaffection.

peak of influence, in the 1870s, the Klan saw itself as an 'invisible empire' ruled by a 'grand wizard'. Each state's complement of members was termed a 'realm' and was under the command of a 'grand dragon'. Smaller territorial units based on counties or groups of counties were headed by 'grand titans' or 'grand giants'. Individual members were 'ghouls', and there were official posts – treasurer and so forth – designated by terms such as 'nighthawk' and 'goblin'.

The founder of the KKK was a Freemason and former general in the Confederate army, Nathan Bedford Forrest. The nonsensical name of his organisation is a corruption of the Greek word *kuklos*, meaning circle, plus the word 'clan' deliberately misspelled to underline the alliteration. The first members of the organisation were all demobilised southern officers, men humiliated and enraged by the peace that the victorious northern states had imposed upon them. They vented their fury and frustration on the weakest of their enemies – the black people who, until recently, had been the personal property of themselves and their neighbours.

The primary activity of the KKK in this first phase of its existence was nothing more nor less than terrorising the emancipated slaves in murderous pogroms. The Klan was effectively suppressed in the 1880s but revived after the First World War and again during the civil rights struggle of the 1950s and 1960s. In more recent decades, American neo-Nazi parties have provided a focus for people who still subscribe to the KKK's violent and racist philosophy but are put off by the risible terminology of the old Klan organisation.

NAZI DAYDREAMERS

The Nazis themselves – or certain elements within the Nazi movement – were fond of the same kind of esoteric myth-making that seems to be part of the appeal of secret societies. In the years after the First World War, several characters who would later be leading figures in the Nazi Party were members of a Munich-based organisation called the Thule Society (*die Thule-Gesellschaft*). This group, which had the appearance of a kind of genealogy club or book group, was in fact an extremely nationalistic, anti-Semitic, quasi-academic cabal with an interest in the entirely unhistoric idea of a proto-Germanic Aryan race. Rudolf Hess, Hitler's deputy, was a

1 · 9 · 1 · 9

Thule-Gesellschaft

K K K

"if your heart's true
it calls to you"

devotee, as was Alfred Rosenberg, the muddle-headed 'philosopher' of Nazism. The society made use of ancient symbols such as the swastika and took as its motto, 'Remember that you are a German; keep your blood pure!'

In the chaotic political situation that held sway in Bavaria after the First World War, the Thule Society forged links with the DAP (German Workers' Party), which evolved into the NSDAP (the National Socialist German Workers' Party, or Nazi Party). This factual connection between the organisations has led to the back-to-front view that the Thule Society is somehow the germ or origin of Nazism, when, in fact, there is nothing more than an overlap in some of their extreme views plus the unsurprising fact that some individuals belonged to both organisations.

Adolf Hitler never went to a Thule meeting, and was rather disapproving of their woolly occult obsessions. He objected to the idea that the Thule Society had somehow paved the way for him or shaped his thinking on race and history: he wanted to take all the credit for his own original world-view. Once Hitler was in power, he had all Germany's abundant esoteric organisations closed down, along with the country's many Masonic lodges.

The eternal lie

The Protocols of the Elders of Zion are perhaps the most pernicious forgery of the modern age, and they are a woefully bad example of the forger's art. Yet this amateurish anti-Semitic calumny has been taken seriously for more than a century, and it has caused incalculable harm.

In May 1920, *The Times* of London ran an article about a book, recently published for the first time in English. The book was called *The Jewish Peril*, and it purported to be the political programme of a secret Jewish group known as the Elders of Zion. That programme took the form of 24 'protocols' – the minutes, so to speak, of a meeting held perhaps two or three decades previously. It was not clear who these elders were, or exactly when and where their clandestine congress had taken place, but their goals as stated in the text made for chilling reading.

According to the book, the aim of the Elders of Zion was nothing less than world domination, the establishment of a global state controlled by them and their appointees. This goal was to be achieved by manipulating the global financial system, undermining Christian values and civilisation, and seizing behind-the-scenes control of governments one by one. Other subtle tools included the infiltration of the press, the dissemination of pornography and the perversion of the education system. It seemed to *The Times* that some elements of the Elders' programme had already been realised in the recent catastrophe of

the Great War and in the emergence of a militant communist regime in Russia.

That alone seemed reason enough to take the document seriously. One of the protocols read: 'We must know how to confiscate property without hesitation, if by so doing we can obtain subjection and power.' That looked like a description, not to say a prophecy, of the Bolshevik victory in Russia. The Bolshevik leadership, *The Times* pointed out, contained 'a high percentage of Jews'. Another passage read: 'We will create a universal economic crisis with the help of gold, all of which is in our hands.' This seemed to be gloating acknowledgment of the worldwide preponderance of Jewish financiers, super-rich families such as the Rothschilds and others. In a word, the text explained the baffling paradox whereby Jews came to be over-represented both in the upper reaches of capitalist enterprise and in the lower depths of the revolutionary movement. It was all part of one ancient and hitherto undreamed-of Jewish conspiracy.

The Protocols of the Elders of Zion were taken from the work of a Russian mystic named Sergei Nilus. They appeared as a rather incongruous appendix to a

CHRISTIAN

E PERIL JUIF

LES PROTOCOLES DES SAGES DE SION

that *The Protocols* were taken from the safe of an organisation called The Society of Zion, 'located in France', that they were leaked to his source by a delegate to the first Zionist Congress in the Swiss city of Basel in 1897, and, more salaciously, that a certain lady stole them from a high-ranking French Freemason (having spent the night with him, Nilus implied).

THE INTERNATIONAL JEW

After the First World War, *The Protocols* found their way out of eastern Europe. They were published in Germany in 1919, in a lavishly annotated edition, and were avidly read by Adolf Hitler. They also found their way to the United States, where they made a deep impression on the industrialist Henry Ford. Two weeks after *The Times* expressed its concern about the Jews' plans for a global takeover, Ford commissioned a series of articles entitled *The International Jew: The World's Foremost Problem*, which ran in his own newspaper, the *Dearborn Independent*. The articles appeared every week for nearly two years, and when they were finished, they were turned into a four-volume book, which sold for a dollar the set. (This collection was massively subsidised by Ford himself.) The newspaper series and the books contained the complete text of *The Protocols*, along with a detailed commentary on how they related to the contemporary political situation in America and elsewhere. 'They fit with what is going on,' said Ford.

But by now, some people were smelling an anti-Semitic rat. About a year after *The Times* published its original piece, it ran a story by one of its foreign correspondents, Philip Graves, proving that *The Protocols* were a forgery. Graves was based in

book of religious meditations entitled *The Great Within the Small*, published in 1905. Very soon *The Protocols* appendix was hived off into a separate book, and translated into other languages. Nilus often wrote tailored introductions for these new editions, in which he explained the origins of the remarkable document. But his explanation changed from one version of the book to another. He said variously

Constantinople, which was crammed with anti-Bolshevik Russian emigrés. One day in 1921, a Russian acquaintance handed him a scoop in the form of a battered book. It was in French, and its title page was missing. Graves's contact said it was part of a job-lot of books that he had bought from another Russian, a former member of the tsarist secret police. Graves could tell by the typography that the book had been published in the 1860s or 1870s. The word 'Geneva' was handwritten on the preface.

The astonishing thing was that the book bore an obvious resemblance to Nilus's *Protocols*. In fact, it was clear that large sections of *The Protocols* were copied or minimally adapted from this unidentified French book. But the original had nothing to do with a Jewish conspiracy; it did not even mention the Jews. It consisted of an imaginary conversation between the medieval Italian diplomat Niccolò Machiavelli and the 18th-century French thinker Montesquieu. In their discussion, Machiavelli details all the cynical methods that a ruthless ruler or government might use to control the populace. His ironic remarks are an obvious and (for its time) witty lampoon of the regime of Napoleon III. But the author of *The Protocols* had stripped the text of its ironical intent, put words into the mouths of the so-called Elders, and passed the whole thing off as a serious blueprint for world domination.

A little detective work in the British Library established that the 'Geneva dialogues', as Graves tentatively called them, were in fact a book called *Dialogues in Hell*, written in 1864 by a certain Maurice Joly. He was a French satirist – and was not Jewish, nor indeed anti-Jewish. He would have been appalled by the use to which his political parody had been put.

Graves's thorough analysis showed beyond doubt that *The Protocols* were a crude forgery. He hazarded a guess – correctly, in fact – that they had been cooked up 20 years earlier by the Russian secret police. Their immediate purpose, the reason they had been passed to the gullible and dishonest Nilus, was to discourage Tsar Nikolai II from proceeding with reforms foisted on him in the wake of the Russian Revolution of 1905. If the tsar could be persuaded that the despised Jews were behind the ongoing political upheavals, he might then resist constitutional change.

IN PRAGUE CEMETERY

But not all of the text of *The Protocols* is an adaptation of that earlier work by Joly. Since his book has nothing whatever to do with the Jews, the idea of a secret cabal of Jewish plotters had to come from elsewhere. Almost as soon as *The Protocols* became available in German, that other source was recognised. In 1868 a German named Hermann Goedsche, writing under the unconvincing English pen name Sir John Retcliffe, had published a novel named *Biarritz*. Goedsche was a convicted forger, a political activist and a virulent anti-Semite. His novel contained a lurid chapter entitled 'In the Jewish Cemetery in Prague', describing a midnight meeting of the heads of the twelve tribes of Israel. At this event, which the novel says takes place once every 100 years, the Jewish leaders report on progress made in the course of the past century: how Christianity has been undermined, the masses whipped up in revolution, Christian womanhood corrupted. At the end of this business part of the meeting, the Jewish leaders offer worship to a golden calf that rises from the grave of a rabbi. Then they kneel down before Satan himself.

Goedsche's fevered fantasy did not remain buried in his novel. The cemetery episode was extracted, the lurid context was edited out and the twelve reports recast as a single monologue. In this form it made its way to Russia, where it was widely published as a pamphlet entitled *The Rabbi's Speech*. There was no indication in these editions that the speech was a work of fiction; it was presented as an entirely factual document. So *The Rabbi's Speech* was both a prototype of *The Protocols* and a source for it. It was often distributed on the streets as a prelude to the pogroms that were a feature of Jewish life in the Russian Empire at the start of the 20th century. The mobs would first read up on the Jews, then smash their synagogues, defile the Torah scrolls and beat their scheming Jewish neighbours to death.

ON TRIAL IN SWITZERLAND

The essential truth about *The Protocols* was well known by the mid-1920s. But this did not stop them circulating. In 1934 the publishers of the Swiss edition were sued by a Jewish lawyer for publishing 'obscene literature'. The judge in the case, Walter Meyer, minutely examined the evidence about the origins of the book, and declared at the end of the trial: 'I hope that a time will come when nobody will understand how a dozen sane and reasonable men could torment their brains over the authenticity of these so-called *Protocols*, which, despite the harm they have done and may yet do, are nothing more than ridiculous nonsense.'

That should have been the end of *The Protocols*. But, tragically, they were just receiving a massive boost. At the time Judge Meyer pronounced his verdict, the Nazis had been in power in neighbouring Germany for two years. They distributed millions of copies of *The Protocols* to schoolchildren, who were taught that this book was a historical document that told them everything they needed to know about the Jews. In Germany *The Protocols* became a justification for mass murder.

The truth about The Protocols was well known by the mid-1920s.

Yet even the defeat of Nazism could not kill off *The Protocols*. After the creation of the state of Israel, they circulated in Arabic throughout the Middle East. An illustrated edition came out in Spain in 1964. They were published in Bombay in 1974, under the title *International Conspiracy Against Indians*. They appeared for the first time in Japanese in 1987. Russian neo-fascists re-issued Nilus's original in 1992, soon after the dissolution of the USSR. (About that time, Russian scholars finally put a name to the man who had concocted *The Protocols*. He was Matvei Golovinsky, a lowly secret-police functionary.) In 1994 Christian fundamentalists in Australia printed a new English edition. And today the plans of the Elders of Zion are available in almost any language on the internet, where each of the 24 protocols can be easily accessed via a hyperlink.

Nearly a century has passed since *The Protocols* were exposed as a cack-handed, small-minded, plagiaristic fake – but still they won't wither away. They have become the indestructible slander, a lie as indelible as an Auschwitz tattoo.

The Lebensborn legacy

Adolf Hitler dreamed of a world ruled by a pure Aryan master race. *Heinrich Himmler, head of the SS, took the Führer at his word and set up a series of maternity homes – first in Germany, later in countries occupied by Germany during the Second World War – where illegitimate Aryan babies could be nurtured. The consequences for those babies have been traumatic.*

From the time he wrote *Mein Kampf* in the early 1920s, Hitler vigorously promoted the ideal of racially pure Germans: blond, blue-eyed Aryans. But there was a practical problem – many of Germany's fittest young men had been killed in the First World War, and the German birth rate was low. In addition, because of a lack of men to marry, German women were entering into illicit relationships with married men, and the resulting pregnancies were being terminated in their thousands each year. Many of these would have been born the offspring of 'racially valuable' Aryan parents. One of the first measures introduced by the new Nazi government in 1933 was to outlaw abortion, under the slogan 'No German babies should go unborn'. Doctors who contravened this ruling faced the death sentence.

Meanwhile, Heinrich Himmler actively promoted procreation among his men, all of whom had been racially screened. He wanted them to father as many children as possible, not just with their wives but also with other Aryan women. The dubious morality of this policy was justified by Nazi racial theory, and fully accepted by its most ardent supporters. To promote the strategy, Himmler founded an organisation called Lebensborn, meaning 'fountain of life'.

The first Lebensborn maternity unit, equipped to the highest standards, opened in 1936 in the village of Steinhöring, near Munich. SS members' wives could have their babies here, but it was also a place where unmarried, 'racially pure' mothers could come discreetly to give birth. Their babies were, for the most part, adopted by SS families. Nine further Lebensborn clinics were built in Germany in the 1930s, and about 8,000 babies were born in them.

ARYANS ABROAD

After 1939 the Nazis began to export their racial policies to occupied countries. German soldiers were prohibited from having relationships with the women of eastern Europe, where the population was 'tainted' with Slav blood. But wherever the local population was deemed to be Aryan, relationships were actively encouraged. This was so in Norway, where the Nordic traits of the people were particularly

HITLER'S BABIES *Brand-new perambulators are lined up in the sunshine, tended by a nurse in a crisp white uniform. By the standards of maternity hospitals in the 1930s, the Lebensborn clinics offered model conditions. Only the flag, bearing the SS insignia, hints that all is not as innocent as it seems.*

admired by the Nazis. Between 1941 and 1945, between nine and 15 Lebensborn homes operated in Norway. About 8,000 babies born to Norwegian women and fathered by Germans were registered with the Lebensborn authorities. Perhaps 4,000 more were born but not registered.

Despite some rumours to the contrary, there is little evidence that this was a coercive breeding programme. Rather, young women – enduring the tough conditions of foreign occupation – were often drawn to the protection and material comforts that fraternising with German soldiers could bring. When pregnant, giving birth at a Lebensborn home would have seemed an attractive option, not only for the quality of the care that they provided, but also because the homes acted as a shield against the disapproval of the Norwegian population. Many of the German fathers were married men, after all. Others were posted to Norway only briefly, on leave from the Eastern Front, so there was little possibility that relations between Norwegian women and German soldiers would be legitimised by marriage.

Consequently, a large number of the babies were taken to Germany for adoption or to be brought up by their German grandparents. But many remained in Norway with their mothers. Their world collapsed when the Germans withdrew from Norway in the closing stages of the war. The Norwegians, who had suffered great privations during the occupation, turned on women who had collaborated with the Germans. A *tyskerhore* (German whore) would be paraded in the streets with shaven head, spat upon and beaten, sent to an internment or labour camp for months and then, on release, shunned. Some women were assigned to mental hospitals, as doctors pronounced that they must have been mentally deficient to fraternise with the occupiers. Their children were not spared. The *tyskerbarna*

(German children) were bullied at school, by teachers as well as by fellow pupils. Sometimes resented by their own mothers or rejected by their own families, many were beaten and abused. Some of the Lebensborn children were assumed to have inherited the supposed mental defects of their mothers and spent their entire childhoods in mental institutions. Some of those being brought up in Germany were repatriated to Norway, and suffered the additional difficulties of integrating into an unwelcoming family, while having no knowledge of Norwegian.

So the Lebensborn children, aged four at most when the war ended, were brought up in an unloving world, carrying the blame for something they had not done, seen as symbols of national shame. They found it difficult to make sense of their treatment. Mothers refused to talk about the past; few would speak of the father, whose identity and fate often remained obscure. Often deprived of a proper

education, the Lebensborn children were unable to pursue career paths that might otherwise have been open to them. As a result of their upbringing, some have been unable to forge stable, loving relationships of trust. Throughout their lives, many have been treated as second-class citizens.

THE LEBENSBORN ADULTS

Although complete wartime records for the Lebensborn children were held by the Norwegian government, they were not declassified and made public until the 1990s. These documents have allowed some Lebensborn survivors, now reaching retirement age, to resolve questions about their own family history and find out who their fathers were. Some of the fathers turned out to be still living in Germany, but reunions, when they occurred, often proved fraught and embarrassing, and did not produce the hoped-for sense of closure.

Only in the 1990s did the Lebensborn survivors being to emerge from years of isolation and go public about

Aktion T4: the Nazis' euthanasia programme

The Lebensborn programme was just part of the Nazi policy of racial purification. While its maternity wards looked after the offspring of 'racially valuable' couples, an effort was being made to eliminate all those who were not valuable. To the Nazis, anyone with a mental handicap or hereditary disability was considered an agent of racial degeneracy. To preserve the purity of German blood, the SS set up the innocuous-sounding Charitable Foundation for Cure and Institutional Care. Doctors were obliged to register all patients who fell into the targeted categories. From September 1939, citing the need to free up hospitals for wounded soldiers, such patients were removed to collection centres. Their families were told they were being assessed for treatment. In fact they were being executed.

This programme was codenamed Aktion T4, after the address of its headquarters at number 4 Tiergartenstrasse, Berlin. It began with handicapped children, then encompassed adults. In the space of two years, around 5,000 children and 65,000 adults were 'granted a merciful death'. Hitler had unofficially sanctioned the operation but with instructions that he must not be associated with it. He feared a public outcry, especially from Germany's large Catholic population. But so many people were involved in the programme, or affected by it, that information leaked out. In the face of vehement protest – almost unheard of in Nazi Germany – the authorities were obliged to suspend Aktion T4 in August 1941. Its staff were redeployed to eastern Europe, where they applied the same processes and techniques to the extermination camps of the Holocaust.

their experiences. They have formed associations to create a lobbying platform, hoping to bring some public recognition of their suffering. Many blame the Norwegian government for turning a blind eye to their plight, but in 2000 they achieved some official acknowledgment when the prime minister made a public apology for the way that they had been treated. Since then, financial compensation has been paid to some, but such payments remain controversial. Many Norwegians complain that their families have received no payment for the damage and loss that they suffered while patriotically opposing the German occupation.

It has been hard for the Lebensborn Norwegians. Although thousands of children were born to German fathers in other occupied countries during the war – Lebensborn homes were established in Denmark, the Netherlands, France and Belgium – in those countries they were fewer in number than in Germany and Norway. There was not therefore the same perception of them as a group, so they avoided the Lebensborn label. Only Germany itself – with 8,000 Lebensborn children and ten homes – paralleled Norway's statistics. Here, however, the SS destroyed almost all of their documents in the final stages of the war, so the Lebensborn survivors are unlikely ever to uncover their genealogical past. Even now, some continue to feel haunted by the fear that their fathers may have been SS killers or war criminals.

'Mutter–Kind–Heim' was the name given to the Lebensborn clinics: mother, child, home. In the 1930s, when the homes were founded, few would have objected to those positive, life-enhancing, innocent-sounding values. And few would have been able to predict the lifetime of misery that lay ahead for the children born in those pristine SS hospitals.

The sealed train

In February 1917, Russia erupted in revolution. This was the moment that Bolshevik leader Vladimir Lenin had been waiting for all his life – but he was in Zurich, stranded in a neutral country as war raged all around. He had to get to Petrograd, no matter what the cost or political risk.

Every day of his exile in Zurich, Lenin went to the public library to read the newspapers, scouring the pages for scraps of news from war-torn Petrograd. On March 15, 1917, he came back home to Spiegelgasse for lunch, as usual. He was still there, in the tiny room next door to the shoemender's, when a Polish comrade named Mieczyslaw Bronski came banging on the door. 'Have you heard?' exploded Bronski. 'There's been a revolution in Russia.' Inside an hour, a dozen or more Poles and Russians were crammed into Lenin's room, loudly discussing what the news meant, how it fitted in with Marxist theory, and when they could all go home.

But it was not that simple. Lenin was ruefully aware that the European war had created the conditions for revolution in Russia but, ironically, that same war made it well-nigh impossible to get there. There was no obvious way for a Russian to cross German territory. Even if there were, it would be unthinkable to traverse the front line between the German and Russian armies. He knew that Britain and France, Germany's other enemies, would not allow him transit through their territory,

since they viewed all revolutionaries as troublemakers who would distract their allies in the Russian government from the vital business of fighting Germany.

ESCAPING SWITZERLAND

Over the next few days, various desperate schemes were mooted. Perhaps the party could get hold of an aeroplane to fly Lenin over the heads of the warring armies and into Russia. But where to find a sympathetic socialist pilot? Or maybe Lenin could sneak into England in disguise, then make his way to Russia through Holland and Scandinavia. But what if the British caught him? He would be interned and out of action for the duration of the war. Maybe someone could find a Swedish deaf-mute who bore a passing resemblance to Lenin? If that person could be persuaded to swap identities, then Lenin could get into Russia on a Swedish passport without betraying the fact that he knew not one word of the language. But Lenin, his wife pointed out, constantly talked in his sleep.

It was the Menshevik leader Yuli Martov who came up with the idea of

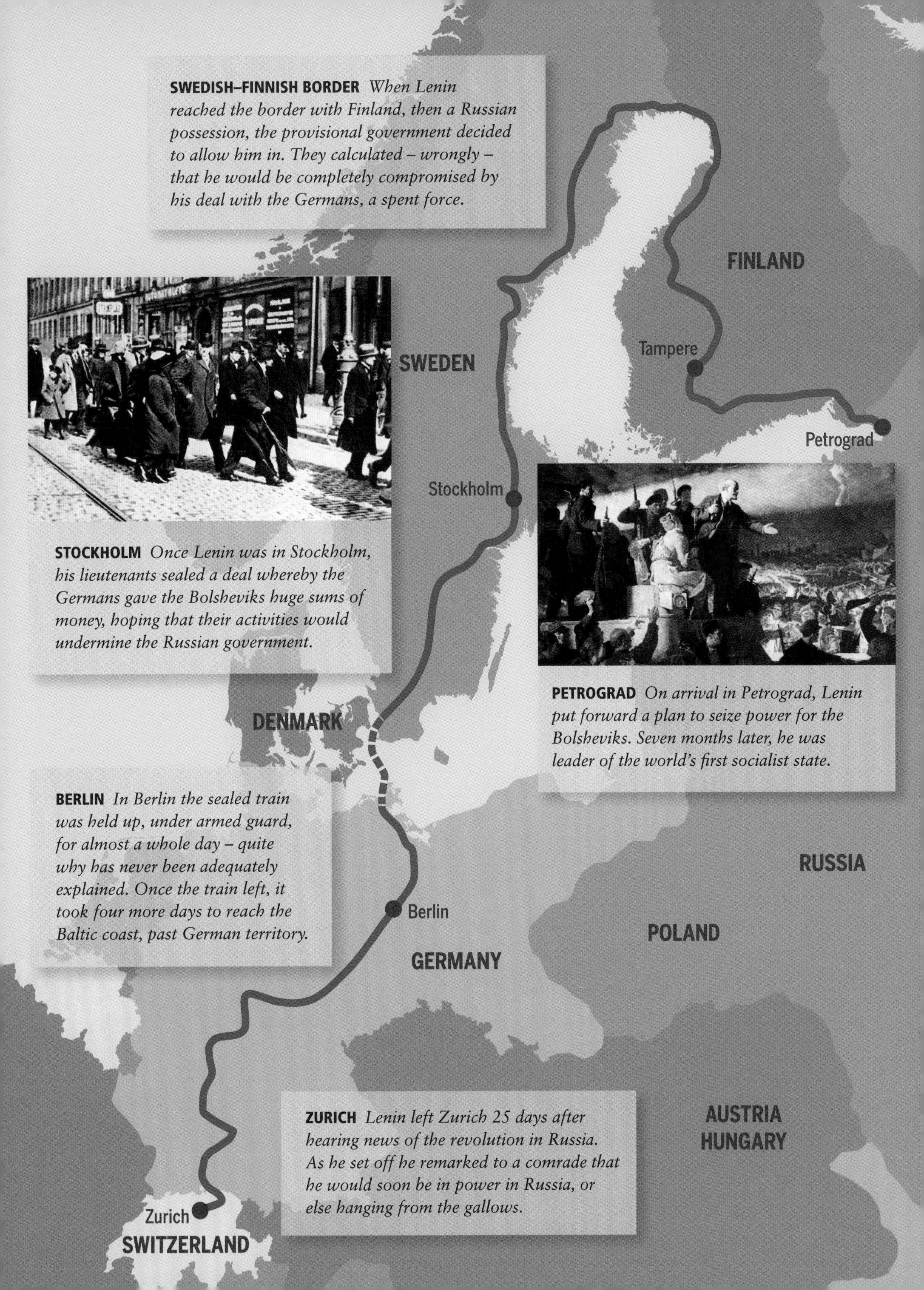

SWEDISH–FINNISH BORDER *When Lenin reached the border with Finland, then a Russian possession, the provisional government decided to allow him in. They calculated – wrongly – that he would be completely compromised by his deal with the Germans, a spent force.*

FINLAND

Tampere

Petrograd

SWEDEN

Stockholm

STOCKHOLM *Once Lenin was in Stockholm, his lieutenants sealed a deal whereby the Germans gave the Bolsheviks huge sums of money, hoping that their activities would undermine the Russian government.*

PETROGRAD *On arrival in Petrograd, Lenin put forward a plan to seize power for the Bolsheviks. Seven months later, he was leader of the world's first socialist state.*

DENMARK

BERLIN *In Berlin the sealed train was held up, under armed guard, for almost a whole day – quite why has never been adequately explained. Once the train left, it took four more days to reach the Baltic coast, past German territory.*

Berlin

GERMANY

RUSSIA

POLAND

ZURICH *Lenin left Zurich 25 days after hearing news of the revolution in Russia. As he set off he remarked to a comrade that he would soon be in power in Russia, or else hanging from the gallows.*

AUSTRIA HUNGARY

Zurich

SWITZERLAND

approaching the German High Command and boldly asking for safe passage through Germany. He reasoned that the Germans would want to send the revolutionaries home for precisely the reasons that the British would want to keep them out. Karl Radek, another Polish comrade, later wrote that the Germans saw Lenin and his followers as a kind of political 'bacillus' – a disease that they could inject into the Russian body politic and so weaken the new provisional government to the point where it would withdraw from the war.

A few voices in the crowd shouted 'Pigs!', 'German spies!'

To keep Lenin free from taint, an approach was made to German diplomats through a series of intermediaries. The main mover was Alexander Parvus, a pro-Bolshevik arms dealer. He assured the German ambassador in Copenhagen that Lenin was 'far crazier' than Alexander Kerensky, head of the provisional government, and predicted that Lenin would be running the country within months. The German authorities responded swiftly, agreeing to Russian demands that, for example, there be no passport checks along the way. The Petrograd soviet of workers' deputies, meanwhile, sweetened the deal by promising to expedite the repatriation of German prisoners of war. All parties seemed to be getting what they wanted.

The Russian revolutionaries and their families – 32 men, women and children – left from Zurich station on April 9, 1917.

There were many well-wishers, but also a few voices in the crowd shouting abuse: 'Pigs!', 'German spies!' At the border with Germany, Swiss customs officials relieved the Russians of their carefully husbanded supplies of sausage and chocolate, much to the travellers' dismay. Arriving on the German side of the border, the travellers were ushered onto a train consisting of one carriage divided into three second-class compartments and five third-class. The Germans had insisted that two officers travel on the train. These enemy soldiers were to keep to their side of a chalk line drawn on the floor. One side of the line was deemed to be Germany; the other side was a Russian enclave, rumbling inexorably towards Petrograd.

BOLSHEVIKS ON THE MOVE
Contrary to myth, the train was never sealed in the sense that the doors were locked or the windows blacked out. It was Lenin who insisted that the occupants be isolated from the outside world, that no German comrades – however politically sound – be allowed on board during halts in the journey. That way, he could say that he never fraternised with the enemy en route. Lenin also refused to leave the train at any point, so that he could claim never to have set foot on German soil. That is not to say that there was no contact with the outside world. Some of the Russians opened the windows and shouted revolutionary slogans at bewildered German troops as they passed slowly through junctions. And the Swiss communist Fritz Platten, by virtue of his citizenship a neutral in the Great War, was delegated to get off the train at stops to buy beer and newspapers.

Such home comforts notwithstanding, conditions in the train were uncomfortable. Everyone insisted that Lenin and his wife Nadezhda have a compartment to themselves, so that he could work along the way. The rest of the party was jammed into the seven other compartments, the single men spending their days and nights on hard third-class benches.

Karl Radek, who was known for his wit, made it his job to keep the others amused with a constant stream of jokes and stories. One female comrade, Olga Ravich, shrieked with laughter at his every remark – so much so that Lenin himself came into the compartment and wordlessly frogmarched her down to the far end, where she would be out of earshot. There was a certain amount of friction between factions on the train – not Bolsheviks and Mensheviks, but smokers and non-smokers. Lenin – who hated tobacco – had banned pipes and cigarettes: smokers were allowed to indulge their habit only in the toilet. But this had led to arguments with those who were forced to wait to use the toilet for other purposes. So Lenin tore up some paper and instituted a system of tickets, one sort for smoking, another for toilet use, both strictly rationed. It was a comradely solution to the problem, and it involved exactly the kind of top-down regimentation of group behaviour that would become a mark of the Soviet regime.

After four days on the slow-moving train, the party reached the Baltic coast. They boarded a steamer for the crossing to Sweden and then another train – without the German officers or any other constraint – to Stockholm. Here Lenin was greeted as an honoured guests by the mayor of the city. Lenin was prevailed upon to buy a new suit of clothes to replace the threadbare jacket and the hobnail boots that he had been wearing in exile. He thought this was a sinful waste

of party funds. 'I am not going back to Russia to open a gentleman's outfitter's,' he grumbled. But he relented. Radek even persuaded Lenin to invest in a respectable homburg (not the proletarian peaked cap that he later adopted).

It was in this bourgeois attire that Lenin completed his journey. That last leg took him up through Sweden, then down through the Russian province of Finland and into Petrograd. His supporters in the city, alerted by telegram to his imminent arrival, arranged for flags and crowds and a military band to play 'The Marseillaise' as his train drew in at the Finland Station. A welcome such as this was becoming customary for returning revolutionaries, but the Bolsheviks in Petrograd put on a show that far outstripped any previous homecoming, and that was designed to demonstrate the (largely imaginary) popularity of their leader.

AFTER THE FINLAND STATION
Leninists and left-wing sympathisers have allowed the triumph of Lenin's arrival at the Finland Station to mask the uncertainty of the moment. As soon as he caught his breath, Lenin promulgated a bold strategy to seize power that struck all his comrades as wrong-headed and hopelessly out of touch with the political reality. Yet Lenin is such a towering figure in communism that it seems unthinkable that his revolutionary comrades might ever have disagreed with him. Still more unconscionable is the possibility that he might have been subject to self-doubt. With hindsight, it is hard to countenance the fact that Lenin, by collaborating with the Germans, might have squandered his chance of power before he even set foot in Russia – that he risked everything on the episode known to history as the 'sealed train'.

Moonshots and murder plots

We are all constantly being lied to – or so many people believe. It is widely claimed that governments and shadowy state organisations are hiding the truth about matters such as the deaths of President Kennedy and Princess Diana, and the missions to the Moon. Is there any truth in these stories? Or is there a different, altogether deeper truth that explains them?

All the best-known and most successful conspiracy theories have certain things in common. In a nutshell, they are all predicated on the idea that a damaging truth has been covered up by certain vested interests (usually national governments). The alleged cover-up is always sloppy or incomplete – and that is what makes it possible, for those who are determined enough, to piece together 'clues' and find a hidden historical truth behind the supposedly cooked-up 'official' version.

The most elaborate of all conspiracy theories has been woven around the assassination of John F. Kennedy in 1963. The official version says that the president was killed by a lone assassin, Lee Harvey Oswald. But according to the various conspiracy theories, the murder was a professional hit carried out on the orders of a group of international bankers, or else the FBI, or the CIA, or Cuban leader Fidel Castro, or anti-Castro Cuban exiles, or Kennedy's deputy Lyndon B. Johnson, or Texas oil interests, or the Israeli government, or the Soviet Union – and these are just some of the candidates.

One point on which nearly all Kennedy conspiracists agree is that Oswald was not the only gunman in Dealey Plaza that sad day. Either he was part of a team, or else he was a decoy whose unwitting function was to distract attention from the real assassins. Theorists say that it would be impossible for one marksman, however proficient, to fire three accurate shots in the timeframe of a few seconds, as Oswald is said to have done. Crucially, they say that the injuries suffered by the president and by Texas Governor John Connally (who was sitting in front of Kennedy in the car) cannot be explained by the contention that two shots hit the passengers from behind.

HISTORICAL ACCIDENTS

Down the years, many plausible experts have cast doubt on the lone-gunman idea, and hundreds of complex experiments have been carried out to prove it wrong. But nearly all of the reconstructions and closely argued rebuttals have been based on misunderstandings and misinterpretations of the available facts (*see* box, opposite).

The myth of the magic bullet

All conspiracy theories about the Kennedy assassination boil down to a discussion of the so-called 'magic bullet'. Conspiracists say that for one bullet to have struck Kennedy in the throat, then Connally in the shoulder, and to have ended up embedded in Connally's left leg, it would have had to have zigzagged impossibly in the air. Therefore, there must have been other shots fired. But it is not impossible for one bullet to have injured both men if their exact relative positions are taken into account. Connally's jump seat was not directly in front of Kennedy's, but closer to the centre of the car. It was also about 8cm (3in) lower than Kennedy's. And he was not facing forward, but was twisted in his seat to speak to the president. Given these facts, the single bullet makes perfect sense. It made just a slight deflection as it passed through Connally's body – as one would expect.

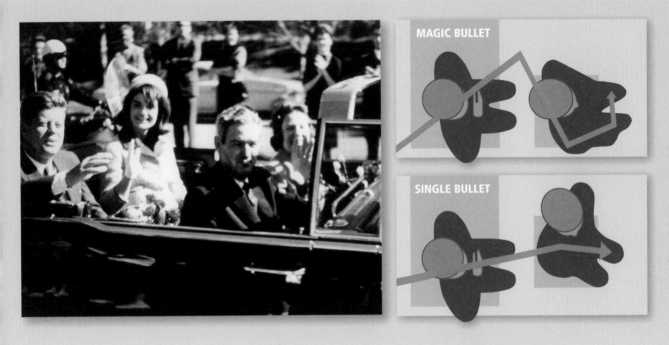

MAGIC BULLET

SINGLE BULLET

And yet millions of people remain deeply attached to the idea that the true story of Kennedy's murder has been hidden from us. It is as if we cannot bring ourselves to believe that a life so promising, that such a spectacular arc of history, can be obliterated by one deranged and otherwise insignificant individual.

In retrospect, all the facts of history appear to be inevitable and somehow pre-determined. From the vantage point of the present day, it always seems that the events and processes of the past were moving inexorably towards a particular outcome, that things could not have turned out any other way. But the unsettling fact is that tiny circumstances can make huge differences to real-life outcomes, and do so all the time – almost invariably without our noticing. Imagine, for example, how different the Second World War would have been without Stalin, Churchill or Hitler at the helm of their respective countries. Yet each of them had fought in other wars and might easily have been killed in action as younger men.

THE LANDING CRAFT *Conspiracists say there should be a blast crater beneath the landing craft; since there is none, the ship must have been placed there. But the craft landed gently, on rock. Any dust raised by touchdown soon settled.*

THE STARLESS SKY *No stars are visible in any of the photographs, so it must be a painted backdrop. But the Apollo astronauts took all their pictures in the sunlight of the lunar morning. The stars were not bright enough to be captured on film.*

THE SHADOWS *Some of the shadows in the photographs point in different directions, so they must have been lit by studio lights rather than by the Sun alone. Not so: all of the apparent anomalies in the shadows can be explained by the uneven lunar surface.*

THE ASTRONAUTS *The fact is, there is certain proof that men have been to the Moon. It lies in the traces they left behind. Photographs taken from space by the Lunar Reconnaissance Orbiter show apparatus abandoned by successive manned missions – as well as those much-debated footprints, made long ago by the first walkers on the Moon.*

THE FOOTPRINTS *Such clear imprints could only be made in a damp substance, such as wet sand; since there is no moisture on the moon, this moonscape is fake. But moondust particles are tiny, like flour. This consistency allows for sharply defined prints.*

If that had come to pass, we would not now think it strange that they were absent from the record. They would simply never have become part of history.

As for assassinations, lone gunmen are often the culprits. One man acting alone (but known to others) murdered President Abraham Lincoln in 1865; John Kennedy's brother Robert was killed by a lone gunman in 1968, as was John Lennon in 1980, and Britain's sole assassinated prime minister, Spencer Perceval, in 1812. Why should Lee Harvey Oswald not belong to this sorry roster? After all, a matter of months before Kennedy's murder, Oswald had attempted to assassinate an army general by shooting him, anonymously, from a distance. He was a proven lone gunman before he ever settled into his sniper's nest on the sixth floor of the Texas School Book Depository.

DEATH OF A PRINCESS

A similar aversion to the heartbreaking randomness of life lies at the root of the conspiracy theories surrounding the death of Princess Diana in 1997. People die in cars every day; the mere fact of a well-known person having a fatal crash is not remarkable in itself. But Diana's untimely death – because she was so famous and so loved – seemed like an unthinkable occurrence, something too extraordinary to be an accident. And yet the driver of her car had been drinking (without doubt), he was driving too fast in order to outrun the pursuing paparazzi, and Diana was not wearing a seat belt. In any other instance, these things would be seen by all reasonable observers – experts and laypeople alike – as factors that contributed to the fatal outcome. Conspiracists assert that the seat belt had

been tampered with as part of a carefully choreographed murder attempt, but there is no evidence for this.

In the end, the simple cause-and-effect explanation of an event is always infinitely more likely to be true than a profoundly complex and convoluted explanation. Conspiracists would maintain that that is precisely what 'they' want you to think – but it is true nevertheless.

UFOS AND MOON MOVIES

A common element of many conspiracy theories is the belief that governments routinely lie to their citizens. This is the essential background to the largest-scale conspiracy theory of all, the assertion that the Earth has been occupied, or at least visited by, beings from other planets.

The immense size of the cosmos makes that theory highly unlikely, and yet there is a body of serious-minded literature describing the many species or types of alien – greys, Andromedans and others – that have made contact with our world. Various theories have been advanced to explain the myriad cases of close encounter, alien abduction and 'flying saucers'. But since UFOs and aliens only really began to be reported in the late 1940s, a more probable explanation is that they represent a fear of hostile foreigners ('enemy aliens', as they were termed in the Second World War). They are, most likely, a hobgoblin of the cold-war mindset, and all the sightings and meetings down the years have entirely terrestrial explanations.

Another implausible claim believed by some is that the manned Apollo missions to the Moon were a hoax. According to the theory, no astronaut ever went there. Instead, the landings were staged in a studio in order to score an apparent victory over the Soviet Union in the cold-war space race, or else as a propaganda stunt directed at the American people. The evidence cited for this claim consists mostly of doubts about the photographic and film evidence. It is said, for example, that the moonscape is demonstrably identical in locations that were ostensibly miles apart, suggesting that the footage was shot on a small movie set; that the photographs have been lit from various angles, as if with an array of spotlights; that the US flag on the surface flutters as if in a slight breeze, when there can be no air movement on the Moon.

> Despite their cloak of reason, conspiracy theorists are as superstitious as the astrologers of old.

All of the objections have been shown to be based on mistaken premises about conditions on the Moon. The fluttering of the flag, for example, is the result of residual movement that came about in the moment that the flag was planted. The flag continues to flap for an inordinately long time because the absence of an atmosphere on the Moon – the very thing that conspiracists say makes it impossible for a flag to flutter – means that there is no air resistance to slow the flag's oscillation to a standstill. As for the photographic anomalies, they can be explained by the fact that sunlight is reflecting in surprising but entirely reproduceable ways.

Even if one ignores the shakiness of the visual evidence, the moonshot conspiracy theory is untenable. For the hoax to succeed, thousands of people would have to have been complicit, and to have kept it secret for the rest of their lives. Is it likely that no one – no cameraman, no false astronaut, no insider politician – would ever have spilled the beans? In the end, it would actually have been harder for the US government to pull off the hoax than to do what it in fact did: land a manned ship on the lunar surface.

THE CONSPIRATORIAL URGE

No disproof of a conspiracy theory will ever satisfy the true believers. Their theories are unfalsifiable, because those who undermine them can always be cast as stooges, as agents of a new and even deeper level of conspiracy. It has often been pointed out that conspiracy theory is like a communicable form of paranoia that can now spread more quickly than ever before because of the unfiltered conditions created by the internet. It has never been easier to publish conspiracy ideas to a global audience, and they look convincing because they seem to be using sound science and strict detective-like procedures to make their case.

And yet, despite their cloak of reason, conspiracy theorists are as superstitious as the astrologers of old. They look at vast, haphazard constellations of events and try to join up the dots, to impose some order and significance on what they see. Sadly, they are looking in places where there is at best very little order or meaning, and most likely none at all to be found. The truth really is out there, but – disappointingly, perhaps – it is usually much simpler and more prosaic than some people would like it to be.

Paul isn't dead

One of the most absurd episodes in the annals of conspiracy theory concerns the supposed death of Paul McCartney in 1966. The 'clues' are multiple and everywhere – like scattered pieces of a mysterious Beatles jigsaw.

According to the theory, Paul McCartney stopped his car one night and offered a lift to a young woman named Rita (later the subject of the song 'Lovely Rita'). She accepted, not knowing at first who the driver was. When she realised the truth she threw her arms around Paul, causing him to lose control of the car and crash. To conceal the fact of his death, McCartney was replaced in the band by a man named William Campbell, who had previously won a McCartney lookalike competition. Campbell could play bass, but had to be trained to play left-handed.

This secret switch allowed the surviving Beatles to continue their lucrative careers. But for reasons that are never addressed by the conspiracy theorists, they filled their songs and album covers with clues to Paul's death. The group shot on the cover of *Sgt Pepper's Lonely Hearts' Club Band*, for example, is said to portray a graveside gathering, featuring – among other hints – a wreath in the shape of a bass guitar. On the cover of *Magical Mystery Tour*, Paul is dressed as a walrus, which was said to be the Greek word for a corpse (it isn't).

The cover of *Abbey Road* is supposed to be full of references to a funeral. John, in his white suit, was said to represent a priest (though priests generally wear black); Ringo in his dark suit was an undertaker; Paul, out of step with the others, is barefoot – which (conspiracists said) is how corpses are buried in Italy; George in his denims represents a gravedigger. The number plate on the car in the background – significantly, a Beetle – reads 281F, a clue that McCartney would have been '28 [years old] IF' he had lived – though in fact he was 27 at the purported time of the crash.

COVER VERSION *What is the meaning of the black police van on the* Abbey Road *cover? Why is left-handed Paul carrying a cigarette in his right hand? Is it proof that it isn't him?*

The idea that there is symbolism in the clothes that the four Beatles are wearing on the *Abbey Road* cover originated in a spoof review of the album written for an American college magazine. The author of that review, a student named Fred LaBour, was astonished when his joke was picked up by serious news organisations and made the centrepiece of the 'Paul is Dead' evidence. If the McCartney conspiracy proves anything, it is that any material can be used to support a nonsensical idea, so long as the theorisers insist, above all, that their theory is true.

Der Staatsanwalt

des Bezirkes/Kreises

Strafsache

Chapter 2
INFORMATION IS POWER

Throughout history, people have known that possession of a secret is a form of strength, that a well-crafted lie can confer an advantage, and that the plain truth is sometimes best kept hidden.

The heresy police

The Spanish Inquisition was a unique institution in the history of the Catholic Church. Though it was staffed and run by monks, it answered not to the Pope in Rome, but to the Spanish monarch. It functioned, in effect, as a kind of early secret police, and it used some surprisingly modern, totalitarian methods to root out its supposed enemies, and so control the populace.

Five hundred years after its terrifying heyday, the reputation of the Spanish Inquisition can still chill the blood. One historian working in the 1960s described the Inquisition as 'the earliest version of the Nazi Gestapo', though it was founded as long ago as 1478. Another writer used the title *Red Inquisition* for a book on the Cheka, the bloodthirsty secret police organisation that evolved into the NKVD, then the KGB in Soviet Russia. Such comparisons recognise that the Spanish Inquisition foreshadowed the nightmare realities of both Nazism and Stalinism, and that its aims and techniques were ominously similar to those of the most oppressive regimes of the 20th century.

One strikingly modern aspect of the Spanish Inquisition was its use of what we would now call 'social espionage', the practice of compelling ordinary citizens to spy on their neighbours by making them fear the consequences of not doing so. This was a standard means of control in both Stalinist Russia and Nazi Germany, where failing to report an enemy of the state was deemed equivalent to *being* an enemy of the state. In 16th-century Spain, the Inquisition was mainly concerned not with unorthodox Christian belief (as had been the case with an earlier inquisition in France) or with witchcraft (as in Germany) but with 'Judaizers' – Jews who had been forced to convert to Christianity but secretly carried on observing the Jewish faith. These hidden Jews were seen as an enemy within, a fifth column. The fevered attitude of the Inquisition to *conversos* (converted Jews) has been likened to the anti-communist hysteria in the USA during the McCarthyite era of the 1950s, when thousands of Americans were denounced as traitors on very little evidence.

THE USES OF TERROR

The Inquisition's work always followed the same pattern. Its agents would come to a city and announce their presence at a special mass. Judaizers were invited to reveal themselves during a 'period of grace'. Those who did so were promised lenient punishment for their sin. Judaizers uncovered after the period of grace were subject to the full force of the Inquisition's

MEN ON TRIAL *In this painting of an Inquisitorial court at work, the accused wear the 'sambenito', the hat and penitential robes that denoted a condemned man. The artist, Francisco Goya (1746–1828), had reason to despise the Inquisition. Just before its demise he attracted its attention by painting nudes, at that time banned as obscene.*

powers, which included confiscation of all property, imprisonment and torture as a means of extracting a confession. The final sanction was 'relaxation to the secular arm', that is, to be handed over to the civil authorities and burned at the stake.

Not surprisingly, the Inquisitors usually persuaded their prisoners to say what was required. But a straightforward recantation of Jewish practices was not sufficient on its own. A confession was not deemed sincere unless the victim provided names of other Judaizers. Under torture, or the threat of it, prisoners named anyone they could think of – thereby providing a fresh crop of victims. The process was self-perpetuating

and all-encompassing, and in this respect was exactly analogous to the Great Terror that engulfed the USSR in the 1930s. And, as in Stalinist Russia, where show-trial victims claimed fantastical crimes for themselves, the frightened people of Inquisitional Spain admitted to ludicrous misdemeanours. In the town of Alcalá in 1564, for example, a 33-year-old woman denounced herself, having remembered that in her teens she had remarked that, 'You don't see me in misery in this world, nor will you find me suffering in the next.' She had realised, she said, that she had inadvertently blasphemed against the doctrine of the immortality of the soul.

The Inquisition let the woman off with a two-day fast and four Hail Marys. She was not a *converso*, after all, still less a Judaizer, and so was not the kind of sinner that interested the Inquisition.

THE SIGNS OF A SINNER

The Inquisition issued an Edict of Faith, a lengthy document that spelled out how to recognise a sinner. This was usually read out at a gathering of the entire local populace. A person should be denounced, says a typical edict, 'if they celebrate the Sabbath, wear a clean shirt or better garments, spread a clean tablecloth, light no fire, eat food which has been cooked overnight in the oven, or perform no work on that day; if they eat meat during Lent'. The edict goes into great detail: 'if they celebrate the seventh night after the birth

The list of suspicious signs ran to thousands of words.

of a child by filling a vessel with water, throwing in gold, silver, pearls, and grain, and then bathing the child while certain prayers are recited; if they throw a piece of dough in the stove before baking; if they wash their hands before praying, bless a cup of wine before meals and pass it round among the people at table ...' Other suspicious signs include: 'if they pronounce blessings while slaughtering poultry, cover the blood with earth, separate the veins from meat, soak the flesh in water before cooking, and cleanse it from blood; if they eat no pork, hare, rabbits, or eels; if they give Old Testament names to their children,

or bless the children by the laying on of hands; if the women do not attend church within forty days after confinement ...' The rituals of death are not spared: 'if the dying turn toward the wall; if they wash a corpse with warm water; if they recite the Psalms without adding at the end "Glory be to the Father, the Son and the Holy Ghost"...'

This is a just short extract. The full list of incriminating behaviours runs to thousands of words. And, though the practices described are mainly concerned with known Jewish rituals, there were grey areas that could place absolutely anyone under suspicion, especially acts of omission such as 'not eating eels'.

The sheer number of signs made them impossible to recall in detail, and this fostered an attitude of mind where any quirk of behaviour, the smallest departure from the norm, might be interpreted by some frightened, confused soul as a mark of heresy – leading to a denunciation. So it was that people were reported to the Inquisition for urinating against a church wall, or for smiling at the mention of the Virgin Mary, or for expressing the opinion (commonplace even then) that fornication is not a sin.

In Barcelona, in 1666, a priest was prosecuted for saying that 'he would prefer to be in hell beside a Frenchman than in heaven beside a Castilian'. In the city of Córdoba, a young theologian named Membreque was arrested for mentioning the doctrines of the Jews in a sermon; all 107 members of his congregation were brought before the Inquisition for having listened to it. This is the same spirit of fear and uncertainty, the same mass psychosis, that in the 1930s saw people in Russia denounced as wreckers and Trotskyites for such trivial offences as failing to cut photographs of Stalin out of *Pravda* before using it for toilet paper.

The Inquisition did not rely just on the cooperation of the ordinary population. It had a vast machinery for seeking out enemies. This included a network of specially built jails (on a smaller scale, these were not unlike the urban HQs of the NKVD, or the political prison camps of the Nazi regime). The Inquisition also had its own army of informers known as *familiares*. These collaborators were not clerics like the Inquisitors, but laypeople who enjoyed certain privileges as a result of their association with the Inquisition – not least a reduced likelihood of becoming victims themselves.

Belongings confiscated from victims of the Inquisition – some of whom were very wealthy indeed – officially became the property of the state, though in practice some were siphoned off by individual Inquisitors. Once again, it is easy to see the parallel with Nazi Germany, where the treasures and heirlooms of many a prominent Jewish family ended up in the homes of high-ranking party members.

THE STATE CENSOR

The parallels do not end there. The Inquisition – like 20th-century secret police from East Germany to China – took responsibility for monitoring the influx of information into the country. It was, among other things, a political censor. The Inquisition banned certain books, prohibited authors deemed hostile to the Church or to the Spanish state, and insisted that permitted works were edited according to its own sensitivities. It cut a single, bafflingly innocent sentence from *Don Quixote*, perhaps the greatest work of Spanish literature. That sentence read: 'Works of charity performed negligently have neither merit nor value.' The Inquisition had a kind of border police,

the *Inquisición de los Puertos de la Mar* (the 'Inquisition of Ports and Sea'), which searched foreign ships at dock for printed material, its operatives as strict and capricious as any North Korean border guard. In 1575 an English sailor in Seville was arrested for possessing a devotional tract entitled *The Treasury of Gladness*.

The Inquisition wanted to eradicate 'thoughtcrime'.

In the end, the apparatus of oppression, and the suppression of free thought, slowed Spain's political development, cutting it off from the enlightened ideas that swept Europe in the 17th and 18th centuries. In attempting to keep Spain ideologically 'pure', the Inquisition succeeded only in holding it back. It resembled the worst police states of the 20th century in that it was interested not just in how people behaved but in *what they thought*.

The Inquisition, it might be said, was determined to eradicate the dissident attitude of mind, the very 'thoughtcrime' that George Orwell identified much later in his novel *Nineteen Eighty-Four*. Its insistence on public recantations and secret denunciations was designed to deprive people of every vestige of a personal inner life, to leave people without even a tiny corner of their soul that they could call their own. They were startlingly ahead of their time because they wanted all their victims to love Christ (or their vengeful vision of him) in the same unquestioning way that Orwell's anti-hero Winston Smith ends up loving Big Brother.

EUREKA *A painting by Joseph Wright acknowledges the debt of modern science to alchemy in its title:* The Alchymist, in Search of the Philosopher's Stone, Discovers Phosphorus *(1771).*

| 16TH CENTURY | EUROPE

The mystic art

Turning base metals into gold and creating the Elixir of Life to *achieve immortality – these were the most famous, and notorious, goals of alchemy. But many alchemists were also seeking answers to the deep, spiritual mysteries of life. It was from this arcane and secretive world of visionaries and charlatans that the modern science of chemistry emerged.*

In 1507 John Damian de Falcius strapped on a pair of wings made of chicken feathers and threw himself from the parapet of Stirling Castle in Scotland. His intention was to fly to France, but instead he crashed in a dung heap just beyond the castle gardens and broke his thighbone.

Damian was widely mocked, but he was no fool. He was a respected thinker who had the patronage of King James IV of Scotland, an enlightened Renaissance prince who spoke six foreign languages, established Scotland's first printing press, and granted a charter to the Edinburgh College of Surgeons. James also set Damian up in a laboratory, paid him generously and made him Abbot of Tongland.

James believed – as did many educated people of his day – that base metals such as lead could be turned into gold through the processes of alchemy. It just needed someone to crack the formula. John Damian claimed to be that man, but, like thousands of alchemists before and after him, he was trying to achieve the impossible. It may be that his courageous attempt at flight – echoing the recent

experiments of Leonardo da Vinci in Italy – was a desperate stunt designed to divert attention from his failure to produce gold. If so, he need not have worried. James IV remained loyal to his faith in alchemy and kept the 'Flying Abbot' in his pay.

ALCHEMICAL ENIGMAS
Alchemy can be traced back to a body of mystical writings known as the *Hermetica*, said by the Greeks to have been penned by a shadowy figure named Hermes Trismegistus. The work became a byword for an esoteric approach to knowledge – a mixture of secret symbols and occult rituals that only the initiated could interpret, and which were believed to be the keys to great hidden truths.

The secretive, mystical nature of Hermeticism set the tone for medieval alchemists, who knew the works through translations from the Arabic. The first European alchemists also benefitted from original work by Muslim scientists. The very word 'alchemy' comes from the Arabic *al-kemiya*. The same Arabic word is also the root of 'chemistry', which is the modern study of the nature of matter. In medieval times, all European scholars subscribed to Aristotle's view that every substance is a fusion of four elements: earth, water, air and fire. But the Arabs had begun to chip away at this concept, largely through experiments in pursuit of practical goals, such as metal refining and medicine. The eighth-century scholar Jabir ibn Hayyan, known as Geber in Europe, is hailed as 'the father of chemistry' because he insisted on controlled and systematic experimentation to achieve repeatable results. He used early forms of standard benchtop instruments, such as the retort and alembic for distillation, and is credited with discovering how to make acids – a key means of reducing substances to their constituent elements.

GOLDEN WORKS OF GOD

For European scientists in medieval times, the attraction of alchemy was that it held out the promise of revealing how the Earth was formed. This pursuit was accepted as legitimate by the Church at first, because its intention was to reveal a truth about God's work. But there was another, less pious, prospect. If alchemists could discover how substances could be broken down into their constituent parts, could they not then use this knowledge in reverse and turn one substance into another – for instance, lead into gold?

Today it seems obvious that the transmutation of base metals into gold is impossible, but to medieval alchemists it appeared tantalisingly feasible. All they needed, it was supposed, was the 'philosopher's stone', a magical solvent or catalyst that could reverse the creative process. It was envisaged not so much as a lump of rock but as a powder, more specifically a red powder such as red

sulphur. For some alchemists, all this was a kind of metaphor. The true alchemy was something spiritual, and the alchemical manufacture of gold equated to the purification of the human soul.

Whatever its deeper meaning, the search for the philosopher's stone became a central quest for alchemists, an inquiry that called upon every branch of study from medicine to religious belief, hermetic ritual and astrology. Alchemy taught that human beings were linked in an all-encompassing universe of chemicals and elements, plants and planets, each with their symbols and correspondences. The philosopher's stone was associated by extension with the 'Elixir of Life', a potion that could bestow eternal life upon whoever drank it, and which could be a panacea, capable of curing all disease. This was as much a religious idea as a scientific or proto-scientific one.

Despite the religious overtones of alchemy, or perhaps because of them, the established Church turned against the practice. Figures such as the Franciscan philosopher William of Ockham declared that belief in God should be founded in faith alone, and any efforts to discover how God had achieved the Creation were disrespectful. In 1403 Henry IV of England banned the pursuit of alchemy except under licence. With a pragmatism typical of the English, however, this was not for religious reasons but for fear that if the transmutation of base metals into gold were achieved, the whole financial structure of the world would come crashing down.

Under pressure from the Church and the state, alchemists became ever more secretive. They wrote in code and secret symbols, at least in part to obscure what they were doing from the authorities. Their methods could readily be confused

Isaac Newton, physicist and magician

Sir Isaac Newton is justly famed for his theory of gravity as well as his ground-breaking contributions to mathematics, optics, the laws of motion and astronomy. What is less well known is that he also devoted a vast amount of energy and time to the secret pursuit of alchemy. Profoundly religious in an unconventional way, Newton hoped that a deeper spiritual understanding would help to unlock the laws of nature and so reconcile humanity to the knowledge that God, Creator of all things, had withdrawn after the Fall of Adam and Eve. Newton's extensive notes – much of them obscure and encoded – remained unpublished and virtually unknown until a sale in 1936. One of the buyers was the economist John Maynard Keynes. In 1947 Keynes published an essay that revealed this arcane side of Newton's work, and much more has been established since. In Keynes's view, this placed Newton in an entirely new historical perspective: 'Newton was not the first of the age of reason,' wrote Keynes. 'He was the last of the magicians.'

with sorcery or even interpreted as satanic practices. Alchemy became the stuff of lurid stories. The legend of Faust, for example, is based on a real character in early 16th-century Germany, Johann Faust. He was a magician, astrologer, necromancer and alchemist, who was said to have made a pact with the devil.

ALCHEMY AND CHEMISTRY

Alchemy was beginning to divide into two strands: spiritual and practical. Both still had gold in their sights. In the late 16th century, the English alchemist John Dee (*see* page 82) hoped that angels, summoned through his crystal ball, would deliver Christian purity to his soul and also vouchsafe to him the secret of gold.

Some alchemists, meanwhile, had begun to apply a systematic and practical approach to chemical experimentation, and the more rigorous methodology of modern chemistry was beginning to emerge. Slightly before Dee's time, the Swiss physician known as Paracelsus rejected occultism and magic in favour of experiments and careful observation, largely in his pursuit of chemical-based

medicines. Yet despite this scientific approach, his fame was linked primarily to a rumour that he had found the Elixir of Life. European kings continued to sponsor alchemists, who toiled beside their furnaces in the bowels of castles, inhaling the poisonous fumes of lead, mercury and sulphur, always in the hope of making some great discovery.

The alchemists were, in effect, striving to be scientists. Modern chemistry was born of medieval alchemy, and showed at last that alchemy was closer to superstition than it was to science. One might say that chemistry bears the same relationship to alchemy as astronomy does to astrology. In both disciplines, discoveries about the mechanisms of the universe were rooted in an earlier belief system. But in chemistry and astronomy, the truth could not have emerged without the work of people who hoped to find spiritual meaning in areas where the scientific facts were impersonal and had no human dimension. This is how knowledge progresses. To paraphrase the physicist and alchemist Isaac Newton: we see further, because we stand on the shoulders of giants.

Three men with a map

The leaders of the three main Allied nations – Winston Churchill, Joseph Stalin and Franklin D. Roosevelt – *came together only twice during the Second World War. But those two top-secret meetings led to a redrawing of the European map, and affected the fate of millions of people.*

Conferences between the three leaders of the Grand Alliance, as Churchill liked to call it, were a distinctive feature of the Second World War. For the first time in history, it was possible for a national leader to travel great distances in order to hold talks face to face. Churchill met Roosevelt and Stalin separately on several occasions, but only twice were all three men together in the same room: at Tehran in 1943, and at Yalta in 1944. Each leader came to the conference table like a slick cardsharp, aiming to play the hand that the war had dealt him as skilfully as possible. The prize that they were playing for was power and influence in the postwar world.

In October 1944, after Tehran but before Yalta, Churchill flew to Moscow for private talks with Stalin. His aim was to settle a few matters of European interest by means of what he himself described as a 'naughty document'. In his first meeting with Stalin, he made some notes on a scrap of paper (according to some Soviet accounts, he produced it already written from his pocket). Churchill's note consisted of a list of European countries where British or Soviet troops were then engaged, along with a percentage split, representing the postwar share of influence for Britain and the USSR. In Romania, the figure was 90:10 in Russia's favour; in Greece, 90:10 with the larger share going to Britain; Hungary was a straight 50:50; Bulgaria, 75 per cent Soviet Union, 25 per cent Britain. Stalin inspected the piece of paper. He then picked up a blue pencil and drew a big tick on one corner, then pushed it back across the table to Churchill – who now seemed to suffer a pang of conscience. 'Might it not be thought rather cynical,' he said, 'if it seemed we had disposed of these issues, so fateful to millions of people, in such an offhand manner? Let us burn the paper.' 'No, you keep it,' said Stalin.

THE POLISH QUESTION

Not a word was said about how these divisions of influence were to be managed or measured. And nothing was said about Poland, the USSR's neighbour to the west, and the country in defence of which Britain had declared war on Germany in the first place. But Poland's postwar fate was of vital interest to all the Allied leaders. It was discussed at a separate meeting, and

THE BIG THREE *The postwar world was taking shape by the time Churchill, Roosevelt and Stalin sat for pictures at Yalta. Stalin was gaining control of eastern Europe; Roosevelt, meanwhile, had declared himself unwilling to prop up Britain's empire.*

once again Churchill found a dramatic way of presenting his case. His took three matches out of a box and placed them on the table to represent the prewar borders of Germany, Poland and Russia. He moved all three matches to the left to demonstrate the idea that the USSR should be allowed to take a slice out of eastern Poland, while Poland took a compensatory slice out of eastern Germany. His suggestion was that the whole country be shifted to the west (*see* maps, overleaf).

But how far should Poland be moved? This question was much discussed by the Big Three at Tehran and Yalta. Stalin insisted that the USSR's border with Poland be set at the so-called Curzon Line, the frontier imposed by the British foreign minister Lord Curzon and the French

prime minister Clemenceau at the end of the First World War. He also demanded that the line be diverted in the south so that the largely Polish city of Lwow (now Lviv) should become Soviet territory. 'Do you want me to tell the Russian people that I am less Russian than Lord Curzon?' he said – and Roosevelt and Churchill gave way. There was little else they could do, since by the time of the Yalta conference Soviet troops were in possession of all the territory that constituted prewar Poland.

As for Poland's western border, the Big Three set this at a line corresponding to the Oder and Neisse rivers. But there are two rivers in Germany called the Neisse, and until Yalta no one had specified which one was meant. Stalin favoured the western Neisse, saying that would give more

1938   **1945**

POLAND REDRAWN *In 1945 a slice of prewar eastern Poland was ceded to the USSR, and a piece of Germany was grafted onto Poland in the west. Stalin refused Roosevelt's request that Poland's borders take in the ancient Polish city of Lwow (see dotted line on map): it became the Soviet city of Lvov (now Lviv). German Danzig, meanwhile, became Polish Gdansk.*

territory to the new Polish state. Churchill remarked that 'it would be a pity to stuff the Polish goose so full of German food that it got indigestion', meaning that it would be hard to relocate all the Germans in that territory. The matter was not resolved at Yalta, but Stalin got his way in the end. The line was ratified in July 1945, by which time the war was over and Soviet troops had advanced far beyond the western Neisse. There was nothing to stop Stalin fixing the border where he wanted it.

THE TWO EUROPES

Germany, consequently, was much reduced in size. Austria was hived off as a separate country, as it had been before the war, and the core German territory was split into occupation zones: British, American, French and Soviet. As for Churchill's percentage plan, it came to nothing. Despite the terms of the 'naughty document', Stalin's share

of influence was 100 per cent in all the countries occupied by his troops: Bulgaria, Romania, Hungary, Czechoslovakia, the newly reconstituted Poland and the Soviet zone of Germany, which became the German Democratic Republic. In all these countries, communist governments were installed, while the western occupation zones of Germany were welded together to form the Federal Republic of Germany.

This was the new map of Europe, forged around a table by three powerful men, each of them doing his best to cajole, persuade, bluff and stall the others. Stalin was the clear winner in this geopolitical game. For the first time in Russian history, Moscow had influence at the very heart of Europe and, more importantly, it had a buffer zone 900km (560 miles) wide: no enemy would be able to launch a surprise invasion from the west. The USSR was as secure as a medieval castle, and eastern Europe was its uncrossable moat.

The last secret of Yalta

At Yalta, Stalin made a side-deal concerning the fate of Russians who *found themselves in the western zones of occupation at the end of the war.*

In the first days of the Nazi invasion of the Soviet Union in 1941, many captured Soviet soldiers chose to join the German army rather than starve to death in a POW camp. Some of these soldiers were still fighting three years later: Georgians and Ukrainians were among those who faced the Allied invasion of Normandy in 1944. Those men had changed sides in a desperate attempt to stay alive; others had gone over more willingly. There was, for example, a mounted unit, the XV Cossack Cavalry Corps, that served in Russia as part of the Waffen-SS. And there was a formation known as the Russian Liberation Army, consisting of three divisions under the command of a Russian general, Andrei Vlasov. It fought briefly against the Red Army in Germany in 1945.

To Stalin, any ethnic Russian who had opposed the USSR was a traitor – and he wanted them all back, including rank-and-file deserters, and also men such as Pyotr Krasnov, anti-communist commander of the Cossack cavalry, who had never been a Soviet citizen. The repatriation deal also applied to civilian slave workers who had been deported from Nazi-occupied territories to work in German factories. Churchill and Roosevelt agreed to hand them all over to Stalin – and to keep the arrangement secret.

The 'forcible repatriations' were carried out by British and American troops in 1945 and 1946. Between 1.5 and 2 million Russians and other eastern Europeans were transported to the Soviet zone of occupation. Many of those who had served in the Wehrmacht were shot or hanged on the spot. The rest were consigned to the gulag, the prison camps of Siberia. Few came out alive, but some survived long enough to tell their tale. The writer Alexander Solzhenitsyn met some *vlasovtsy* – men of Vlasov's army – while he was in the camps. He wrote that their fate was 'truly the last secret, or one of the last, of the Second World War'. As for General Vlasov, he was captured by American troops, handed over to the Russians, and taken to Moscow. He spent a year in prison, and was executed in August 1946. The British arrested General Krasnov and likewise delivered their prisoner to the Russians. He too was hanged in a Soviet prison.

HITLER'S COSSACKS *Many Cossacks saw communism as the enemy of their traditional freedoms, and so fought with the Wehrmacht in the hope of bringing down communist rule.*

The corpse that lied

One morning, in the midst of war, the body of a British officer washed up on the coast of neutral Spain. He had drowned, it seemed, after the plane carrying him crashed into the sea. Chained to the body was a briefcase full of secret documents. Nazi agents in Spain were desperate to get their hands on the briefcase – and British intelligence was praying that they would succeed.

In the spring of 1943 the Second World War reached a turning point. Allied troops were on the verge of defeating the Germans in North Africa – 'the end of the beginning', as Winston Churchill would call it – and in the Soviet Union the *Wehrmacht* was on the retreat for the first time in nearly two years. The military initiative was with the British and Americans, and their obvious next move was to strike north from Africa into southern Europe. This would open up the Mediterranean Sea for Allied shipping, and would force the Germans to fight on a new front. Militarily, the best place to land invasion troops was the island of Sicily, off the toe of mainland Italy, and a relatively short distance from the Allies' platform on Africa's Mediterranean coast.

THE SICILY PROBLEM

But the strategic good sense of an attack on Sicily was as self-evident to the enemy as it was to the Allies. 'You'd have to be a bloody fool not to know it was Sicily,' remarked Churchill at the time – and his commanders told him that the Germans were already beginning to reinforce the island with big guns and fresh troops. But what if the Germans could be persuaded to doubt the obvious truth? If Hitler could be made to believe – or at least suspect – that the invasion force was going to land elsewhere, then he would have to spread his forces and so thin out his defences in Sicily. British intelligence had people whose job it was to plant that kind of doubt in the mind of the enemy, to play tricks that would lead German commanders into strategic errors. The hub of that network was the Twenty Committee – so called because 20 in Roman numerals is XX, that is, a 'double cross'.

One of the members of the Twenty Committee, a naval intelligence officer named Ewen Montagu, was asked to consider the Sicily problem. He first turned to a memorandum written by a fellow officer named Ian Fleming (later to achieve fame as the creator of James Bond). In 1939, at the outbreak of war, Fleming had compiled a list of 51 *ruses de guerre*, potential schemes for feeding false information to the Germans. Idea number 28 read: 'A suggestion (not a very nice one) … a corpse dressed as an airman, with despatches in his pockets, could be dropped on the coast, supposedly from a parachute that had failed. There is no difficulty in obtaining corpses but, of course, it would have to be a fresh one.'

This caught Montagu's eye. He dismissed the parachute part of the idea but saw that the underlying principle might work. What if one were to craft a top-secret document to make it seem that the coming invasion force would be landing somewhere other than Sicily – Greece, say? One could plant that document on a dead body, then have it fall into German hands. But everything would have to be plausible: the state of the corpse, its apparent identity, the confidential paperwork, the manner in which the information came to the Germans' attention. This would be hard to pull off, but Montagu knew – as all good conjurors do – that many an illusion

succeeds because the dupe cannot credit the lengths that a trickster will go to. He put the plan forward, and Churchill swiftly gave it his go-ahead. The codename that Montagu chose for the operation was fittingly macabre: Mincemeat.

THE SEARCH FOR A BODY

Montagu was teamed up with Charles Cholmondeley, an army officer attached to MI5. The first task of their joint enterprise was to find a suitable corpse – a part of the plan that Ian Fleming thought would be easy. It turned out to be fiendishly difficult. Montagu and Cholmondeley had already decided that their man was to be found floating in the sea off Spain, as if he were the victim of a plane crash, so they needed a male of military age who had died of a cause compatible with drowning. This alone was tricky enough: even in wartime, young men do not just drop dead, and there was no easy way for Montagu to know when one did. And if the right kind of corpse were found, how was it to be commandeered from the relatives of the deceased? Montagu needed a usable body, and he needed it soon. He began to consider the option of graverobbing, but at the same time approached Sir Bentley Purchase, coroner of St Pancras in central London. Sir Bentley was completely trustworthy, and he soon found what Cholmondeley and Montagu were looking for.

INVENTING MAJOR MARTIN

One cold night early in 1943, Glyndwr Michael, a 34-year-old Welsh vagrant, took his own life by ingesting rat poison in a disused warehouse in King's Cross, close to St Pancras. Sir Bentley alerted Montagu that the perfect candidate had arrived in his morgue. There was a sad but fortuitous bonus: the dead man had no next of kin, so there was no one who wanted to bury him. The Mincemeat team made discreet enquiries of an eminent pathologist, who told them that rat poison would not show up in a standard autopsy. If this body were pulled from the sea, a workaday pathologist would find no reason to think that the man had died of a cause other than drowning.

The corpse was put on ice while Cholmondeley and Montagu set about creating a plausible identity for the man. First they made a sailor of him. If word leaked back of an army officer dead at sea, too many people among the British top brass might wonder and ask questions, but a drowned naval officer was not news, not in wartime. So he became a navy man, though that created a new problem. Naval officers wore tailored uniforms, and having the frozen dead body measured and fitted would be both ghastly and impractical. Montagu therefore made Martin a Royal Marine; he would still be the responsibility of the Royal Navy, but he could wear off-the-peg battledress like a soldier. A new uniform was ordered from the quartermaster, and Cholmondeley wore it for a month to give it a slightly lived-in appearance.

THE GIRLFRIEND
Major Martin's fiancée Pam was, in fact, Jean Leslie, a secretary in MI5, whose day job was analysing intercepted German signals. Montagu came to believe in his fiction so completely that he always addressed Jean as 'Pam'.

The dead man was now given a name: William Martin. There were several Martins in the Marines, and this fact might add a touch more verisimilitude to the deceit. Moreover, it was known that German Intelligence had a copy of the army list – the complete roll-call of British officers – but only as far as the letter L. They would not be able to check against their list to corroborate the identity of the body. Martin's rank was set as acting major – about right for his age, and senior enough for him to have been entrusted with confidential documents.

> *They provided Martin with a fiancée and named her Pam.*

The next problem was an identity card. Cholmondeley and Montagu tried photographing the dead visage of Glyndwr Michael, but that didn't look right: he was too obviously cadaverous. They needed a convincing lookalike, and they took to scouring the streets of London, hoping to bump into someone with the same lean features, the same receding temples. The search was fruitless until, one day, an officer dropped by Naval Intelligence who was the very spit of the deceased Mr Michael. His photograph was soon on Martin's ID card. The card was stamped as a replacement – as if the major had mislaid the original – and this explained its recent issue.

But Major Martin needed more than a military background, he needed a personal life. Montagu and Cholmondeley dreamed one up for him as if he were a character in a book. And, like first-time novelists, they worked hard to make their creation believable, three-dimensional. They provided Martin with a fiancée named Pam. One of the young women working as an analyst in Naval Intelligence donated a photograph of herself for Martin to carry in his wallet. A different woman, the elderly chief secretary of MI5, wrote love letters purporting to be from Pam: 'That lovely golden day we spent together … oh, I know it has been said before, but if only time could stand still for just a minute …'

Bill and Pam were due to be married: among the items procured for him was a receipt for an engagement ring bought at a London jeweller's. It was an expensive one – but Major Martin was rather careless with money, as a sharp letter from the manager of Lloyds Bank made clear. It informed Martin that his overdraft had reached the unacceptable level of more than 37 pounds. These and other artefacts, such as a St Christopher's medal, were gathered together, ready to be tucked into his wallet or the pockets of his uniform.

THE FALSE LETTER

So this was the Major Martin that Mincemeat wanted to sell to the Germans: a man in love, perhaps absent-minded, financially embarrassed, nominally Roman Catholic. He was also a capable and reliable staff officer – because he had been entrusted with hand-delivering a highly sensitive document. A great deal of thought went into the contents of that document. It had been decided that it would take the form of a personal letter from General Archibald Nye, Vice-Chief of the Imperial General Staff, to General Harold Alexander, the British commander in Tunisia. The letter began: 'My dear Alex, I am taking advantage of sending

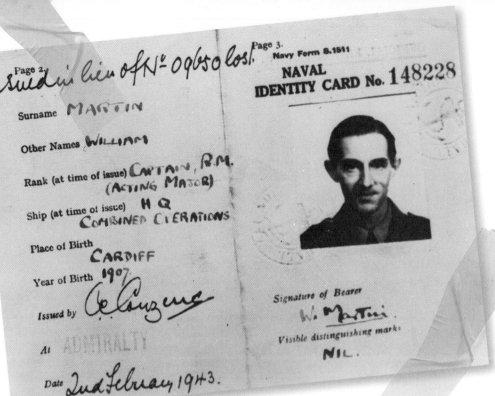

NAVAL
IDENTITY CARD No. 148228

Surname MARTIN

Other Names WILLIAM

Rank (at time of issue) CAPTAIN, R.M.
(ACTING MAJOR)

Ship (at time of issue) H Q
COMBINED OPERATIONS

Place of Birth CARDIFF

Year of Birth 1907

Issued by *(signature)*

At ADMIRALTY

Date 2nd February 1943.

Signature of Bearer
W. Martin.

Visible distinguishing marks
NIL.

THE MUGSHOT
The major's identity card was one of the most difficult parts of the deception to pull off. But no one guessed that the man in the picture was not the man in the Spanish morgue – not least because his face was beginning to decompose.

you a personal letter by hand of one of Mountbatten's officers …' and waffled on about matters such as the Americans' unfortunate practice of awarding Purple Hearts to British soldiers wounded while serving with them. It then named two landing sites in Greece for the invasion, and mentioned Sicily just as a 'cover target for HUSKY'. Husky was the genuine codeword for the planned Mediterranean invasion – not of Greece, as the letter implied, but of Sicily, which the letter specifically ruled out.

The letter was placed in a briefcase that was attached to Major Martin's body with a chain. He was ready to go. But the body had by now been in cold storage for some weeks, and this created an unexpected last-minute snag. His feet were frozen stiff, and it was impossible to get his boots on. Cholmondeley and Montagu had to thaw his ankles with an electric heater until they were pliable enough to slide the boots on. The body was then packed into a cylinder filled with dry ice and driven overnight to Scotland. Here it was loaded onto a submarine. On the night of April 29, 1943,

HMS *Seraph* surfaced a kilometre (half a mile) off Huelva, on Spain's Atlantic coast. The crew brought the canister on deck, where the body was unpacked. *Seraph*'s captain, by way of an afterthought, read the 39th Psalm as the body slipped into the water: 'I was dumb with silence, I held my peace … I opened not my mouth …'

MINCEMEAT SWALLOWED

And so the floating body was found by fishermen returning from their night's work. They handed it over to the Spanish navy, who delivered it to the local mortuary. The Spanish authorities alerted the local British consul and invited him to attend the autopsy. This was an unpleasant affair, as Major Martin was rapidly decomposing. The consul (who was in on the Mincemeat plan) suggested to the Spanish doctors that they call a halt – and they readily agreed. The dead Englishman was a Catholic after all, and post-mortems were frowned on by the Roman Church. The cause of death was recorded as drowning, and the body was released to the consul for burial.

D for Deception: Operation Fortitude

Operation Mincemeat was not the only time that Allied sleight of hand fooled Hitler. The same principle, but with a different bag of tricks, kept the Germans guessing about the D-Day landings of June 1944. As with the invasion of Sicily in 1943, there was no hiding the fact that an attack on France was coming. American troops had been massing in Britain for months, and vast quantities of ships and trucks had been spotted by German reconnaissance planes. Given that the invasion was undisguisable, the Allies did their best to keep the Germans guessing about its exact time and place. This was Operation Fortitude.

The Nazis did not know that all their agents in Britain had been captured. Some of them had been turned and were now sending radio messages to their controllers suggesting that the main force was heading for the Pas de Calais (where the distance across the Channel is shortest). German intelligence was also fed false information to the effect that a large diversionary force might land in Normandy (where the real landing beaches were). All this was backed up by manufactured physical evidence: balsawood planes and rubber tanks that looked real enough in aerial photographs, and a blizzard of radio signals between non-existent army units in Kent, the closest point to Calais. These measures persuaded the Germans to hedge their bets even after the invasion began: for weeks they held Panzer divisions back to meet the expected Calais invasion.

To reinforce these deceptions, the Allies invented an entirely fictitious US Army Group, to be commanded by the real General George Patton. The Germans knew Patton, and feared him above all commanders. When he did not appear in France in June, this strongly suggested that the Normandy landings were a mere diversion. Even genuine war activity was used to deceive: for every bomb dropped on targets in Normandy, two were directed at the Pas de Calais. They were a violent but eloquent way of persuading the Nazi war machine to look the wrong way.

As for the crucially deceptive documents, they were handed back to the Spanish navy for safe-keeping. Spain, though neutral in the war, was very much pro-Nazi. The success of the plan depended on the Spanish authorities flouting diplomatic custom and passing the documents to Germany's agents. Honourably, but unaccountably, the Spanish navy refused to do so. Instead they sent General Nye's letter and all of Major Martin's effects to Madrid. It was some time before Germany's chief agent in Spain could persuade his contacts to let him see the contents of Major Martin's briefcase – and all the while the British ambassador made a noisy show of demanding that they be passed to him unopened. Photographs of the documents were made in haste and flown to Berlin. In May, Nye's letter was brought to the attention of Hitler himself. 'No doubts remain regarding the reliability of the captured documents,' noted the accompanying communiqué. 'Examination as to whether they were intentionally put into our hands shows that this is most unlikely.'

Hitler was convinced. He pored over his maps, and began to move units away from Sicily – from all over the European theatre, in fact – to shore up defences in Greece. When Sicily was invaded in July 1943, Allied casualties were surprisingly light. Major Martin – the unhappy and unsung Glyndwr Michael – had done his posthumous duty, and saved many lives.

The Stasi files

The secret police was the largest employer in communist East Germany. *In the 1980s it had 91,000 employees and 174,000 informers, and it kept files on more than 5 million people – about a third of the population. Those files tell a story of state paranoia and petty everyday betrayal.*

In the autumn of 1989, the Berlin Wall began to crumble and the communist German Democratic Republic entered its death throes. During those strange and hopeful days, citizens in towns across the country noticed odd phenomena in and around offices belonging to the Stasi, the East German secret police. Palls of smoke hung in the sky above its faceless grey buildings, and convoys of trucks were heading out from Stasi HQs into the countryside. It soon transpired that the lorries were carrying documents to paper mills, to be pulped. The Stasi was destroying huge amounts of evidence of its repressive activities over the past four decades; it was attempting to cover its tracks. The process continued even after the Wall came down in November; in December and in January the following year, people stormed Stasi headquarters in Erfurt and Berlin, among other cities, to stop the shredding and burning of files.

The Stasi was modelled on the KGB and, like the Soviet secret police, it was responsible both for foreign espionage and for covert surveillance within the state's borders. But in proportion to the civilian population, the Stasi was far larger than the KGB or any other secret police service in eastern Europe. In fact, by the same measure, the Stasi was about seven times bigger even than Hitler's secret state police, the Gestapo. It has been estimated that the files amassed by the Stasi, and preserved by the action of democratically minded German people, occupy a total of 178km (110 miles) of shelving.

ENEMIES AND INFORMERS

Much of this vast mountain of material is made up of case files on individual East German citizens. The files on prominent dissidents or critics of the regime run to ten or more bundles; others contain just a few sheets of paper. But almost every file contains information provided by informers – friends, work colleagues, even family members of the person under observation. To the Stasi, these low-level internal spies were known as *inoffizielle Mitarbeiter,* unofficial co-workers, or IMs for short. Though they were unpaid and untrained, they were a key element of political control in the East German police state. 'The unofficial co-workers,' stated a manual for Stasi officers, 'are the most important factor in the fight against the

SHELF LIFE *The records of the Stasi contain millions of written documents, along with photographs, tape recordings and other forms of evidence. The Stasi even stole clothes samples from suspects, which they stored in sealed jars, so that the owners could be pursued by tracker dogs if they tried to escape to the West.*

secret activities of the class enemy'. This army of amateur spies was immense. It has been said that there was a part-time Stasi agent in every classroom and lecture theatre, every factory, every office, every social club and church congregation, in absolutely any collective of any size.

The IMs were not usually volunteers. In the first instance, they were approached by Stasi and invited to inform. Some agreed readily out of political conviction, because they wanted to 'protect the GDR'. Others were flattered by the importance that the Stasi was always careful to attach to the task. A small minority of informers

were press-ganged by being confronted with some past or present misdemeanour, such as illegal contact with people in the West. New informers had to sign an oath of silence and were allowed to choose their own codename. Many opted for cute or slightly dashing names: Angel, Artist, Sugar, Notary or Cherry.

A Stasi controller was empowered to help his IMs in various ways – clearing bureaucratic obstacles to a new flat or a promotion, for example. This had the effect of binding IMs to the organisation by debts of gratitude. A Stasi controller might come to be seen as an influential friend, and the operational meetings a kind of secret tryst. 'One should not forget to offer female unofficial employees something sweet to eat,' recommended the Stasi manual.

Even in the German Democratic Republic, the most Orwellian of states, it was not possible for the police to watch everyone. The Stasi concentrated its attention on dissident intellectuals and their circles, on church groups, and on any affiliation, however informal, that looked

Some informers used the Stasi to settle personal scores.

like it might have social change as its goal. Ecological clubs were a special Stasi obsession in the 1980s. And it was also interested in moral weakness – evidence of drunkenness or adultery, say – since these things could be used against a person. It tried to undermine pastors and priests by putting sexual temptation in their way. But most of the information gathering was passive; it consisted of IMs listening to what people said, writing it up, and handing it in like homework.

Some informers, uneasy with what they were doing, deliberately fed the Stasi boring accounts of insignificant incidents, or went out of their way only to say positive things about the people they had been asked to spy on. Such unhelpful co-workers were usually spotted and decommissioned. Yet even enthusiastic IMs were generally undiscriminating. They had to produce something to keep the Stasi happy, so quantity of information was more important

than quality. One informer in Gransee in the 1960s told his controller that he heard someone in a café say that their TV set could receive 'capitalist' channels; another customer, he wrote, showed a friend photographs of his trip to West Germany. All this was duly noted and filed away.

A university lecturer wrote in a report that his son had told him about a child at school who had admitted going to church. He added proudly that his son 'knew enough to tell the teacher'. Some informers used their Stasi connection in an attempt to settle personal scores. A lawyer in Perleberg denounced the cleaner in his office, saying that she took a suspicious interest in Soviet troop trains. The case officer looked into it, and discovered that the lawyer had made a pass at the cleaner and been refused; her trips to the freight yard were to see her lover, a railway worker.

INFORMATION OVERLOAD
So the IM data was not always reliable, but then the intelligence gathered by Stasi professionals was often banal and useless too. The writer Erich Loest, for example, was under surveillance round the clock. His file contained endless dull (but nonetheless chilling) passages along the following lines: 'L kissed his wife. L then went to the kitchen and made a cup of tea. L returned to his study with the tea …'

The sheer mass of data provided by informers was, in the end, unmanageable. It was impossible for the Stasi to sift a potentially significant incident from the mass of unnecessary detail. But in a sense that was not the point. The power that the Stasi exercised was not contained in the files: it was a function of the mistrust that 'informer culture' sowed in society. Not everybody was being watched or reported on, but everyone knew that they might be

Stasi records as personal history

In 1991 the new united German government passed a law allowing citizens to have sight of their own Stasi file. By the end of 1994 about a million Germans had applied to do so. Many were deeply shocked to uncover how thoroughly their lives had been penetrated by the Stasi – and to find out who had been informing on them. One well-known activist learned that 50 acquaintances had reported on her. The trauma that was often engendered by the contents of Stasi files led some to question the wisdom of preserving them. Perhaps the material is too raw, they said, and it would be better (as in some other former communist countries) to lock them away for a generation at least. That way, they would be painless historical documents by the time they were examined. One church leader even suggested that a huge bonfire be made of the archive.

Meanwhile, tens of thousands of Germans applied to see their Stasi file only to find that they had never had one. This too was traumatic in its way: to believe that one was involved in the righteous struggle for political freedom, then to find that one's contribution was so insignificant as to be invisible to the all-seeing secret police. The one-time dissident poet Lutz Rathenow has called this unhappy feeling 'file envy', and in its way file envy is as likely to cause a person heartache as the discovery of a fat file filled with intrusion and treachery.

Occasionally the files revealed a silver lining. Some people found on reading their own case notes that people they had suspected of spying on them never did any such thing, and this knowledge has come as a happy relief, a form of closure. And the singer Wolf Biermann, whose political songs got him expelled from the country, was overjoyed to find in his file a letter from his deceased mother, written decades before but never delivered to him because it was intercepted by the Stasi and filed permanently in his dossier – until he came to read it.

being watched, and so an entire population – with some brave and honourable exceptions – lived in an environment where they dare not speak, let alone act, because of the risk attached. This uncertainty was a poison that the Stasi drip-fed into East German society. It induced a kind of political paralysis that kept the state safe from its own citizens. The Stasi itself understood this and – with exquisite irony – sometimes planted a rumour that a subject was a Stasi agent when they were no such thing, so as to undermine a 'hostile-negative' circle.

Viewed like this, the files themselves are a mere by-product of the Stasi's long years of surveillance activity. But they are powerfully toxic nevertheless, and still have the power to destroy lives and relationships. So, for example, a leading church activist named Vera Wollenburger learned from her Stasi file that her husband had enrolled as an IM years before they met and reported on her throughout their married life. The revelation led swiftly to divorce, though he claimed that he was only ever trying to change the Stasi's opinion of his wife, to influence their thinking. And the actor Ulrich Mühe – after playing a secret policeman in *The Lives of Others*, an acclaimed film about Stasi surveillance – discovered that his wife had been an informer. This came as a huge shock to the German public, as the Mühes were a well-loved celebrity couple. Before the story broke, Ulrich Mühe had been asked how he prepared for the role. He said, 'I remembered.'

Astrologer royal

With his long white beard and flowing robes, Dr John Dee was one of the strangest personalities in the court of Elizabeth I. He was also one of the most brilliant, but his indulgence in occult practices gave rise to rumours that he was in league with the devil. Much of his life remains a mystery – perhaps because he was not only a magician, he was also a spy.

Success came early to Dr John Dee. While still in his 20s, he was feted throughout Europe as a man of prodigious intellectual gifts. In 1542, at the age of 15, he had entered St John's College, Cambridge, and he became a founding fellow of Trinity College aged 19. He lectured in advanced algebra and geometry at Erasmus's university in Leuven (now in Belgium) and also at the University of Paris. He was a renowned mathematician who could turn his mind to practical matters such as navigation. One of his collaborators was the innovative Flemish cartographer Gerardus Mercator.

Like many scholars in the heady days of the Renaissance, Dr Dee had a hungry sense of curiosity about everything, not just spheres of knowledge that we would now think of as scientific. In an epoch when little distinction was made between observable, testable truths and magic, he pursued studies in astrology and alchemy, searching for a deeper understanding of the forces that control our lives.

Dee's precocious advancement was due in part to his family connections. His father had been a minor courtier during the reign of Henry VIII, and so Dee was brought up within the orbit of the royal household. He served as tutor to the young Edward VI, and when Edward's half-sister succeeded to the throne as Mary I in 1553, Dee was appointed astrologer to the new queen.

LIVING DANGEROUSLY

Two years later, however, Dee was in trouble. He had cast a horoscope for Princess Elizabeth, Mary's younger half-sister, in order to predict when the queen's reign would end. Clearly this was an act of treason, and might have cost Dee his head. In 1555 Dee was imprisoned at Hampton Court, but for some reason was not sent to the block. After a few months he was mysteriously released with a full pardon. This episode appears to have endeared Dee to Elizabeth – and she retained an interest in him when, in due course, she became England's queen. Elizabeth's steadfast support was his lifelong protection. And he needed it, because it was already being whispered that Dee was meddling with dangerous, satanic powers.

Dee became Elizabeth's trusted adviser on matters of science, and he was also her personal astrologer. He used charts and horoscopes to divine a favourable date for her coronation. He also acted as adviser and tutor to many leading ministers and courtiers, including William Cecil, Lord Burghley; Robert Dudley, the queen's powerful favourite; and Sir Francis Walsingham, Elizabeth's principal secretary – and spymaster.

He was asked to advise the Queen about toothache.

It is not known exactly what services Dee performed for Walsingham, but it seems likely that when Dee travelled to other European courts, to draw up horoscopes or dispense his wisdom, he gathered politically useful information that he passed back to the principal secretary. His fame as an astrologer made him welcome in high places, and this was a perfect cover for espionage. Dee had a keen interest in ciphers and secret writing that chimed with his esoteric preoccupations and his penchant for hidden knowledge. His notebooks were full of coded jottings, and the ability to hide a message in impenetrable symbols was, of course, a very practical skill for a spy. Dee had a more open involvement in England's early empire-building. He acted as consultant on the crucial science of navigation, and assisted the departing voyages of many of the great maritime explorers of the day – men such as John Cabot (Giovanni Caboto), Walter Raleigh and Martin Frobisher.

For his own part, Dee was driven to explore the boundaries of human knowledge rather than the fringes of the known world. In 1565 he moved to a large and rambling waterside house at Mortlake, on the River Thames, to the west of London. Here he assembled one of the largest private libraries in Europe, along with a major collection of globes and mathematical, astronomical and scientific instruments. He pursued what we would now think of as conventional studies, publishing in 1570 one of his most successful works: a preface, designed for the general reader, to a translation of *Elements*, the classic work by the ancient Greek mathematician Euclid.

Dee's house in Mortlake was well situated for the royal palaces of Richmond, Hampton Court and Windsor. Queen Elizabeth would visit him at home, often unannounced, when travelling by river (she turned up on the day his wife died and was apparently much amused by a concave mirror that turned her reflection upside-down). Dee, meanwhile, was a frequent visitor to the royal palaces. He went to Windsor to discuss the appearance of a comet, and in 1578 advised Elizabeth about a toothache. When it did not respond to treatment, he was asked to travel to Germany to consult other physicians – and may have done some undercover work for Walsingham while there.

CONVERSING WITH ANGELS
All the while, Dee continued his occult pursuits. To his mind, these were not incompatible with his scientific studies. He believed that mathematics, the deep wonder of numbers, was at the heart of divine magic. And his search for spiritual, otherworldly truth was about to take a great leap forward.

WISE OLD MAN *A portrait of John Dee painted in about 1594, when he would have been 67 years old, and most of his life's work was behind him. 'There is nothing,' he wrote, 'the works of God only set apart, which so much beautifies and adorns the soul and mind of man as does knowledge of the good arts and sciences.'*

In 1581 Dee had a powerful, life-changing vision. The angel Uriel appeared to him bathed in shining light, and called upon him to use a crystal ball to communicate with other angels. So he began 'scrying', crystal gazing to contact the angel realm. He soon found that he could not do this alone: he needed someone else to scry for him while he noted down the words of the angels. In 1582 he met a younger alchemist named Edward Kelley. He was in

all probability a trickster and a charlatan, but to Dee he seemed to be the perfect collaborator in his new angelic enterprise. Using a crystal ball and a polished obsidian mirror, Dee and Kelley embarked on a long series of 'spiritual conferences', as they called their encounters with angels. They claimed that the angels spoke to them in a form of 'celestial speech' now called Enochian. It is not clear where this language came from – Dee might have invented it, perhaps as a code. The angels apparently communicated to him in this language by tapping out letters on a board, as in a seance. Dee recorded hundreds of conversations. He hoped that the ethereal beings he had contacted would pass on their secret knowledge of the celestial world, that they would reveal to him the hidden meaning of the universe.

Though carried out in utmost secrecy, this activity caught the attention of the clergy, who assumed that Dee and Kelley were indulging in black magic. In 1583 they were forced to flee abroad, taking their families with them. This at least was their story, but their true motives remain unclear. In any case, they now began a six-year tour of eastern Europe in search of sponsors. Dee had a considerable reputation to trade on, but both he and Kelley could also offer a rich protector their knowledge of alchemy and claim that they were on the verge of acquiring the secret of turning base metals into gold.

Members of the nobility who were initially happy to invest in the pair soon tired of being asked for more money without any sign of gold. Dee and Kelley travelled through Poland and then on to Prague as guests of Rudolf II, the Holy Roman Emperor. At this point the Pope intervened, demanding that Dee and Kelley be expelled, or else burned at the stake for heresy – such was Dee's reputation. The pair fled back to Poland, before settling for two years in Třeboň in Bohemia, at the invitation of Count Vilem Rožmberk.

Throughout their travels, Dee and Kelley continued to record conversations with angels. Some of their notes, written in Enochian, were sent back to London – to the office of Sir Francis Walsingham. Dee was accompanied by his second wife, who was some 28 years his junior. In 1587,

when Dee was 60 and she was 32, Kelley reported that the angel Uriel wanted them to share everything, including their wives. Dee was so convinced about the spiritual worth of their work, and the personal integrity of Kelley, that he accepted a *ménage à trois*. Two years later, Dee and his wife parted company with Kelley, never to see him again.

LAST DAYS IN MORTLAKE

Dee's name had by now acquired a number of damning epithets such as 'companion of the devil' and 'provoker of imps and demons'. He might have shrugged off such insults, but when he returned to England he found that his precious library and collection of instruments had been ransacked by a mob that suspected him of satanism. Queen Elizabeth took pity on her old friend, and in 1595 appointed him Warden of Christ's College, Manchester.

When Elizabeth died in 1603, Dee's luck seemed to run out. Elizabeth's successor, James I (James VI of Scotland), was deeply hostile to occult practices. Then, in 1604, Dee's wife and several of his children died of plague. He returned to Mortlake, where he died in 1608, at the age of 81.

Dee's life remains hard to fathom. Was he a seeker of spiritual and scientific truth, an angel-obsessed lunatic, an undercover spy or (as his association with Kelley suggests) an innocent dupe? The biographer John Aubrey, writing a lifetime after Dee's death, saw him in a positive light, as a wizardly figure. 'Dee had a long beard as white as milke,' wrote Aubrey. 'He was a great peacemaker, and if any of the neighbours fell out, he would never let them alone till he had made them friends. He was tall and slender. He wore a gowne like an artist's gowne, with hanging sleeves. A mighty good man he was.'

The stars and Nancy Reagan

Ronald Reagan's schedule was controlled by an astrologer, at the behest of his wife. This sensational claim was made by Donald Regan, the president's former chief of staff. It was, he wrote, 'probably the most closely guarded domestic secret of the Reagan White House'.

On March 30, 1981, Ronald Reagan had a brush with death: outside the Washington Hilton Hotel, would-be assassin John Hinckley Jr fired a volley of pistol shots, one of which ricocheted off the president's limousine and hit him in the chest.

Following this event, Nancy Reagan contacted Joan Quigley, an astrologer whom she had met previously. She asked if Quigley could have foreseen the assassination attempt, and Quigley replied in the affirmative. She showed the first lady charts to back up her claim. From this time on, Nancy was regularly in touch with Quigley about the president's schedules, asking her to judge which days were propitious or otherwise.

The president's diary soon became ruled by the conjunctions of the stars. If Quigley said that a particular day was astrologically unfavourable, appointments would be dropped or rescheduled. Days were ranked as good, neutral or best avoided. Quigley's influence could also affect the fine detail. In December 1987, when Ronald Reagan signed the Intermediate-Range Nuclear Forces Treaty with the Soviet premier Mikhail Gorbachev, the ceremony in the White House took place at precisely 2pm, because Quigley had studied both men's horoscopes and had deemed that hour auspicious.

When Donald Regan became White House chief of staff in 1985, he was shocked to find that Nancy Reagan was controlling the schedules on the advice of an unnamed 'friend'. But he was unable to do much about it, and in the end it was Nancy who won out. According to Donald Regan, she engineered his resignation after two years. The catalyst for his removal was the scheduling of a press conference about the Iran-Contra arms scandal. For Regan, the timing of this conference was crucial – but the astrological readings prevented him from arranging it according to his own political judgment. Regan was unable to control his frustration, and the president made it clear that he should leave.

To some degree Donald Regan got even. He published his revelations in 1988, the year before Ronald Reagan's term of office was due to end. From that time, Quigley ceased to be consulted. President Reagan insisted that astrology had never affected policy, but Nancy was called upon to explain herself. She pleaded that astrology was just her way of mitigating the worry that she felt every time her husband went out and faced the public. And astrology, she suggested, could be seen to have been effective: there had, after all, been no further assassination attempts.

The hermit state

North Korea is the world's most secretive nation. No foreign journalists are allowed to report from there, and the country has very few visitors of any kind. Only the most privileged citizens are allowed to go abroad. This almost pathological aversion to outside influence is not just a reflex of the communist regime; it is rooted in the country's Confucian past.

At Panmunjom, on the border between North Korea and South Korea, a bizarre military ritual takes place every day. Across the Military Demarcation Line, tense, rigorously disciplined soldiers from South Korea and US troops from the United Nations Command eyeball their counterparts in North Korea, standing just yards away. This is the focal point of the Demilitarised Zone or DMZ, an alleyway 4km (2.5 miles) wide that divides the Korean Peninsula in two. It is a no-man's-land lined by chain-link fences topped by coiled razor wire and sown with tank-traps and mines. Only light arms are permitted in the DMZ, but on either side of it the two armies face each other with tanks and missiles and thousands of troops, on constant alert.

Panmunjom is where the armistice was signed at the end of the Korean War in 1953. The ceasefire came after three years of bitter fighting between North Korean communists and their Chinese allies on the one side, and, on the other, South Korean nationalists supported by an American-led coalition of UN troops. The 1953 armistice has never been converted to a peace treaty, and so for more than half a century North Korea and South Korea have continued to be technically at war. Panmunjom remains the most heavily militarised spot on Earth.

The relationship between the two nations is a kind of persistent microcosm of the old cold-war antagonism between the United States and the Soviet Union. North Korea, after all, is the last outpost of hardline communism, a totalitarian state that exercises absolute control over its citizens. South Korea, meanwhile, has a capitalist – that is free-market – system. And while South Korea has become integrated into the global community, North Korea is a recluse among nations. The hostile face it shows to the world can be seen as a defensive attitude, the bristling panoply of tanks and missiles as a massive, unmistakable KEEP OUT sign.

A LONG HISTORY OF INVASION

The immediate cause of North Korea's armoured xenophobia is the trauma of the Korean War, with its fierce incursions by foreign troops, but the mistrust of

미제를 몰아내고 조국을 통일하자!

MIGHTIER THAN THE SWORD *A North Korean poster shows serious young citizens fighting off foreign enemies with a giant pen. The imagery and the rhetoric are contemporary and communist, but the hostility towards foreigners and mistrust of their motives is far older than the present totalitarian regime. It goes back centuries.*

outsiders goes back much further. The Korean Peninsula has been repeatedly overrun, by the Chinese in the 6th and 7th centuries, the Khitans of Manchuria in the 10th and 11th centuries, Mongols in the 13th century, Japan in the 16th century, the Manchu Chinese in the 17th century. After this, Korea's rulers decided to accept Chinese suzerainty and closed its borders to all others.

In the course of the 19th century, however, Korea witnessed the collapse of the Chinese Empire in the wake of intrusion by Western merchants and missionaries. Korea attempted to avoid the same fate by vigorously resisting aggressive trade initiatives by the USA, Britain and France. Some of those commercial ventures were little short of acts of war. In 1866 an American ship, the *General Sherman*, arrived off the Korean coast hoping to sail up the Taedong River to the capital, Pyongyang, and open trade negotiations.

Korean officials boarded the ship as it proceeded upriver to tell the visitors that they were unwelcome – but were taken prisoner. When the officials did not return, civilians on the banks of the river began to shoot arrows at the ship, upon which the American captain gave orders to fire the ship's guns. The ship then turned back, but ran aground in shallow water. A Korean force stormed aboard, rescued their people and slaughtered the ship's crew. An American force despatched to find out what had become of the *Sherman* was embroiled in a brief conflict known in the West as the Korean–American war, and in Korea as 'the American disturbance'. It cost few lives but exacerbated Korean mistrust.

There were other episodes. Soon after the *Sherman* incident, a German merchant tried to steal the remains of the father of Korea's regent from the grave, thinking that he could use it as a bargaining chip. If the regent agreed to open Korea's ports to trade, he could have his father's body back. Korea's ruler responded by harassing foreign missionaries, since they were the countrymen of Korea's tormentors, and by persecuting Korean converts for practising their alien religion. But this policy of retaliation merely angered the Western powers still more, and provided them with new pretexts for interfering in Korea's internal affairs.

Korea's understandably cool attitude to Western advances earned it a reputation as the 'hermit kingdom', a term that first appeared in a 500-page book on Korea written by an American missionary in Japan who never visited the country. But in the end, the pressures of Westernisation proved too great, and Korea could not maintain its isolation or its independence. Late in the 19th century, it was drawn into the international power play of eastern Asia. In the early 20th century it became the stepping-stone for Japanese expansionism into that region, and Japan dominated Korea in the first part of the 20th century. To the North Koreans, the involvement of UN forces in the civil war of 1950–3, and the perceived influence of the USA on South Korea after the war had ended, are just yet more examples of foreign intervention, and conform exactly to the pattern of Korean history.

THE CONFUCIAN FACTOR

So the stand-off between the two Koreas looks like a strange and dangerous vestige of the 20th-century cold war, but in fact it goes much deeper than that. By the same token, North Korean society appears on the surface to be a version of 20th-century state communism, but here too this simplistic explanation ignores Korea's history. The unique form of North Korean communism can be seen as a grotesque parody of the Confucian ideal of a well-ordered society that was central to Korea for centuries.

For more than 500 years – from 1392 until the Japanese takeover in 1910 – Korea was ruled by one dynasty, known as the Joseon or 'morning calm'. The founder of the dynasty, Yi Song-gye, completely overhauled the way in which Korea was ruled. He was a follower of the Chinese thinker Confucius, who had lived 2,000 years earlier, and he introduced Confucian ideas of good government in much the same way that 20th-century revolutionaries introduced Marxism when they came to power.

> *Kim Jong-Il was credited with sinking 11 holes-in-one the first time he ever played golf.*

Confucian philosophy came to dominate Korean political structures for centuries, and it suffused Korean society. At the heart of Korean Confucianism was respect for superiors, for the head of the family. In the Confucian order, every individual knows his station and accepts that some people are more 'virtuous', and so worthy of respect and obedience. Ideas such as equality were anathema to Confucius. In his worldview, rank is everything, and all good things flow down from the very few people at the top of the pyramid towards the mass of people at the bottom. 'As soon as there was heaven and Earth, there was the distinction between

Kim Il-Sung: darling of the diplomatic world

The International Friendship Exhibition Hall, near Pyongyang, displays more than 220,000 diplomatic gifts presented to Kim Il-Sung and Kim Jong-il by foreign leaders and dignitaries. Among them are a crocodile-skin briefcase donated by Fidel Castro, a stuffed bear's head from Nicolae Ceaușescu, a bullet-proof limousine from Stalin, a basketball signed by Michael Jordan from US Secretary of State Madeleine Albright, plus numerous once state-of-the-art electronic gadgets such as a Sony Walkman, a 1980s Chinese boombox and an early Apple computer. This huge, oddball time capsule, displayed in some 400 marbled halls, is one of the nation's most popular visitor attractions: North Koreans come here daily in their thousands. The gifts are interpreted as proof of the high esteem and affection in which their leaders are held by the 180 or so donor countries around the world.

above and below,' he wrote. 'When the first wise king arose, the country he occupied had the division of classes. The ancient kings established the rules of proper conduct and divided the people into nobles and commoners, so that everybody would be under someone's control.'

This vision of the ideal society could almost be a description of the relationship between the Great Leader, the Party and the people in North Korea today. The state-endorsed hierarchy, and the total conformity that North Korea imposes on its citizens, can be understood as a continuation, albeit a distorted one, of Korea's medieval past.

The most striking aspects of life in North Korea are the all-pervasive political regimentation of the populace, and the extreme cult of personality centred on the leader. Kim Il-Sung, who ruled from 1948 until his death in 1994, is still revered as the 'Eternal President'. Kim Il-Sung's son and heir, Kim Jong-Il, received almost as much adulation as his father. When Kim Jong-Il died in 2011, he was succeeded by his son, Kim Jong-Un. North Korea had become a hereditary communist monarchy.

The first two Kims are ingrained on the minds of all citizens through countless statues, murals, films and news footage, as well as through popular myths and songs, learned in infancy. One story concerning Kim Jong-Il says that a double rainbow and a new star appeared in the heavens at the time of his birth. He was also credited with sinking 11 holes-in-one the first time he ever played an 18-hole golf course.

For North Koreans, Kim Jong-Il was semi-divine. They knew nothing of his humble birth in a Soviet refugee camp, his penchant for expensive French cognac or his collection of 20,000 DVDs. They might have heard tell of such things if they had access to information from the world outside North Korea, but only the highest ranks of the carefully groomed elite have clearance for that. Foreign broadcast signals are jammed, and the North Korean internet is in fact an intranet, a closed computer network with no link to the World Wide Web. So, in many ways, the social control and leader worship that distinguish North Korea are Confucian as much as they are Stalinist. Kim Il-Sung gave a name to the system he introduced to his country. He called it *juche*, or self-reliance. North Koreans, oppressed and kept in ignorance by *juche*, are brought up to believe they live in the happiest land in the world, and they thank Kim Il-Sung and Kim Jong-Il for their good fortune.

Secret writings

Codes and ciphers have been used for at least 2,000 years, and there has always been a race between codemakers and codebreakers to stay one step ahead. The business of keeping written messages secret was once the preserve of specialists such as military planners, financiers, diplomats and politicians. But codes are now a feature of everyday digital communication.

When Mary Queen of Scots was beheaded in 1587, she had good reason to curse the codebreakers. A plot to assassinate her cousin, Queen Elizabeth I of England, establish Mary on the throne and restore the Roman Catholic faith had been exposed by her letters, which had fallen into the hands of Elizabeth's agents. The letters were written in a complex code, but it was cracked by codebreakers working for Elizabeth. Once the secret was out, Mary's execution was inevitable.

Strictly speaking, the system that Mary tried to use was a mixture of code and cipher. In a code, words, numbers or symbols are used to signify agreed words or entire sentences. For example, a spy might use the word 'rose' to convey the idea: 'Meet tomorrow at the usual place.' Such systems are cumbersome as they require each operator to have full knowledge of all the codewords, perhaps kept in a dictionary-like codebook. In a cipher, each letter in a message is substituted by other letters, numbers or symbols, so as to obscure the meaning. To unscramble the message, the recipient needs to have a 'key' to the substitutions, but a cipher is more flexible than a code because the parties are not restricted to a prearranged set of messages.

The history of cryptography is really the story of ciphers, the striving to cloak the written word in a veil of secrecy. There have been innovations and counter-innovations; walls of verbal obfuscation have been built and then breached. The process amounts to a kind of intellectual arms race, a war of ingenuity between those who make ciphers and those who break them.

LETTERS AND NUMBERS

Julius Caesar used a very simple method of letter substitution to encipher his messages. Each letter in the message was moved on a fixed number of places – three, say – through the alphabet. So every letter A might be written as a D, every B as E, C as F – and so on. This method, known as the Caesar shift, worked well enough in a world where most people were illiterate, but even a Roman-era codebreaker would not find it too hard to crack. The number

General Heinz Guderian, commander of German tank forces, stands in a command-post vehicle that is equipped with an Enigma machine (in the foreground). As one soldier types into the machine, a second notes down the encrypted text one letter at a time. The process was cumbersome, but it seemed secure. Right to the end of the war, the Germans believed that their system could not be broken quickly enough to influence events.

of keys, or possible solutions, to the code is quite small, because it is equal to the number of possible shifts. It would not be too laborious to test for each possibility – 25 in all in the modern English alphabet – to see if a decoded message emerged.

Maximising the mathematical possibilities has always been part of the encoder's aim: the more potential solutions there are to a cipher, the harder it is to decrypt. If the number of solutions is so great that they cannot each be tested individually, then the codebreaker is left hopelessly searching for a needle in a cryptographic haystack. In a substitution cipher, one simple way to increase the

number of solutions is to randomise the relationship between the plain letters and their encrypted equivalent: A might be D, but B and C need not be E and F; they could be any other letter. The message is still perfectly easy to read by a recipient with a key, but there are many millions of different ways of mixing 26 letters, far more than any decoder could ever hope to check.

For hundreds of years, random letter substitution constituted an unbreakable cipher. But around AD 850, an Arabic scholar named Al-Kindi found a way past the huge numerical obstacle that it posed. He noticed that there are patterns in the frequency with which letters of the alphabet occur in a text. In an English text of any length, for instance, 'e' is almost bound to be the most common letter. Also, certain letters occur frequently in combination, for example 'ch' and 'oo' and 'th'. By counting the frequency of encrypted letters and looking for repetitive patterns in encrypted text, it is possible to get to the point where guesses can be made based on knowledge of the language. Frequency analysis, as this is now called, was a foot in the door, and it rendered all substitution ciphers breakable. The encoders needed a new and better idea.

In the 1460s, the Italian Renaissance architect Leon Battista Alberti realised that the way to defy frequency analysis was to use not just one cipher alphabet, but several. He produced an instrument now called the Alberti cipher disk. Two alphabets (and some numbers) were inscribed on two concentric wheels. By turning the inner wheel, the letters would line up with different letters on the outer wheel, allowing the sender to change the cipher alphabet several times in the same message. To decipher a message, all the recipient needed was a 'priming key', showing how and when to turn the wheel. This was the codemaker's state-of-the-art tool until the 19th century. By then Alberti's idea had evolved into a more sophisticated form – the Vigenère cipher – in which the key could be changed with each letter of the text by using sets of tables.

But a skilled cryptanalyst could still detect frequency patterns in the Vigenère cipher. It was breakable because it was, in the end, a recurrent set of substitution alphabets. Though the key changed with every letter, it re-occurred after a set number of letters. If you could find a repeated cluster in a text, you could potentially work out how many letters were in the key. And if you could do that, you could do a frequency analysis on each letter of the key, and so – eventually – crack the code.

The British mathematician Charles Babbage, inventor of the first mechanical computer, demonstrated in 1854 that the Vigenère cipher was breakable – but no one seems to have noticed. And nobody could have known that the calculating machines that Babbage envisaged were the future of codebreaking. It was ceasing to be a mental puzzle to be teased out through inspiration and insight, it was becoming a branch of computer science.

CODING MACHINES

In the 20th century, cryptography became the work of machines, not men. A key invention of the age was Enigma, brainchild of a German engineer named Arthur Scherbius. It looked like a strange typewriter. Inside it were a number of removable rotors, linked to electrical circuits that scrambled each letter as it was typed. The beauty of the machine was that the rotors clicked on every time a key was pressed, so the code changed in an apparently random way with each keystroke. The encrypted letter lit up on a lampboard, and had to be noted on paper. This scrambled message was sent telegraphically, and the receiver, whose machine would have to be set up in exactly the same configuration as the sender's, would key in the encrypted text to receive the plain-text message.

Enigma was adopted by the German army. A number of refinements were added, and, by the time the Second World War broke out, it was so sophisticated – the number of possibilities it generated so astronomically high – that the German armed forces were confident that their coded communications were unbreakable. But in fact Enigma had long since been cracked. In 1932 a group of Polish cryptographers had learned how to decrypt military codes by bundling together sets of Enigma machines. Five weeks before

The 'unbreakable' Enigma had long since been cracked.

the outbreak of the Second World War, they passed their findings to British intelligence. The Polish breakthrough made possible the work of the secret army of cryptographers at the British decryption centre, Bletchley Park. Here, engineers built Colossus, a huge conglomeration of valves and tubes that could test encrypted German traffic, transcribed onto punched tape, against hundreds of possibilities per second. Colossus could not decrypt messages automatically. But the head start it provided meant that the incisive minds gathered at Bletchley could test hunches quickly. They knew, for example, that German operators often began messages with the phrase 'Heil Hitler', so they could test for this phrase against hundreds of settings to see if the solution came up.

Colossus is now acknowledged to have been the world's first programmable computer, albeit one designed for a narrow task. Nowadays, secure communication is unthinkable without the vast calculating power of digital machinery. Virtually all internet communication, from emails to online shopping and banking, makes use

of a mathematical device called the RSA algorithm, named after Ron Rivest, Adi Shamir and Len Adleman, who described it in 1978. In the RSA system, messages are encrypted using very large prime numbers. These are easy to create but extremely hard to decode, or 'factor', because the key is so long (unlike the word-length keys used in the Vigenère cipher). The system is considered unbreakable, but the safety bar is forever shifting upwards as computer power increases. Digital brains, unlike human ones, really can test every one of millions of possibilities, so the 129-digit numbers used in 1978 are weak by today's standards. The current 616-digit numbers would take thousands of years to crack, even with the most up-to-date technology.

DIGITAL DEFENCES

Every modern cryptographer knows that it is only a matter of time before any code is broken. All our secrets are time-limited. Computer hackers are today's front-line cryptographers, and they deploy an armoury ranging from 'social engineering' (persuading users to hand over vital details) to 'brute force attacks' that use programs to probe digital defences for every conceivable weakness. Governments and businesses are constantly alert to hackers, who may damage or steal a database, raid bank accounts, or close down whole systems. The hackers tend to be people who simply enjoy the challenge of testing their computing skills against the security measures of corporations or government agencies. Some are even employed by these very organisations to test their security. Cryptography in the 21st century remains a fascinating mindgame, though the players are no longer wordsmiths and linguists, they are invariably software engineers, mathematicians and programmers.

The president's sickness

Franklin D. Roosevelt was confined to a wheelchair for 24 years, including the 13 during which he served as US president. But almost nobody knew that he could barely stand unaided. His disability was concealed from the American public because Roosevelt and his advisers felt that his physical infirmity might look to voters like political weakness.

The year 1920 was a punishing one for Franklin Delano Roosevelt. He was then a young politician, 38 years old, and held the post of assistant secretary of the navy. In that role he had to deal with a political storm concerning the existence of a homosexual network at a training station in Newport, Rhode Island. Roosevelt was widely criticised for sanctioning the use of *agents provocateurs* to investigate the situation, and that criticism was still ringing in his ears when he resigned the navy job in order to accept the Democratic Party's nomination for the post of vice-president of the United States. A gruelling campaign was followed by the disappointment of electoral defeat, and then a series of politically damaging appearances before a court of inquiry relating to the Newport affair. By July 1921 Roosevelt was utterly exhausted, and looking forward to a long holiday in Canada.

A SUDDEN ILLNESS

On August 10, Roosevelt went sailing for part of the day. On his return to shore he happened upon a brushfire, which he beat out with evergreen wands, hastily chopped from nearby trees. Then he swam for an hour in the cold water of Glen Severn, before yomping the 3km (2 miles) home in his wet swimsuit. He went to bed that night complaining of a slight backache. When he woke up in the morning he could not use his left leg; by night his right leg had also collapsed underneath him, and he was running a high temperature. The following day he was paralysed from the chest down.

A string of doctors came to see him and made various diagnoses – first a cold, then a blood clot. Everything suggested the condition was minor and temporary. Then, on August 20, a doctor called Samuel Levine came from Boston and said that without a doubt Roosevelt had contracted polio. As it happens, this too was probably wrong – it is now believed that Roosevelt had fallen prey to the much rarer and then little known Guillain-Barré syndrome – but the prognosis was right enough: the paralysis of his legs was irreversible.

In the 1920s there was a dread attached to disability, a lack of understanding that is now hard to credit. Some American cities

had ordinances forbidding disabled people from even appearing in public. Chicago's so-called 'Ugly Law', contained in section 36034 of the Municipal Code, stated that 'no person who is diseased, maimed, mutilated or in any way deformed so as to be an unsightly or disgusting object or improper person to be allowed in or on the public ways or other public places in this city'. Such rules were aimed primarily at beggars rather than disabled people, but they were a stigma all the same, a reflection of the attitudes of many able-bodied people.

So the loss of the use of his legs was not just a devastating personal blow for Roosevelt, who had always prided himself on his athleticism, it also seemed to be the death knell for his promising career. He was a rising star, despite his defeat in the 1920 election, and there was every reason to believe that he would follow his cousin Theodore Roosevelt all the way to the White House. But it was hard to see how the American public could be persuaded to give him their backing now that he was – to use the parlance of the time – a cripple. To govern a country like the United States, a man had to be seen to be strong and fighting fit. Surely no one would vote to see America led from a wheelchair?

DOCTORS OF SPIN

Almost as soon as Roosevelt fell ill, the people closest to him began to talk down the seriousness of his condition. His friend and adviser Louis Howe kept the press at a distance while Roosevelt was taken from his holiday home to hospital in New York. The *New York Times* reported that Roosevelt was 'ill of poliomyelitis', and quoted someone at the hospital as saying 'that the attack was very mild and that Mr Roosevelt would not be permanently

crippled'. The family doctor told the newspaper that Roosevelt was 'regaining the use of his legs'. The medical men already knew that this was not true, and so, deep down, did Roosevelt himself.

But the lie that Roosevelt was on the mend had now been told, and the myth that he had 'beaten polio' would be maintained for the rest of his life. In the years that followed his first bout of illness, Roosevelt's entourage went to enormous lengths to keep his disability secret. This involved a supreme physical effort on the part of Roosevelt himself. In March 1922 he was fitted with metal braces, each of which weighed more than 3kg (6lb 6oz) and encased his powerless legs from ankle to hip. Wearing these supports, Roosevelt learned to walk again – or at least to move upright – by swinging his torso and using a cane to keep his balance. But it was painful and tiring, and he could never do more than a few steps at a time.

On presidential campaigns, Roosevelt always made his speeches at a heavy, specially strengthened lectern that he gripped with both hands for support. Newsreels show that he never gestured with both hands, and only occasionally with one hand. Instead, he used his head for emphasis – nodding or shaking it as he spoke. On one occasion, he fell flat on his face as he moved away from his lectern, but the press corps was respectful and sympathetic, and the incident was not reported. Cartoonists – whether they were for Roosevelt or against him – always portrayed him as an able-bodied man, energetically striding across the American political stage.

Once Roosevelt was elected president in 1932, the White House machinery was there to help to maintain the illusion of wellness. Roosevelt moved around in a

Roosevelt remembered

Franklin D. Roosevelt is the only disabled person ever to have been US president. But the statue of him in his wheelchair (right), is a late addition to his monument in Washington DC. The original statue (which is still there, at the heart of the complex) shows him seated in an ordinary chair, wrapped in his cape. When the memorial opened in 1997, some people were troubled that the depiction of him disguised that fact that he was disabled – just as Roosevelt himself hid it in his lifetime. It was felt that this representation told less than the whole story. And, from a modern perspective, it seemed wrong not to acknowledge his disability openly. President Clinton agreed and had commissioned an additional figure even before the monument opened. In 2001 a new 3m (10ft)-high statue, one that showed Roosevelt in his wheelchair, was added to the ensemble.

LARGER THAN LIFE *The statue of FDR in his wheelchair was designed by artist Robert Graham. On the wall behind it are inscribed some words from Roosevelt's wife Eleanor: 'Franklin's illness gave him strength and courage he had not had before. He had to think out the fundamentals of living and learn the greatest of all lessons – infinite patience and never-ending persistence.'*

light, manoeuvrable wheelchair of his own devising but was never photographed in it. If ever a press photographer did snap him in his chair, the film was confiscated by secret service agents. In advance of any public appearances, White House personnel checked that the president would not be required to climb stairs – impossible in his leg braces. He never got out of the presidential limo in sight of the public, since this required him to be physically lifted from the car. He was, however, often photographed standing up on the rear platform of the presidential train carriage. Every detail was attended to: even the clasps on the bottom of his steel leg braces were painted black, so they did not catch the eye.

Such measures sustained President Roosevelt's public image through three terms of office. He was elected for a fourth term in 1944, but by this time his health

problems were multiplying. He was in fact a dying man, and the secrecy around the state of his health was increasingly difficult to maintain. In November 1944, at a Thanksgiving dinner attended by dozens of guests, he looked profoundly sick, coughing and shaking as he carved the turkeys and tried to tell cheery stories. At his inauguration in January 1945, he could barely stand, despite the long-serving lectern. And yet, when Roosevelt died in April 1945, having suffered a massive cerebral haemorrhage, people were surprised as well as saddened. The majority of the American public had no idea that he was anything less than hale and hearty, that the man who had guided America through the great Depression and marched the nation to the brink of victory in the Second World War, had in all those years never walked a single step.

Strong leaders, failing powers

Roosevelt is by no means the only world leader to have *concealed an infirmity or manufactured a glowing impression of his physical state of health. The practice is widespread, even today.*

There was a time when political leaders – kings and princes – were required to be strong in body, because part of their function was to lead armies into battle. For centuries now, strength of character has been far more important than actual muscle, but still leaders feel the need to display physical prowess – or at least to conceal weakness.

In the last years of the Soviet Union, it was common practice to alter official portraits of the geriatric leadership to make them look younger or better. Leonid Brezhnev, a bewildered 76-year-old at the time of his death in 1982, looked a vibrant 50 in his pictures. His image was boosted in other ways that had as much to do with personal vanity as political expediency. For example, his unreadable ghosted wartime memoir was awarded the Lenin

MEDAL MAN *In his latter years Brezhnev was rarely filmed or photographed, because his slow manner and slurred speech betrayed how senile he had become. Instead, flattering official portraits made much of his four 'Hero of the Soviet Union' stars, his eight 'Orders of Lenin', and the dozens of other honours he had awarded himself.*

Prize for Literature, as if he were one of the leading Russian writers of his generation.

When Mikhail Gorbachev was promoted to the Politburo of the Communist Party in 1980, the distinctive birthmark on his forehead was airbrushed out of his portrait as if it were a stain on his character. And a good ten years were shaved off the apparent age of Yuri Andropov, the man who succeeded Brezhnev in the Kremlin. Andropov fell seriously ill within months of taking office, but right up to his death the Soviet media insisted that he was suffering from nothing more than 'a heavy cold'. Russians knew that there was more to it than that. And when, one night in February 1984, the lights in the Kremlin's offices remained on all night, people swiftly concluded that a silent change of regime was underway. Sure enough, it was announced soon after that Andropov had died.

President Kennedy was in pain every day of his time in the White House.

In modern Russia, there is still a need for the man in the Kremlin to look like he is physically as well as politically powerful. Vladimir Putin, variously president and prime minister of the Russian Federation, has become known for staging regular photo opportunities designed to boost his macho image: he has been shown riding a Harley-Davidson trike with the so-called 'Night Wolves' biker gang, arm-wrestling at a youth camp, exploring the Siberian countryside bare-chested and on horseback, hunting on the steppe and diving for treasure in the Black Sea. The subtext is always the same. The pictures say: I am a strong and fearless man, and the right person to tame this large and rowdy country.

This kind of manipulation of a statesman's public image is easier to manage in a totalitarian state, where the government has control of the media. But, as Franklin D. Roosevelt's case shows, it can also work in democratic countries with a free press. In fact, it happened again in America within a generation of Roosevelt's time in office. John F. Kennedy was portrayed as the very model of a fit and energetic young politician, but he suffered from Addison's disease – a serious malfunction of the adrenal gland that forced him to have a life-threatening operation on his back before his election in 1960. In the two years between 1955 and 1957, he spent time in hospital on seven separate occasions – for back pain and also for intestinal problems. As with Roosevelt's illness, Kennedy's medical condition was treated as top secret so as not to endanger his chances of securing the White House.

During his time as president, Kennedy was often in excruciating pain from his spinal problems, and would sometimes have multiple injections of painkillers before going out to face a press conference or a public meeting. In the latter part of 1962, he was taking a range of pills every day for his various ailments: codeine, Demerol and methadone for pain (as well as injections of procaine); Ritalin, a stimulant used to treat depression and irregular heartbeat; meprobamate, librium and occasionally Stelazine for anxiety; barbiturates as sleeping pills; thyroid hormone for the Addison's condition; and injections of gamma globulin that may have been intended to combat infections.

President Kennedy was a sick man for much of the time, and it seems likely that he was in pain every day of his time in the White House. Sometimes he needed help to dress, because he could not bend his legs. He endured his illnesses stoically, but the silence around them was also a deliberate public-relations ploy. For sound political reasons, Kennedy was only ever presented to American voters – falsely and by various deceitful means – as the epitome of youthful rude health.

Chapter 3
POLITICS AND WAR

War, it has been said, is the continuation of politics by other means. Both spheres of activity involve intrigue and betrayal, courage and cunning. And both can be dangerous and cruel.

The fugitive king

In July 1651 Charles Stuart, the future King Charles II, marched into England at the head of a Scottish army, hoping to crush the new parliamentarian republic. But Charles's army was defeated at Worcester, and he was reduced to the status of an outlaw on the run. His escape hung on disguise, a network of safehouses and the clandestine help of friends.

The most dangerous episode in the life of Charles II began at the Battle of Worcester. This was the last major engagement of the English Civil War. Charles, then 21 years old, had marched with an army from his base in Scotland, where he was still recognised as the rightful king. He had hoped that Englishmen would rally to his flag as he passed through England, but after a decade of civil war the country was tired, and many were indifferent or opposed to his cause.

A Roundhead army under the command of Oliver Cromwell engaged Charles's weary Scottish force at Worcester on September 3, and Charles's army was crushed. Charles retreated inside the city walls, but then – as Cromwell's soldiers poured through the gates – he had to take flight. According to one account of that day, he slipped out of the back door of a house as a Roundhead colonel burst through the front. Certainly he escaped from the town by the skin of his teeth.

As the last skirmishes took place, Charles met up with a large group of cavalrymen and courtiers – the remnants of his defeated army – on the road just north of the city. The consensus among his retinue was that they should ride and fight their way back to Scotland. Charles saw that this was a forlorn hope, that a large force was sure to be tracked and destroyed within days or hours. His only chance of evading capture was to become invisible, or at least totally inconspicuous.

FIRST DAYS ON THE RUN
At a fork in the road, the king's men went left; the king himself went to the right. Charles took a favourite courtier along with him, Lord Henry Wilmot. At 39, Wilmot was almost twice Charles's age, and the younger man looked up to him. Wilmot was witty, dissolute, devoted to the Royalist cause and to Charles personally. Unfortunately, he was also something of a buffoon, and – ominously for the matter in hand – he loved drawing attention to himself. He was so vain that he absolutely refused to don a disguise or travel on foot, even after the king himself had cut his hair and dressed in a woodman's clothes. In the six nerve-wracking weeks that followed

GILDED YOUTH *Charles, aged 20. In later life he often told the tale of his escape from England after the Worcester defeat.*

Wilmot had a habit of making blundering interventions into delicate and carefully laid plans. He was, in short, a liability – though he acted throughout as if he were the guiding genius of the escape.

Charles, though he was adrift and at large in enemy territory, had some natural allies among the population: the Roman Catholic minority. England's 'recusants' – Catholics who refused to abandon the old faith – tended to be Royalist in sympathy. They could be relied upon to shelter the king, and they knew how best to do it:

after 60 years of religious persecution, they were practised in the arts of subterfuge and had ways of hiding their secrets – and their people – from the government's eyes.

The Giffard family were recusants in this mould. They owned an estate called Boscobel, which was 45 miles (75km) from Worcester, in the midst of thick woodland. This is where Charles headed first. On reaching Boscobel in the small hours of the morning, Charles was welcomed by the Penderell brothers, Catholic tenants of the Giffards. They disguised him, and had him dirty his face with soot from the grate. It was too dangerous for him to stay in the house: Roundhead soldiers were a mile or two away, and they were sure to come searching the house soon. So Charles spent his first day as a wanted man sheltering alone in the depths of Boscobel wood.

By now he had a plan. He would head for the town of Madeley, where there was a crossing over the River Severn into Wales. The populace was largely Royalist there, and the soldiers of the parliamentary army were few. He set off at night, with one of the Penderell brothers as his guide. It was a 9 mile (15km) walk, and every step was painful for Charles, as the only shoes that could be found for him were too small. All the more galling, then, that the trip was in vain: the bridges and ferries over the Severn were closely guarded. Charles had no choice but to head back to Boscobel.

But Charles urgently needed to get away from this part of the country, which was still swarming with enemy soldiers. He spent the daylight hours hiding in Boscobel woods again – this time up an oak tree. The parliamentary search parties came so close

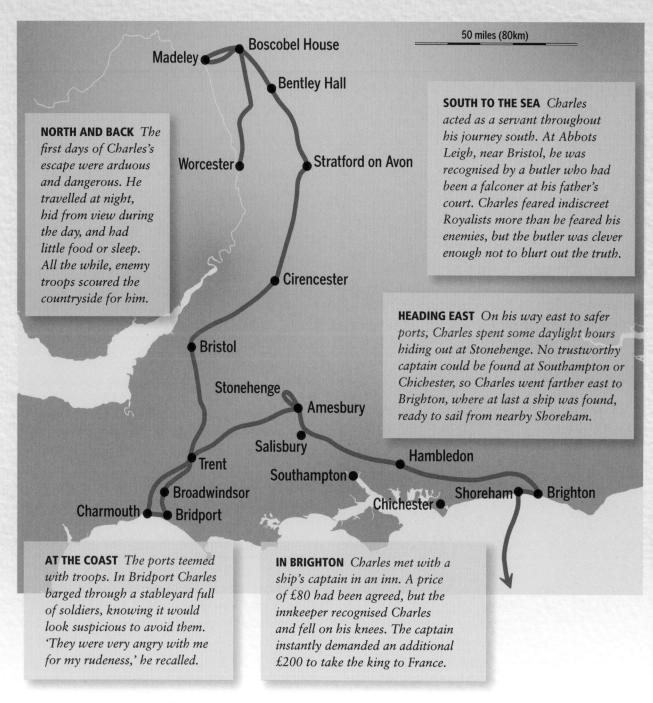

50 miles (80km)

Boscobel House

Madeley

Bentley Hall

SOUTH TO THE SEA *Charles acted as a servant throughout his journey south. At Abbots Leigh, near Bristol, he was recognised by a butler who had been a falconer at his father's court. Charles feared indiscreet Royalists more than he feared his enemies, but the butler was clever enough not to blurt out the truth.*

NORTH AND BACK *The first days of Charles's escape were arduous and dangerous. He travelled at night, hid from view during the day, and had little food or sleep. All the while, enemy troops scoured the countryside for him.*

Worcester

Stratford on Avon

Cirencester

HEADING EAST *On his way east to safer ports, Charles spent some daylight hours hiding out at Stonehenge. No trustworthy captain could be found at Southampton or Chichester, so Charles went farther east to Brighton, where at last a ship was found, ready to sail from nearby Shoreham.*

Bristol

Stonehenge

Amesbury

Salisbury

Hambledon

Trent

Southampton

Broadwindsor

Shoreham

Brighton

Charmouth

Bridport

Chichester

AT THE COAST *The ports teemed with troops. In Bridport Charles barged through a stableyard full of soldiers, knowing it would look suspicious to avoid them. 'They were very angry with me for my rudeness,' he recalled.*

IN BRIGHTON *Charles met with a ship's captain in an inn. A price of £80 had been agreed, but the innkeeper recognised Charles and fell on his knees. The captain instantly demanded an additional £200 to take the king to France.*

that Charles could see them through the canopy of the tree. He returned to the house after dark and spent the night in a cramped priest-hole. Then, in the morning, he set off for Bentley Hall, the home of a former Royalist officer, Colonel John Lane.

Charles's intention was to make his way to London inconspicuously on foot,

then find a boat to take him to the safety of France. But at Bentley a better option arose. Colonel Lane's sister had a permit to visit a friend near Bristol who was due to have a baby. If Jane Lane were to take the king with her, in the guise of her servant, then perhaps he could escape to France from Bristol – like London, a major port.

For this leg of the journey Charles adopted the name Will Jackson. He shared a horse with Jane, and they became lifelong friends along the way. The ride to Bristol took Charles out of immediate danger of capture, but there were still hazards. Charles had no idea of a servant's role, and aroused suspicion when he seemed not to know how to operate a mechanical spit. In a neat reversal of the truth, he explained that meat was scarce where he came from. Charles's quick wits and actorly instincts saved him more than once that day. Earlier, he had been required to take Jane's horse to a blacksmith's to be re-shoed. The smith proved to be chatty, and wondered if 'that rogue Charles Stuart' had been captured. 'If that rogue were taken,' replied servant Will, 'he deserves to be hanged more than all the rest, for bringing in the Scots.'

IN SEARCH OF A SHIP

No ship bound for France could be found at Bristol, so Charles headed instead for the south coast. There was by now a price of £1,000 on his head, but the bounty hunters had lost his trail. His whereabouts remained a subject of great interest to the London press, which, in the absence of any solid information, made their stories up. Readers of the broadsides and 'newsbooks' were told that the king had thrown in his lot with a known highwayman named Captain Hinde, and was 'skulking about in some private corners with his guide'. One publication ventured that he was in London, making secret visits to places associated with his dead father. Some pamphlets printed as fact the rumour that Charles, a swarthy young man over 6ft (1.8m) in height, was making his way through the English countryside disguised as a woman.

On the way south from Bristol, Charles stopped at the village of Trent and hid in the home of a Royalist officer named Francis Wyndham. Here, from an upstairs window, he had the unnerving experience of seeing the villagers celebrate the news that he had been killed at Worcester. From Trent, Charles made his way to Charmouth on the south coast. Here Wyndham and Wilmot hired a ship's captain to take the party to France under cover of darkness. But on the appointed night the captain failed to show up. It turned out that his wife, having got wind of the dangerous plan, locked her husband in the bedroom until the tide was out.

It was at Charmouth that Charles's pursuers again got wind of him. Another smith, while fitting a shoe to Wilmot's horse, noticed that the other three were all made in different counties, one of them in Worcestershire. He guessed what this meant and raised the alarm. A party of soldiers set off in pursuit of Charles, who had been seen leaving for Bridport. The soldiers missed him by moments, because he had turned off the main road to head back to Wyndham's house at Trent.

Charles lay low at Trent for two weeks while his aides sought out a ship far along the coast in Brighton. They succeeded in hiring a coal-boat, *The Surprise*, and sent word to Charles to join them. He boarded ship in the nearby village of Shoreham, and at last set sail for France early on the morning of October 15. A couple of hours later soldiers arrived in Shoreham asking if anyone had seen 'a tall, black [dark-haired] man, six feet two inches high'. But Charles was by now out at sea and beyond their reach. Eleven years were to pass before he could return to England – to a royal welcome, and a coronation.

DOWN BY THE RIVERSIDE *Fugitive slaves fording the Rappahannock River in 1862. By this time, runaways could travel under the protection of the Union army.*

The underground railroad

In the decades leading up to the American Civil War, thousands of black slaves fled the southern states to seek liberty in the northern states or in Canada, a British colony. Many were helped on their way by sympathisers who formed a clandestine network known as the underground railroad.

Fugitive slaves travelled mainly on foot, alone or in small groups, along paths through woods and fields, over hills and river crossings, usually at night. Here and there they found people to help them, often freed former slaves, who might give them somewhere to hide during the day and perhaps feed and clothe them before sending them along a back route to the

next safe haven. Secrecy was paramount. Always the fugitives risked betrayal, or running into a posse of slave-catchers, professional hunters with horses, weapons and bloodhounds. Slaves, after all, were a valuable commodity, and their owners promised rich rewards for their return.

Captured slaves were returned to their owners in chains. They faced severe punishment, often administered in public to deter others. But stories of runaways were part of the culture of slavery. Slave children grew up haunted by ghoulish tales of Martha 'Patty' Cannon and her gang, who roamed the Delmarva Peninsula around Delaware on the east coast. They captured runaways and kidnapped freed slaves, then transported them south to be sold. Her victims were concealed in secret rooms, held in leg-irons and whipped mercilessly if they did not comply. Cannon was nearly 70 when the law finally caught up with her. She was arrested after four bodies – including those of two children – were found on her land. She died in prison in 1829, apparently having poisoned herself to avoid trial.

Winter was the best time for fugitives to travel because the nights were longer. And when they reached the broad Ohio River – the boundary line between the southern slave states and the free states of the North – there was every chance they might find it frozen over and be able to cross it easily on foot. Runaway slaves could breathe more easily once they reached the North. Here there were open networks of helpers, free blacks as well as white families, often connected to the numerous 'abolitionist' (anti-slavery) groups and the more radical churches.

All of the states of the North had abolished the slave trade by 1807, largely due to the influence of their religious settlers – Presbyterians, Congregationalists, Baptists, Wesleyans and, above all, Quakers. But, in 1850, under pressure from the powerful slave-owning lobby of the South, the US Congress passed the Fugitive Slave Law, which made it illegal to help runaway slaves even in the northern states. Offenders faced arrest, heavy fines and imprisonment. Suddenly the North was no longer a safe haven. Free black people already in the North also became more vulnerable. The slave-catchers were casual about whom they picked up, and former slaves found it hard to prove their status as free men and women.

As a result of the Fugitive Slave Law, the ultimate goal for fugitives became Canada. Slavery per se (as opposed to trade in slaves) had been abolished throughout the British Empire in 1834. So now the fugitives 'followed the North Star' that much farther than before, travelling across the northern states to the Great Lakes, where they hoped to find a sympathetic ferryboat captain. By 1860 more than 30,000 runaway slaves had reached Canada. Most settled in southern Ontario.

THE SLAVE TRADITION

Slavery in America was almost as old as European settlement. The first slave ship from West Africa arrived in the English colony of Virginia in 1619. At first, the trade grew slowly. But as commercial agriculture developed – first tobacco and rice, then, crucially, cotton – the numbers of imported black slaves shot up. The very low-cost labour of slaves in the late 18th century gave the country a vital competitive edge in international trade. There were some 500,000 slaves

The Mason-Dixon Line

The Mason-Dixon was a demarcation line originally drawn up to resolve border disputes between British colonies. Later it served as the boundary between the southern states that approved slavery (Maryland, Virginia, West Virginia) and those in the north that did not (Pennsylvania, New York and others).

in the American colonies at the time of the Declaration of Independence in 1776. Despite the promised liberties ('All men are created equal'), slavery remained central to America's commercial and social system. But attitudes were changing. As early as 1777 the state of Vermont abolished slavery, and soon a swathe of northern states followed suit. But in the south, where the plantation economy was more firmly established, the dependence on slave labour continued to grow.

By 1800 the nation was split more or less along the Mason-Dixon line. To the north of the line, there was no slavery; in the states to the South of the line, a slave economy prevailed. The aim of every runaway southern slave was to cross the Mason-Dixon line, and so be free. An intricate network of paths and escape routes began to develop from the late 18th century onwards. In about 1830 the expression 'underground railroad' first appeared, a reference to the actual railroads that were then being built in the USA. The term was apparently coined by frustrated slave-catchers who, when their quarry vanished without trace, mused that they must have taken some kind of secret or hidden railroad.

The slave-hunters' rueful joke became a hopeful byword for thousands of fugitives. At the same time, the rather apt railroad metaphor was cheerfully adopted and extended by those involved in assisting the fugitives. Safehouses and sheltering churches became known as 'stations' operated by 'stationmasters'; secret routes were termed 'lines'; those who helped fugitives along the way were referred to as 'agents'; providers of clothes and money were 'stockholders'; those who personally guided fugitives to safety were 'conductors'. As for the fugitives themselves, they were variously referred to as 'passengers' or, more impersonally, as 'packages', 'cargo' or 'freight'. On one occasion at least, the terminology was entirely apposite. In 1848 Henry Brown, a slave from Richmond, Virginia, had himself nailed into a wooden box and despatched to the Philadelphia Anti-Slavery Office. He spent 27 hours in the box, some of them upside-down, before arriving safely and being triumphantly released. Henry 'Box' Brown later became an ardent abolitionist campaigner.

Providers of clothes and money were 'stockholders'.

Generally, the railway jargon was a useful code, but it had another serious purpose. Messages using railway terminology were exchanged to dupe interceptors into thinking that the 'passengers' were actually travelling by train, that the 'packages' were freight. In fact, very few runaways used trains. Most walked, some travelled by wagon or occasionally on horseback. Others travelled on ships from southern ports, or on Mississippi steamboats. Numerous escape routes and methods were covered by the blanket term 'underground railroad'. Most of them threaded through the upper south states of Virginia and Kentucky, bordering the Ohio River. Some routes flanked the Mississippi or passed up the eastern seaboard into the North. Other routes to freedom led in other directions: through Texas to Mexico, or through Florida to the Caribbean islands. Slaves taking the Florida route could rely on the assistance of Native American Seminoles – until they were evicted from their ancestral homelands in the 1830s.

THE RAILROAD WORKERS

Thousands of people, black and white, were involved in the work of bringing slaves to freedom. One of the most celebrated individuals is William Still of Philadelphia, the son of former slaves and a vociferous campaigner. He kept records that formed the basis of a memoir called *The Underground Railroad*, published in 1872. And a Quaker named Levi Coffin helped to turn Cincinnati, Ohio, into the 'Grand Central Station of the Underground Railroad'. He and his wife Catherine assisted more than 2,000 southern fugitives.

In nearby Ripley, on the north bank of the Ohio River, a Presbyterian minister called John Rankin was closely involved, along with his wife Jean and some of their 13 children. Allan Pinkerton, a Scottish immigrant, offered his cabin at Dundee, near Chicago, as a 'station'; he later became famous as the founder of the detective agency that bears his name. Thomas Garrett, another Quaker, openly sheltered fugitives for 40 years at Wilmington, Delaware, and is said to have helped more than 2,700.

Then there was Frederick Douglass, a former slave who ushered refugees through his base in Rochester, New York. He had escaped from the South in 1838 and wrote with great eloquence about the experience of finding himself suddenly free: 'A new world had opened upon me. I lived more in one day than in a year of my slave life. It was a time of joyous excitement which words can but tamely describe ... Anguish and grief, like darkness and rain, may be depicted; but gladness and joy, like the rainbow, defy the skill of pen or pencil.'

Douglass became a well-known face of the abolitionist movement, but the most famous 'conductor' of all was Harriet Tubman. Having escaped from slavery in Maryland in 1849, Tubman travelled back into the South at least 13 times to bring out fugitives. Among the first people she led to the North were members of her own family, including her young nephews and nieces. She became known as the 'Moses of her people'. It was said that she never lost a passenger. Harriet Beecher Stowe kept a station near Cincinnati. Her novel *Uncle Tom's Cabin*, based on the true stories of runaway slaves, was published in 1852 and became an instant best-seller, raising anti-slavery sentiment to fever pitch.

One militant abolitionist decided that passive resistance was not enough, that the time had come for guerrilla tactics. In 1859 John Brown, an ardent supporter of the underground railroad, led a raid on the arsenal at Harpers Ferry, Virginia, to capture weapons for an armed insurrection of slaves in the South. He was captured during the raid, then tried and hanged. The stage was set for a showdown between North and South. The civil war that broke out in 1861 cost 600,000 lives, but victory for the North in 1865 ensured that Abraham Lincoln's decree of emancipation was adopted throughout the United States. All the slaves of the South were now legally free men, and the work of the underground railroad was at an end.

It is not known how many slaves escaped via the underground railroad. The system was necessarily secretive, and few records were kept. Some estimates suggest as many as 100,000, others fewer. Whatever the number, those who escaped constitute just a tiny fraction of the slave population as a whole. But the railroad had a significance that was far greater than the bare statistics convey. It gave America's black population hope that one day they might all make it to the 'freedom lands'.

Saved by the Comet Line

The secret network known as the Comet Line was established in Brussels to help stranded Allied airmen and other servicemen get out of Nazi-controlled territory and return to Britain. Like the underground railroad in the USA, it saved hundreds of people – but at great cost to many of the operators.

During the First World War, Edith Cavell, a British nurse working in Brussels, set up an escape route to the Netherlands for British, French and Belgian soldiers who became trapped behind German lines. In 1915 she was arrested, tried and shot by the Germans. When the Germans again invaded neutral Belgium in May 1940, the 23-year-old Andrée de Jongh determined that she would emulate Cavell and do everything in her power to combat the enemy.

Within a few months she had begun her own network. Using the codename 'Dédée' and working alongside her father Frédéric ('Paul'), she established safehouses in Brussels, hiding servicemen until they were ready to travel. She used contacts in the Belgian resistance to devise routes to get them to British-controlled territory. This usually meant travelling by train, via Paris, right through German-occupied France, then finally – with the help of Basque guides – walking across the Pyrenees into neutral Spain.

'Dédée' herself escorted two sets of British servicemen to the safety of Bilbao on Spain's north coast, late in 1941. At the British consulate in Bilbao she requested help, which was duly provided by British military intelligence. Her network developed fast, but it always retained a Belgian leadership. It became known as the Comet Line because of the speed with which it operated.

Andrée de Jongh personally made 32 trips to and from Spain, delivering 116 evaders, including at least 80 aircrew. But, in January 1943, the Comet Line was betrayed, resulting in the arrest of some 50 of its leading agents. Many of them were tortured and executed; some were shipped to concentration camps such as Buchenwald in Germany, or the camp for women at Ravensbrück.

That same month Andrée de Jongh was herself arrested with three evaders at Urrugne in France, the final stopping point before the border crossing in the Pyrenees. The Gestapo could not believe that someone so young was the founder of this ambitious escape route, so she was spared execution and spent the rest of the war in concentration camps. Her father was arrested in Paris on June 7, 1943, and executed by firing squad. The Comet Line itself survived, delivering the last of some 800 servicemen to safety in Spain in June 1944, as the Allies retook control of France.

SURE GUIDE *Andrée de Jongh was known as 'Little Cyclone' by British intelligence; the codename was a testament to her unflagging energy. After the war she came to Britain to receive the George Medal in recognition of her bravery in helping British evaders.*

The lost man of Mijas

In 1969, 63-year-old Manuel Cortes handed himself in to the police in the Spanish town of Malaga, and claimed amnesty. During the 1930s he had been the socialist mayor of a village called Mijas, then a Republican soldier in Spain's bitter civil war. For the entire 30 years since Franco's victory, Cortes had been hiding – inside his own house in Mijas.

Even as a young man, Manuel Cortes commanded the respect of his neighbours in Mijas. He had a fierce sense of social justice, born of the inequality that he had witnessed all around him as he grew up in the early decades of the 20th century. Spain's rural population was cruelly exploited – by heavy local taxes, unfair sharecropping practices, unscrupulous landowners. The outrage that Cortes felt led him to become a socialist and a union organiser, and to get involved with the village council. His political work made him some enemies, but in March 1936, aged 30, he was elected mayor of Mijas.

WAR AND ITS AFTERMATH

Just three months later, in July 1936, right-wing elements in the military, led by General Francisco Franco, staged an uprising against the elected Republican government. Spain swiftly descended into civil war as the army seized control of some regions. Supporters of the Republic took up whatever arms they could find and made ready to defend their towns and villages against Franco's so-called 'Nationalists'. Cortes, as village mayor, organised the defence of Mijas. In 1937 he joined the Republican army, serving first as a front-line fighter then as a medical orderly. He was still serving in 1939, when the Nationalists triumphed.

Like thousands of defeated Republican soldiers, Cortes was disarmed and told to make his own way back home. But, though the war was over, the killing was not. Everywhere, Republicans and left-wingers were being denounced by their neighbours and purged by the new regime. A signed *denuncia*, backed up by two witnesses, was enough to get someone shot. Early in 1939, several of Cortes's socialist comrades in Mijas were executed as a result of such denunciations. This was before Cortes arrived home, so he knew nothing of it, but some instinct of self-preservation made him take care as he journeyed back to Mijas.

Manuel Cortes reached his home village in the dead of night on April 16, 1939. No one saw him arrive because he made his way across open fields rather than walk down the road. He went first to the house of his foster parents, who told him what deadly peril he was in. Manuel's wife Juliana was called to the house and she brought with her their small daughter, Maria. Manuel took the little girl in his arms for the first time in two years. Maria later said that this was her earliest memory, being held by this stranger whom she somehow knew to be her father.

That same night, Manuel and Juliana hatched a plan for keeping him alive. In the barber's shop belonging to Manuel's father was a dressing room that had been bricked up for so long that nobody in the village would remember that it was there. What if he were to hide out there for a while, until things cooled down or an official amnesty were declared? It would be cramped and uncomfortable, but bearable until it was safe for him to be seen. Over

She put a child's chair in the space – there was no room for any other furniture.

the next couple of days, Juliana prepared the hiding place. She knocked a hole in the wall, an opening big enough for Manuel to climb through, and hung a large picture over it. She cleared the dark space of dirt and rubble and put a child's chair in it – there was no room for any other furniture.

Manuel moved into his hiding place, a couple of nights after his return. He did not know then – how could he? – that he would spend the next two years in this tiny cell, followed by another 28 years

concealed in other dark spaces and locked rooms. For three long decades he would not breathe the fresh outdoor air nor feel the rain or the sun on his face, nor speak to anyone outside his immediate family. He would not visit another town, or even see a different street in his own village. At the age of 33 he was embarking on a self-imposed prison sentence.

SEARCH AND INTERROGATION

The first two years were the worst. No amnesty came, and so Manuel had to stay put. He was tormented by boredom, and filled his long silent days as best he could. He could have taken some pleasure in reading, but Juliana owned few books and dare not suddenly start borrowing the works of political philosophy that Manuel would have enjoyed. That would have looked suspicious – and suspicion was everywhere. It turned out that an acquaintance of Manuel's had seen him on a train as he made his way to Malaga in 1939 and had reported the sighting to the police. Juliana was summoned to the police station every week and interrogated: Have you seen your husband? Has he been in touch? She denied ever having set eyes on him, saying that if he was alive then she was delighted but that she had not heard from him. Her house was searched often, but the police found nothing, of course, because Manuel was holed up in the shop. To Juliana's amusement, people in the village would sometimes take her aside and tell her confidently that they had seen Manuel in Malaga, working as a barber under an assumed name. Good, she would say, then you know more than me.

As for Manuel, he adapted to his bizarre confinement. He read and reread Juliana's romantic novels by candlelight, since they were the only books available.

His re-appearance was a huge sensation, not just in Spain but around the world.

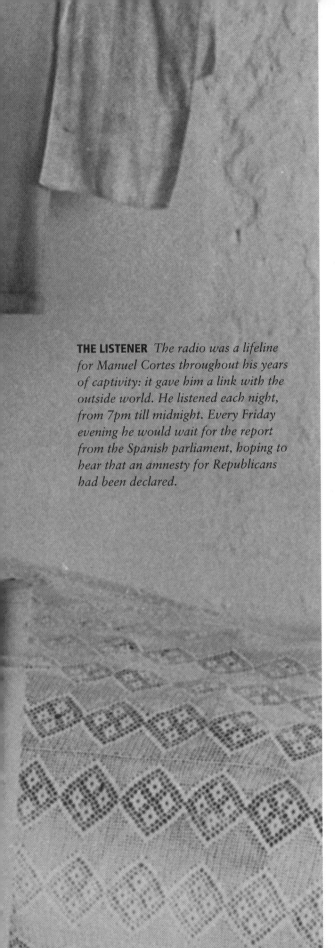

Every day, after dark, he came out through the hole in the wall to stretch his legs, to see his wife, to eat a meal. He gave up smoking because it made him cough, and there was always the possibility that someone might hear him and put two and two together. He had to deny himself the pleasure of becoming re-acquainted with his daughter. Instead, Maria was brought to play in the shop from time to time, and he would silently watch her, peeping out at her from behind the hanging picture. But he did not show himself nor speak to her in those first years. Maria was told that she had dreamed her cuddle with her father that first night, and on some level she came to believe it.

NEW HOUSE, DIFFERENT CELL

In 1941 the family moved house, and Manuel was smuggled to the new abode at night. Once he was installed there, his life became somewhat easier. Though he had a hiding place for emergencies, he could move around the top floor freely during the day – and this alone made him feel like he had been liberated. It was much easier for Juliana to provide his meals, since she no longer had to find a daily pretext to visit the barber's shop.

Manuel discovered that, if he was cautious, he could watch people pass by on the street without being seen. He observed many old acquaintances and got to know new people by sight. Ironically, perhaps, it was easier for Manuel to stay in touch with the global scene, thanks to a radio that Juliana bought him. Most joyfully of all, Maria was let in on the secret. When she was about five years old, she was told that her father was hidden in the house. The revelation came with dire warnings never to tell anyone, that her father would be killed and her mother would go to prison if she breathed a word. She understood the seriousness, and did as she was told. But for years afterwards, well into adulthood, she felt physically sick at the sight of a policeman.

Ten years passed in this way, then the family moved again to a larger house on the same street. Once more Manuel was moved in secret. He was to spend 18 years inside this third domestic jail. The police searches had ceased by now, but there were other dangers. One summer's day Maria, then 10 or 11 years old, was frying vegetables on the patio under a makeshift wooden shelter. The pan caught fire, and the flames quickly spread to the shelter. Neighbours came running with buckets, but the fire was already too strong to douse. Just before the roof caught light, someone grabbed the wooden posts of the burning shelter and tore it down so that the fire would not spread to the house and could be extinguished on the ground. When it was all over, Juliana went upstairs to see Manuel. He was as white as chalk and almost sick with fright.

A DANGEROUS SICKNESS

Juliana lived in dread of Manuel falling ill. She had a vague plan for that eventuality: she hoped that she could smuggle him out of the house to hospital in Malaga, where she could bribe a doctor not to ask questions. But she knew that the chances of making such a scheme work were slim. For common illnesses, such as flu and rheumatism, Manuel took medicines that Juliana bought over the counter in the anonymous surroundings of Malaga. He was also compelled to be his own dentist. 'The thing that plagued me most was my teeth,' he later told his British biographer, Ronald Fraser. 'The number I've pulled out over the years! Nine or ten it must

be, including some of the molars at the back – with my fingers. As soon as I got a toothache I knew that the only cure was to get the tooth out. Often the tooth wouldn't move at all, then it would be days before I could start to shift it. I always got it out in the end, however long it took.'

One day, early in the 1950s, the long-feared illness struck. Manuel woke up with an excruciating pain in his side. For two days he lay in bed, convinced that he was dying. Not daring even to cry out, he buried his face in a pillow to muffle his moans. Juliana began to implement her desperate Malaga plan, but Maria, by now a teenager, volunteered to feign her father's symptoms to the village doctor, so that some kind of treatment could be prescribed straight away. The doctor was called to the house, and Maria acted out the agony that her father was suffering, silently, behind locked doors. The doctor was baffled by the lack of visible symptoms. He would not prescribe the morphine that Maria begged him for – 'Not for a young girl,' he said – but he gave her some lesser analgesics. Miraculously, they did the trick when given to Manuel. His mysterious pain subsided and did not return.

GHOST AT THE FEAST

Just as painful, in their way, were the emotional sacrifices that Manuel had to make to keep his presence hidden. He missed his own father's funeral, sitting upstairs alone while his relatives attended the wake in the kitchen below. Even sadder, perhaps, was the wedding of his daughter Maria. The house was crowded with people on that morning, so Manuel could not take any part in the preparations. But he had arranged with Maria that she would tarry for a moment by the door to the staircase so that he, crouching at the keyhole, could see her in her bridal gown. It was like the old ruse that he had used when she was a toddler, to watch her from behind a picture.

After the ceremony, family and friends gathered at the house to mark the day. None of them suspected that the father of the bride, whom no one had seen in decades, was just a few steps away, weeping bitter tears over the lonely feast that Juliana had prepared for him. Before Maria left for her honeymoon, she found a pretext to slip upstairs to say goodbye, so Manuel did at least get to embrace his only child on her wedding day.

> *Maria's children, like Maria before them, were schooled never to mention their grandfather.*

On the last day of her honeymoon, Maria told her husband Silvestre about the big family secret – the father-in-law hidden upstairs. He was not as surprised as she had expected: he had spent enough time in the house while courting Maria to have noted the odd scrape and cough that sounded through the floorboards. He was one of only five people let in on the secret during the 30 years that Manuel was in hiding. The others were a trusted cousin who had once tried to arrange his escape to France and – in the fullness of time – Maria's three children. Like their mother before them, they were schooled from an early age never to mention their

grandfather in the presence of outsiders. As a precaution, they were never told his name, so that if the word *abuelo* ('grandpa') did fall from their lips, people would assume that they were referring to Silvestre's father. Manuel was a willing babysitter. The grandchildren were human company at last – affectionate, trusted people for him to talk to. He dearly loved his daughter's children, and he was devastated when the eldest, Rosamari, died of leukaemia at 19 months. Once again, Manuel grieved alone while a beloved member of his family was buried.

THE TASTE OF FREEDOM

But the long imprisonment of Manuel Cortes was coming to an end. One day in 1969 he was listening to the radio news, as he did every day, when the newsreader announced a general amnesty for all who had fought for the Republican side in the civil war. He could hardly believe it – in fact, he did not credit it until he had read the full text of the government proclamation in the newspaper. Once he was sure of amnesty, he came out of hiding and handed himself in to an astonished police officer. It was almost 30 years to the day since he had arrived home from the war.

The re-appearance of Manuel Cortes was a sensation – not just in Mijas or even in Spain, but around the world. He was, for a short while, an international celebrity. When asked what it felt like to return to normal life, he would say, 'These shoes are killing me.' He had, after all, been padding around in slippers for half his life. Manuel said that he wanted to enjoy the few years of life left to him. Happily this turned out to be more than just a few. Manuel Cortes died in 1991 at the age of 86, having enjoyed 22 years as a free man.

The Sabbath delight

In 1946 a rusting milk churn was found in a Warsaw basement. It was stuffed with documents – newspapers, photographs, diaries, children's drawings – produced in the city's Jewish ghetto during the Nazi occupation. This extraordinary collection was a cry to the future from Poland's doomed Jews.

Warsaw before the Second World War was the unofficial capital of European Jewry. In the 1930s a third of the city's population were Jews; many of them had roots in the city that went back hundreds of years. And no one knew the Jewish history of the city better than Emanuel Ringelblum, a historian who had written a doctoral thesis on Jewish life in Warsaw during the Middle Ages. Ringelblum was a socialist and political activist. After's Hitler's rise to power in 1933, he devoted much of his

TIME CAPSULES *The metal boxes and milk churns were battered and rusted, but the Ringelblum papers inside were mostly undamaged.*

time and energy to humanitarian work among dispossessed Jews who had escaped or been expelled from Nazi Germany.

The Nazis invaded Poland in September 1939 and took Warsaw within the month. Ringelblum saw at once that a tragedy was about to befall his people, and he responded with a historian's instinct. He knew the supreme importance of primary sources to any understanding of historical events, so he began to document the experiences of Polish Jews under Nazi rule by collecting testimonies and statements from the refugees drifting into Warsaw. He also wrote down his own observations, keeping as complete and accurate a journal of events as he could.

BIRTH OF THE GHETTO

In the first year of the Nazi occupation, Polish Jews were thrown out of their jobs, forbidden to travel, to own wireless sets, or to buy food in non-Jewish shops. At Easter 1940, the persecution turned violent. The Germans, together with Polish anti-Semites, embarked on a full-scale pogrom in Warsaw: over a period of eight days, Jews all over the city were beaten

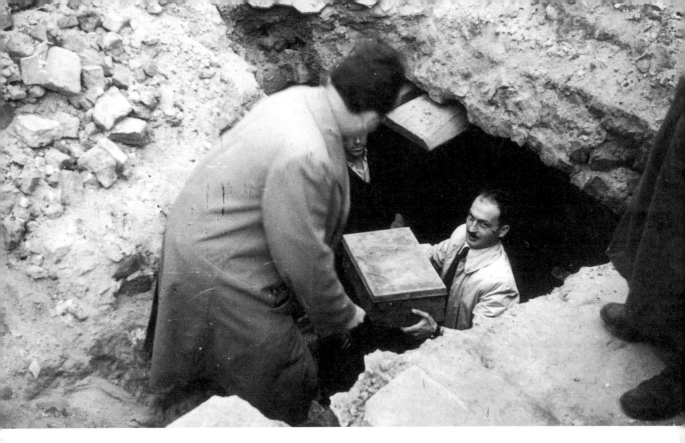

BURIED TREASURE *The papers had been hidden only a few years before but recovery of the archive was an archaeological undertaking. Ghetto survivors helped pinpoint where the boxes were buried.*

and robbed. In November 1940 the Nazis published a decree establishing a *jüdische Wohnbezirk,* a 'Jewish quarter', within Warsaw. Henceforth, all Jews in the city would be required to leave their homes and live within the bounds of a few streets on the left bank of the Vistula river. A map was printed showing the dimensions of the proposed ghetto: about 30 per cent of the population of Warsaw was to be confined to a space that occupied 2.4 per cent of the urban area, roughly 4km² (1½ sq miles).

The confinement of the Jews to the ghetto was carried out swiftly. Very soon, people began to succumb to diseases connected with overcrowding, exposure and lack of food. More than 400 died even before German troops had finished building the perimeter wall, 3m (10ft) high and topped with broken glass and barbed wire. Once the wall was complete and the

ghetto was sealed, the death toll rapidly rose to around 5,000 a month. At the same time, the population was supplemented by Jews relocated here from other parts of Poland. At its height the ghetto held 400,000 people.

HARVESTING HISTORY

Emanuel Ringelblum was inside the ghetto with his wife Yehudit and son Uri. His years of experience as a social organiser were now a valuable asset to the ghetto population. He spent his days working with others to set up soup kitchens and trying to find shelter for the thousands living on the streets, including the growing contingent of orphans. He also continued his documentary work, maintaining a chronicle of life inside the ghetto and gathering news and eyewitness accounts from newcomers so as to build a fuller

HISTORY MAN *Emanuel Ringelblum turned the dry work of historical archiving into a gesture of defiance and an act of heroism.*

picture of what was happening to Poland's Jews. But Ringelblum saw that events were too momentous for one man alone to record: he needed an organisation.

A BAND OF SCHOLARS

Ringelblum called about a dozen people to a meeting, mainly established academics, scholars and journalists. He asked them to conduct interviews, to make notes of things they saw and heard, and to collect copies of the posters, announcements, advertisements and Nazi proclamations that were pasted to walls inside the ghetto. He also wanted ration cards and identity cards, plus examples of the underground

newspapers that represented every shade of Jewish opinion (socialist, communist, Orthodox, Zionist) and all the languages of the ghetto (Yiddish, Hebrew, Polish). He needed accounts of the many cabarets, concerts and political rallies that took place under the eyes of the German soldiery. He wanted stories about people who found ways to get past the wall to trade with Poles on the outside, the little boys who acted as couriers and smugglers. He wanted to document the fact that synagogues were functioning all over the ghetto, and that there was even a church for Jewish converts to Christianity. He wanted to record the deeds of courageous Poles who passed food into the ghetto or helped people escape from it – and of the Jewish collaborators who reported their own people to the police in the hope of a better chance of survival.

Among those Ringelblum recruited for this vast undertaking were Szymon Huberband, a rabbi; Rachel Auerbach, an avant-garde writer; Israel Lichtensztajn, a well-known editor on a Yiddish weekly; and Menachem Linder, an economist. There were also young researchers such as Dawid Gruber, a 19-year-old student. Once work began, the group met regularly to collate and catalogue their transcripts, manuscripts and other finds. Their meetings usually took place on a Saturday afternoon, the part of the Sabbath when – in normal times – an inquiring theological discussion might take place in a Jewish home. The Hebrew term for this weekly event was *oneg shabbat*, 'the Sabbath delight', and Ringelblum now took this phrase as the codename for his ambitious archival project.

Ringelblum had high hopes for the collection. He initially intended that, after the war, he might deposit it all in a new academic institution dedicated to the experience of the Jews in Nazi-occupied Europe. He envisaged a great book, a kind of encyclopedia of the darkest hour in the Jews' long history. At the same time, he understood that his information could serve as evidence in postwar trials of Nazis. He was also aware that the material had urgent political significance. He gathered together the testimonies of those who had witnessed incidents of mass murder and smuggled them out of the ghetto, so that they could be passed to the Polish government-in-exile in London.

THE FINAL UPRISING

Such accounts left Ringelblum in no doubt that the Nazi plan was genocide. In July 1942 SS troops began sweeping through the ghetto, rounding people up and herding them through a gate that led to a railway yard. Here they were loaded into freight trucks and taken directly to the Treblinka concentration camp, 80km (50 miles) away. It was the beginning of the end for the ghetto, and Ringelblum decided that the moment had come to hide the archive. He had it packed into ten metal boxes, which were then concealed in a cellar.

The deportations ceased for a while in the autumn. Inside the ghetto, the Jews used this lull to organise themselves into fighting units. They built bunkers and managed to procure a few pistols and rifles. It was not much of an armoury, but when SS units next entered the ghetto in January 1943, they met fierce resistance. The weeks of the uprising were carefully documented by Ringelblum's team, and a second cache of documents was sealed in two milk churns, then hidden in a separate secret location. A third and final set of documents was buried before the Nazis obliterated the ghetto that April.

In the chaotic days of the uprising it became easier to slip in and out of the ghetto. Before it was razed to the ground, Emanuel Ringelblum escaped with his wife and son and was given shelter outside the ghetto by a Polish family. Together with numerous other Jews, they hid in a cellar in the so-called 'Aryan' part of Warsaw. Here they remained for almost a year until, in March 1944, they were betrayed and arrested. In July Ringelblum, his family, his fellow fugitives and the brave Poles who had sheltered them were led back to the flattened ruins of the ghetto, where they were all shot.

Among the survivors of the ghetto were two of Ringelblum's volunteers, an economist named Hersz Wasser and the writer Rachel Auerbach. In January 1946 they returned to the site of the ghetto and helped to locate the second cache of documents. The first cache was unearthed five years later, in 1950. The third has never been recovered, but it is believed to be somewhere beneath what is now the Chinese Embassy.

Tucked into one of the recovered milk churns was a note written by Dawid Gruber, one of the youngest of Ringelblum's group. He had died in the uprising. Gruber's note makes clear that, for him, helping to preserve the history of the ghetto was an act of resistance every bit as meaningful and powerful as fighting Nazis on the streets. He wrote: 'I would love to see the moment in which the great treasure will be dug up and scream the truth to the world, so the ones who did not live through it may be glad and we may feel like veterans with medals on our chests. May the treasure fall into good hands, may it last into better times, may it alarm and alert the world to what happened. May history attest for us.'

MI9: escape and evasion

Compasses hidden inside pens and collar studs, maps printed on silk handkerchiefs, flexible sawblades disguised as bootlaces. A department of British military intelligence, devoted to helping prisoners of war escape, came up with these devices and many others. Each gadget was designed to give Allied fugitives the best possible chance of avoiding capture.

In December 1939, three months into the Second World War, a new intelligence department began operating out of a large hotel room on Northumberland Avenue in central London. It was given the designation Military Intelligence, Section 9 – MI9 for short – and it had two main tasks: to help Allied prisoners-of-war (POWs) to escape from the camps in which they were held; and to assist people on the run in occupied territory – for example, downed air crews – to reach neutral territory and return home.

The head of this new organisation was a man named Norman Crockatt, a decorated veteran of the First World War who had spent the intervening years

working as a stockbroker. He began by clarifying and refining the remit of his section. To Crockatt, it seemed important to focus on the needs of British personnel in enemy territory, so MI9 swiftly dropped an additional responsibility for the interrogation of enemy POWs held in Britain. That function was passed to another department, MI19. On the other hand, it seemed to Crockatt that RAF officers ought to know how to cope if they found themselves stranded in enemy territory, so his department began training them in escape and evasion techniques – knowledge that they were then expected to pass on to the men in their units.

SAFE HIDING *Hairbrushes and other everyday items were equipped with secret compartments that could hold maps and other small but useful objects. Thousands of escape tools were smuggled into POW camps in this way.*

To this end, MI9 officers routinely debriefed servicemen who had managed to return to Britain from occupied lands. The department then disseminated the intelligence that they gathered to other agencies. One section specialised in devising codes that could be used to pass information clandestinely to and from the POW camps. Above all, Crockatt sought to foster what he liked to call 'escape-mindedness'. He instilled the message that it was a soldier's duty to try to evade captivity. All the prison-camp tunnellers, the men who carved fake official stamps from the heels of shoes or fashioned radios from biscuit tins and bits of wire, or who laboriously sawed through metal bars with razor blades, were acting in the spirit of Norman Crockatt and MI9.

HANKIES AND BOOTLACES

Yet if MI9 is remembered today, it is mainly for the inventions of one of Crockatt's subordinates, an ingenious and energetic individual by the name of Christopher Clayton Hutton. His job was to procure and devise aids for escape and evasion. His gadgets fell into two categories: pre-capture and post-capture. The first were supplied to air crews and other servicemen despatched to hostile territory, and were intended to be used only if things went wrong; the second were smuggled into POW camps in concealed form. All were designed to help those on the run.

Hutton started by getting hold of a copy of every real-life First World War escape story that he could lay his hands on. He had the plots summarised by sixth-formers at Rugby School, where Crockatt had studied. The first conclusion that he drew from the schoolboy abstracts was that maps are vital when evading capture, so he contacted Bartholomews, a well-known

TRUE NORTH *Tiny compasses were concealed in the buttons of airmen's uniforms. Ingeniously, they were provided with reverse screw threads, so that only people in the know were likely to succeed in opening them.*

firm of map-makers, and experimented with printing their products on squares of silk, which could easily be bundled up and hidden. The solution lay in adding pectin to the printer's ink, which then produced a stable impression. Later he achieved good results with rice paper, which was extra thin and did not rustle.

Servicemen on the run in unfamiliar territory needed to be able to orientate themselves, and that meant using compasses. Here Hutton showed particular ingenuity. Tiny devices barely a quarter of an inch (6mm) long were hidden in smokers' pipes, fountain pens and cap badges. Collar studs revealed directional needles when paint was scraped off their bases. Others were sewn into shirt collars and belts. In all, well over 2 million such devices were produced in the course of the war. Some did not even need to be disguised. Hutton experimented successfully with magnetised razor blades that indicated north when hung from a piece of thread.

The stories that Hutton collected suggested that cutting tools were always a necessity, so next he turned his mind to knives. He took his inspiration from the Gigli saws used by surgeons for cutting bones. These consisted of little more than lengths of wire with abrasive edges. Hutton sheathed such wires in textile covers, converting them into bootlaces. He

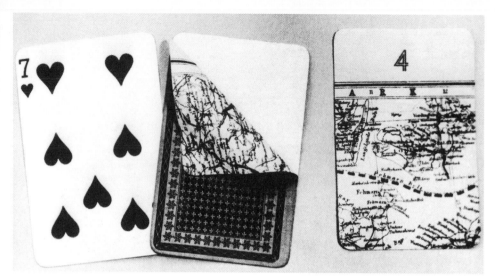

also supplied hacksaw blades that could be suspended on a length of string down the inner leg of a pair of trousers.

Escaped POWs seeking to avoid detection needed suitable civilian clothing. Hutton helped provide it by sending blankets to the camps with tailoring patterns printed on them in invisible ink. These showed up when the blankets were washed, making it relatively easy to cut out the material needed to sew a passable non-military overcoat. MI9 also experimented with convertible boots for flying crews, which came equipped with a tiny knife that could be used to cut away the leggings, thus making the boots resemble everyday walking shoes. The leggings could then be sewn together to make a fleece waistcoat.

HAMPERS FOR FUGITIVES

MI9's most successful product for air crews was the escape box, eventually issued to all those flying over hostile territory. It looked like a cigarette tin and was packed with useful items: boiled sweets and chewing gum, compass, razors, matches, needles and thread, a rubber water bottle, water-purifying pills and even Benzedrine tablets for energy. Hundreds of thousands of these life-saving hampers were produced.

MI9 devoted much effort to finding ways of getting its goods into the camps where Allied prisoners were held. Hague Convention rules, accepted by the Germans as well as the Allies, specified that prisoners-of-war should be allowed to receive letters and parcels. MI9 seized upon this channel, though, scrupulously, they never used the cover of Red Cross packages for such purposes, so as not to compromise that organisation's neutrality.

Screwdrivers were hidden in cricket bats, serrated wires were sealed inside combs and toothbrush handles. When the Germans, growing wise to such ruses, took to X-raying all incoming mail, MI9 found more devious ways to smuggle in supplies. Maps and money, for example, were sandwiched between the inner and outer skins of condensed-milk tins, where they would not show up on the radiographs. In 1941 and 1942 alone, MI9 despatched more than 6,800 packages to POW camps. Almost a quarter of those contained concealed equipment. Coded instructions would be sent in advance, advising prisoners what to expect and where to look.

An estimated 25,000 British and Commonwealth escapers and evaders managed to find their way back home from enemy territory during the course of the war. Many of them would never have made it without MI9 and Christopher Hutton's ingenious devices.

The man who would be Q

MI9 was not the only organisation inventing devices to help individuals to evade the Nazi net. The Special Operations Executive (SOE), created to conduct guerrilla warfare, had its own specialists. Among them was Charles Fraser-Smith, the original of Ian Fleming's gadget-maker, Q.

In the James Bond novels, Q is the otherwise unnamed head of Q Branch, a fictional secret-service division responsible for devising ingenious spying devices. His real-life equivalent in the Second World War was Charles Fraser-Smith, an MI6 operative who had previously been a Christian missionary in Morocco. Officially, Fraser-Smith was employed as a temporary civil servant in the Clothing and Textile Department of the Ministry of Supply. Neither his ostensible boss nor his secretary knew his real job, which was to develop equipment for spies and agents operating in occupied lands.

Fraser-Smith began by buying in props from outside suppliers. One early assignment involved procuring authentic army uniforms for SOE operatives in neutral Spain. But Fraser-Smith was too imaginative to be a mere quartermaster, albeit a secret one. He soon started dreaming up ideas of his own. These included pens containing hidden compasses and shaving brushes with space in the handle to insert rolls of film. In an age when pipe-smoking was common, he created pipes with asbestos-lined stems that could hold secret documents. He called the devices 'Q gadgets', a term he coined by way of analogy with the Q ships of the First World War – heavily armed decoy vessels disguised as unarmed merchantmen, used to lure enemy submarines. Ian Fleming, who had dealings with Fraser-Smith while working for naval intelligence, later borrowed the term for his own fictional gadget-mongering boffin.

Fraser-Smith's job involved oiling the wheels of cooperation for British operatives working alongside local resistance movements. That could

IDEAS MAN *Charles Fraser-Smith kept many examples of his inventions, and in retirement he set up an informal museum of his work at his home. He lived to see himself fictionalised as Q in the James Bond books.*

mean, for instance, providing quantities of Balkan tobacco to raise the spirits of Josip Tito's Yugoslav partisans. He also sought ways of making 'clients' inconspicuous in hostile territory. This led to one of his more bizarre concepts: garlic-scented chocolate for airmen flying missions over occupied France.

Some of his best innovations outlived their immediate purpose. He concealed semi-solid food in toothpaste tubes, developing a method that would be used to package cheese spreads and other comestibles in the postwar years. He was also credited with introducing the use of compressed-air cylinders to inflate life jackets and providing them with a fluorescent dye designed to make downed airmen visible to rescuers.

The fruits of Fraser-Smith's innovative mind remained secret until the 1970s, when he was finally granted security clearance to write about his unique role in the Second World War.

Gallant she-soldiers

In most places and historical eras, warfare has been a largely male affair and soldiers were by definition men. But there are many documented cases of women disguising themselves as men in order to go into battle. Some of these female warriors had distinguished military careers, and spent years on active service without their secret being discovered.

The 19th-century Swiss writer Madame de Staël was once told an odd tale by André Masséna, marshall of France. He was recalling an incident at the Battle of Büsingen, fought in Germany in 1800. He had spotted a lone French artilleryman fighting for his life against a group of Cossacks and Bavarians. 'The young man, who appeared quite a child, defended himself desperately. I despatched an officer with some men to his assistance, but they arrived too late. His body was covered with wounds, at least thirty. And do you know, madame, what this man was. A woman! A handsome woman too, though she was so covered in blood that it was difficult to judge her beauty. She had followed her lover to the army. He was an artillery captain, and when he was killed she defended his remains like a lioness. She was from Paris, her name was Louise Belletz, and she was the daughter of a fringe-maker …'

The marshall believed he had witnessed something unique: a woman masquerading as a male soldier, and fighting as bravely as any man. But every element of the incident – the deceptive cross-dressing, the courage shown in battle, the desire to be close to a lover serving in the army – was an occurrence so commonplace as to be almost a clandestine military tradition.

MUSKET ON HER SHOULDER

About the same time as Louise Belletz was fighting in the guise of a man for France, a woman named Nadezhda Durova was doing the same in Russia. Durova grew up in a military family, surrounded by cavalry officers, and she seems to have wanted to be one of them from childhood. 'My martial inclinations grew stronger with every day that passed,' she wrote. 'I forgot nothing of what I learned from the hussars. I would run round the nursery shouting, "Squadron! Face right! From your mark, forward march!"' In her early 20s Durova ran away from her home and an unhappy marriage to join a Polish light-cavalry regiment. Serving under the alias Alexander Sokolov, she bravely saved the lives of two comrades in the Prussian campaign of 1806–7, and was wounded at the Battle of Borodino in 1812.

CAVALRY MAIDEN *Nadezhda Durova's lively account of her exploits as a cavalry officer is one of the first autobiographies in the canon of Russian literature.*

One of the first documented instances of military transvestism concerns a woman known only as Private Clarke, who fought in the English Civil War of the 1640s. A ballad called 'The Gallant She-Soldier', written in about 1655, told of her exploits. She was, it seems, every inch the trooper: 'With musket on her shoulder, her part she acted then / And every one supposed that she had been a man,' goes the song that lauds her. 'She would drink and take tobacco, and spend her money too / When as occasion served that she had nothing else to do.' Clarke, like Louise Belletz, served alongside the man she loved. She was unmasked as a woman only when, while still a soldier in the ranks, she bore him a son. The fact that Private Clarke gave birth to a child was an unmissable clue to her gender; most she-soldiers did not do anything so revelatory. Certainly not Kit Cavanagh, perhaps the most fearless and accomplished woman ever to serve in a man's army. She did most of her soldiering in the 18th century, in many ways the heyday of the incognito female warrior. Cavanagh was known by various names – Christopher (or Kit) Walsh, Kit Davies and (after she was discovered) Mother Ross.

BRAVE MOTHER ROSS

Kit Walsh first joined the army in 1693 in order to find her husband, who had apparently been press-ganged after getting drunk in a Dublin tavern. Leaving her children in the care of her mother, Kit went to enlist. 'I cut off my hair and dressed me in a suit of my husband's ... I bought me a silver hilted sword, [then] ... offered my service to go against the French ... The hopes of soon meeting my husband added a sprightliness to my looks, which made the officer say I was a clever brisk young fellow. He gave me a guinea enlisting money, and a crown to drink the king's health, and ordered me to be enrolled.'

Within weeks Kit Walsh was in Belgium, taking part in the so-called Nine-Years' War. She fought at the Battle of Landen, where she was wounded and captured. She was exchanged in 1694 and returned to her regiment. By this time she was so deeply in character that she somehow became involved in a dispute with a fellow soldier over a woman. They fought a duel and Kit killed her rival, as a result of which she was discharged from the army. But she was still intent on finding her husband, so she re-enlisted with the Scots Greys, remaining with the regiment for some years without ever revealing her female identity. She was wounded for a

second time at the Battle of Schellenburg in 1704, and fought in the Battle of Blenheim later that year. It was after Blenheim that she finally caught up with her husband, who was propositioning a Dutch woman at the very moment that his wife found him. Richard sheepishly agreed to keep his wife's secret. They claimed to be brothers to explain the fact that they had the same surname.

The fortunes of war led at last to the unmasking of Kit Walsh. She was badly wounded at the Battle of Ramillies, where 'an unlucky shell struck my head and fractured my skull. Though I suffered great torture by this wound, yet the discovery it caused of my sex in the fixing of my dressing, by which the surgeons saw my breasts, was a greater grief to me.'

Kit was discharged – with honour this time – and stayed with the army as a sutler (a civilian merchant) throughout the Spanish War of Succession. Richard Walsh was killed at the Battle of Malplaquet in 1709, and Kit spent a day searching for his body so that she could bury him. Soon after, she married another soldier (a friend of her husband's), saw him killed too, married again and was widowed once more. Though she was now living openly as a woman, and was officially a non-combatant, she could not resist the whiff of gunpowder. One day, while taking food to the front line, Kit stopped to grab a rifle and took a potshot at an enemy soldier. This drew fire from the opposing lines, and Kit was hit in the face. It was her last battle injury: in 1712 she returned to England, where she lived out her days as a Chelsea Pensioner. When she died in 1739, she was buried with full military honours.

But the British army was not long without an outstanding she-soldier. In 1745 a woman named Hannah Snell enrolled in a regiment of foot at Carlisle. Like Cavanagh, she had joined up to find a husband who had deserted her. Hannah's disguise consisted of a suit of clothes loaned by her brother-in-law; she borrowed his name too – James Gray.

In the barracks at Carlisle, according to her own account, Hannah was wrongly accused of neglect of duty and sentenced to 500 lashes. It is almost incredible that she underwent this protracted ordeal without her gender being discovered, so the truth of this part of her story has been doubted. It seems certain, however, that she deserted her regiment and later fetched up in Portsmouth, where she enlisted as a marine. She was shipped with her company to India, where she took part in the siege of Pondicherry (1748). Though she received multiple wounds in the legs during the battle, she managed to avoid detection when she was treated by the surgeons. She allowed them to dress her legs, but did not tell them about an excruciatingly painful musket ball lodged close to her groin. Instead she waited till her other injuries had been seen to, then 'thrust in both her finger and her thumb' and removed the bullet herself.

IN A MAN'S WORLD

Snell's fortitude in a crisis is admirable, but no less amazing is the ingenuity that she and other women soldiers must have constantly displayed in order to remain undetected. At the same time, it is hard to imagine how the men in the ranks failed to spot that they had women alongside them. In the case of Snell and Cavanagh, the thick, baggy uniforms of the 18th century may have made it easier to disguise a womanly figure and achieve a mannish look. The hygiene practices of the time would have helped, too: no soldier in those days would have dreamed of stripping to wash, or of taking off his clothes to sleep. All the same, she-soldiers undoubtedly faced delicate and uncomfortable problems every day of their military service. They had to explain away their remarkable lack of a beard, for example, and several of those who left accounts speak of the unpleasantness and indignity of having to

It must have been troubling for her that she was known as 'the pretty dragoon'.

bind their breasts. Kit Cavanagh claimed to have learned to urinate standing up with the help of a contraption consisting of a 'silver tube and leather straps', a feat that would have added a persuasive edge to her cover story. Nevertheless, it must have been troubling for her that she was universally known in the Scots Greys as 'the pretty dragoon'.

Herein lies another conundrum. She-soldiers were not always masculine-looking; in fact, contemporary sources often remark on their feminine good looks. One of the last and most successful of the she-soldiers was, by all accounts, remarkably beautiful when not posing as a man. She was called Loreta Velazquez, and she served as a Confederate officer in the American Civil War.

While most she-soldiers have found that it is wise not to stand out, Velazquez longed for the recognition and glory that war sometimes confers. She joined up as a scout, having first equipped herself with a fake beard and a false name, Harry Buford. She participated in the Battle of Bull Run (1861), then decided to impress her superiors with some freelance espionage. She crossed the front line into Union territory, changed into her women's clothes, and proceeded to Washington DC, the enemy capital. She gathered intelligence by attending soirées and chatting to Union officers, then made her way back to her own side, donning her uniform and beard along the way.

In 1862, while leading a patrol, Loreta was wounded in the foot. Still in male guise, she withdrew to the Confederate city of New Orleans to recuperate. Here, ironically, she was arrested by the military on suspicion of being a Union spy – and of being a woman in disguise. She chose this moment to tell her whole story, hoping to be commended for her work. Instead she was sent to jail for ten days and made to pay a $10 fine.

Velazquez was unfortunate. Most she-soldiers attracted admiration for their deeds, and some became feted celebrities. Kit Cavanagh's story was written up (and perhaps embellished) by no less

a writer than Daniel Defoe. Nadezhda Durova, whose gender was revealed after her disapproving father sent a tip-off to the military authorities, was granted an audience with Tsar Nikolai I. He gave her a medal and a commission and allowed her to continue to serve as a male officer in the hussars. Hannah Snell came back from the wars with her identity intact, then sold her story to a publisher. When word of it reached the ears of the Duke of Cumberland, under whom she had fought, he awarded her a stipend. She invested the money in a pub that she called The Widow in Masquerade.

She was arrested for being a spy – and a woman in disguise.

For contemporaries, the remarkable thing about she-soldiers was their obvious valour and their appetite for war. They were seen as laudably masculine, as if they had somehow transcended their feminine weakness. In our day women routinely join the armed forces, and we are no longer surprised when they perform bravely in the face of danger or bear pain. The female partisans and resistance fighters of 20th-century wars provide plenty of examples of supreme courage, and we know that women, no less than men, are capable of heroism on the battlefield and elsewhere. The she-soldiers of the past can now be admired simply for being fine warriors. From a 21st-century perspective, it does not seem so odd that Brigadier Preston, Kit Cavanagh's commanding officer, described her as 'the best man I had'.

BEARDED LADY
Loreta Velazquez was a fearless soldier. She fought disguised as a man and spied on the enemy in women's garb. After the American Civil War she sought adventure first as an explorer and then as a gold-miner.

The admirable Doctor Barry

James Barry was a pioneering doctor and one of the finest military surgeons of the 19th century. When he died in 1865 a secret was revealed: he was anatomically a woman.

As far as is known, James Barry was born Margaret Ann Bulkley. Though considered female at birth, it is possible that he was what would now be termed intersex or transgender. He decided at an early age to live life as a man.

While still very young, perhaps in his mid-teens, Barry went to Edinburgh University to study medicine, graduating in 1812. The medical profession was exclusively male, and so Barry is sometimes cited as Britain's first qualified woman doctor. In 1813 he became a regimental surgeon and was posted to Cape Town. Here his appearance and personality attracted much comment. He was very short, barely 1.5m (5ft) tall, and had soft, androgynous features. His manner was rather harsh – sometimes for sound professional reasons, but frequently it seemed through sheer temper. He was often in trouble with his superiors for insubordination or 'conduct unbecoming the character of an officer and a gentleman'.

MEDICAL REFORMER *A contemporary sketch of Dr James Barry, who deserves to be remembered for his pioneering work in sanitation and field medicine. He saved hundreds of lives.*

CHILDBIRTH PIONEER

Some doubted the medical capabilities of a surgeon who looked so childlike, but that was a crass misjudgment. Barry was a remarkable physician, and his career is full of achievements. In Cape Town in 1820, for example, he performed one of the first successful Caesarean sections, saving the life of both mother and baby. In other postings – from Mauritius to St Helena to Canada – Barry strove to improve sanitation and hygiene in the army camps. He fought for better conditions for black prisoners in South African jails and for lepers in their segregated colonies. In all this, his intransigence was a definite virtue. At the end of his career, he took unpaid leave in order to go and tend soldiers wounded in the Crimean War.

James Barry died of dysentery in retirement, worn out by years of tireless work and debilitating tropical illnesses. He had left strict instructions that he be buried quickly in the clothes he died in, but that request was ignored. The charwoman paid to lay out the body of a distinguished military man objected when she found that 'the corpse is a woman's'. The truth was more complex than that, but it is fair to say that Dr Barry was a unique and admirable individual who more than earned his place in medical and military history.

Behind the sultan's throne

In Western imagination, the grand vizier is an unscrupulous and sinister adviser to a weak oriental ruler. In reality, viziers were often men of great wisdom and deft diplomatic skills. But wielding great power from the shadows was a perilous task, provoking great rivalry and jealousy, and the careers of many viziers were cut short by a violent and untimely death.

The Turkish and Islamic Arts Museum in Istanbul is housed in a fine stone palace. This building, erected in 1524, was once the home of Pargali Ibrahim Pasha, grand vizier to Suleiman the Magnificent. Ibrahim's life was a classic rags-to-riches tale, the stuff of legend throughout the Ottoman Empire. The son of a Greek Christian sailor, Ibrahim was seized by pirates as a child and sold into slavery. He was lucky: he worked in a palace that just happened to be the childhood home of Suleiman, and the boys grew up together. Ibrahim became Suleiman's falconer, then rose through the palace hierarchy to reach the position of grand vizier in 1523. He was now second-in-command of the Ottoman Empire. He married Suleiman's sister, and amassed a vast fortune.

THE RULER'S BURDEN
Viziers such as Pargali Ibrahim Pasha were a power behind the throne in the Islamic world. Caliphs and sultans ruled, and lived lives of supreme luxury, but they did not always have the patience or competence to deal with the administration

of government. Responsibility for matters such as official appointments, taxation, education and foreign relations were often delegated to a vizier – the word derives from an Arabic term meaning 'burden-bearer'. With that responsibility came the opportunity to wield extraordinary power. A skilful vizier could carve out a role that combined the functions of kingmaker, chief minister and trusted adviser to the ruler. Later, when the word 'vizier' began to be used for a minister at any level of government, the term 'grand vizier' came into use to distinguish the pre-eminent man in the political hierarchy.

The role of vizier was shaped by Yahya ibn Khalid, vizier to Harun al-Rashid, caliph of Baghdad from AD 786 to 809 (the latter's name has entered legend because of his frequent appearances in tales of *The Thousand and One Nights*). By the 11th century the role of the vizier was well-enough established to be the subject of books and manuals. One of the most celebrated of these instructionals was the *Siyasatnama* ('Book of Government') by Nizam al-Mulk, vizier to the Seljuk

sultans between 1063 and 1092. This enlightened and thoughtful text is full of advice on how to wield power justly, covering such matters as appointing ministers and listening to the troubles of aggrieved subjects.

The long-lived Muslim empires of the Abbasids, Seljuks and Ottomans all had viziers. Some were military leaders, and many were outstanding statesmen or diplomats. Pargali Ibrahim Pasha, for instance, brokered treaties with Francis I of France and with Charles V, King of Spain and Holy Roman Emperor.

The vagaries of foreign diplomacy may well have seemed straightforward compared with life in a sultan's court, which could be a labyrinth of rivalries and jealousies between the sultan and his family, his wives, concubines and heirs. Viziers were players in this deadly power game. The career of Pargali Ibrahim Pasha again provides a prime example. He backed the wrong faction as two sons of Suleiman, Mustafa and Selim,

manoeuvred to place themselves in line for the succession. In the process he made an enemy of Selim's mother, a former slave of Slavic origins named Roxelana. He also became intoxicated with his own authority and awarded himself the title sultan, a gross affront to Suleiman. Despite their long friendship, the sultan had Ibrahim executed in the manner reserved for high-ranking members of the Ottoman Empire: he was strangled with a silken cord.

One of Ibrahim's successors as grand vizier, Rüstem Pasha, was married to a daughter of Roxelana. He naturally favoured his brother-in-law, Selim. Rüstem spread rumours that Mustafa planned to seize the throne from his father. Convinced that this was true, Suleiman invited his son to an audience, then watched as he was strangled with a bowstring by his eunuchs.

FOREIGN INFLUENCES

Many of the early viziers, men such as Yahya ibn Khalid, were Persian – effectively foreigners operating in an Arab environment. Persians had a reputation for sound administration, but that was only part of the reason for installing them in this powerful role. It was thought that a man from a different culture and background might better be able to remain aloof from the tangled ambitions of the ruling family and from harem politics. A foreigner could also function as a political lightning conductor, making hard and necessary political decisions from which the ruler could distance himself. And, of course, foreigners were entirely dispensable: they could be eliminated without a qualm if they fell from favour.

The outsider tradition was embedded in the Turkish Ottoman Empire. Many of the grand viziers were products of the system of recruitment called *devshirme*.

no 1683 den 12
er wider den 12
pott Dneck geschlagen

Jüly dickay: Residenz Statt Wien
Ar: mit verlüßt vnd
Worden

RIGHT-HAND MAN *Kara Mustafa Pasha was the archetypal grand vizier: ruthless, grasping and violent. The sultan had him strangled in 1683, after he failed to take Vienna. His last words were, 'Make sure you tie the knot right.'*

This was a kind of 'blood tax' by which boys were taken from Christian families in conquered lands, converted to Islam and trained to be administrators. As a result of *devshirme*, the chief minister under the Turkish Ottomans tended to be Albanian, Croat, Bosnian, Greek or Italian. One clear advantage of the system was that it promoted advancement by merit rather than birth, and many grand viziers worked their way up from lowly backgrounds. Pargali Ibrahim Pasha fitted this pattern.

HIGH-STAKES GAME

Folk tales might portray viziers as sinister and unscrupulous schemers – the grand-vizier figure in Disney's *Aladdin* is a classic clichéd caricature – but some viziers were popular figures and deservedly so. Nizam al-Mulk founded a chain of higher-education colleges called Nizamiyyah schools, and invited poets and scholars to take part. He thus laid the groundwork for an education system that would later become the madrassah system of religious schools. Some viziers earned their popularity simply for creating order out of chaos. At the same time, many viziers became immensely rich, and not just through the salary provided by the sultan. Officers appointed to senior roles were expected to make payments to the vizier for the favour.

But if viziers became too popular, too powerful or too rich, they made enemies and risked being assassinated or executed. The pattern was established right from the start, in the days of Caliph Harun al-Rashid. When the family of his vizier, Yahya ibn Khalid, became too dominant and ostentatious, power was suddenly ripped from them. In AD 803 Yahya's eldest son Jafar inherited his position. Jafar was gifted and generous, a peacemaker, but

he was accused of having an affair with the sister of Harun al-Rashid, a capital offence. Despite the fact that Jafar was his childhood companion, the sultan ordered his execution. Harun al-Rashid had the executioner beheaded too, as a mark of affection for his friend.

More than eight centuries later, the role of the vizier was still precarious. Kara Mustafa Pasha was the last of the respected Köprülü dynasty of Ottoman grand viziers, but in 1683 he led the humiliating retreat from the Siege of Vienna. He was duly executed by ritual strangulation, and his head was delivered to Sultan Mehmet IV in a velvet bag.

Kabir, the son of a cook, rose to be prime minister.

The last of the viziers came to power in Persia not in Turkey, but his story is in keeping with the vizier tradition. Mirza Taqi Khan Amir-e Kabir was born in 1807, the son of a cook. By his early 40s he had risen to be prime minister under Shah Naser al-Din. He was a thoroughly modern politician who initiated a massive and rapid programme of reform – building factories, modernising the judiciary, setting up a postal system, founding a newspaper and restricting the influence of the clergy. But Kabir had a powerful enemy in the shah's mother-in-law, who arranged for his death in time-honoured fashion: he was set upon in his bath-house, and his wrists were slit. It was the kind of violent end that could have come to any vizier in the course of more than a thousand years.

The devil's chariots

Two years into the First World War, British forces unleashed a new top-secret weapon on the German trenches. It consisted of a fleet of strange metal-plated vehicles that ran on newfangled caterpillar tracks and sprouted machine-guns from the sides. No one realised it at the time, but this, the first deployment of the tank, was the start of a new era in land-based warfare.

TRENCH BUSTER *The first tanks to see action were lightly armed, lozenge-shaped machines that carried a crew of eight men. Four of those men were engaged entirely in driving and steering the vehicle.*

In 1903 the great science-fiction writer H.G. Wells published a short story called 'The Land Ironclads'. The tale envisaged a future war in which victory is won through the use of mobile, armour-plated machines that can navigate ploughed fields without getting bogged down, and crash through defensive earthworks as easily as the metal hull of a warship cuts through a stormy sea. Wells gave them the appearance of 'a large and clumsy black insect ... crawling obliquely to the first line of trenches and firing shots out of portholes in its back.'

Wells was describing a weapon yet to be invented – the tank. But machines uncannily similar to the ones that he imagined (albeit rather smaller) rolled into battle during the First World War, a mere 13 years after his tale was published. The real-life tanks owed nothing to Wells's vision, yet, remarkably, they went from the first sketches on the drawing board to their first appearance on the battlefield in the space of about two years. No weapon in modern history has been developed from scratch so rapidly

Swinton's aim was to combine armour plating with a 'bullet-proof cupola'.

The purpose of the tank was to end the static trench warfare that prevailed on the Western Front. Their first deployment, on the Somme in 1916, was not a great success, but they soon proved their worth on the battlefields of Flanders. Since then, this lumbering weapon, invented for a

narrowly defined tactical situation, has proved immensely diverse. The descendants of the trench-busting tanks became the key strategic land weapon of the Second World War and later conflicts.

When war broke out in 1914, Britain's army was equipped with the latest deadly weaponry but depended almost entirely on pre-industrial methods to move. Each piece of artillery, every shell, had to be drawn into position by draft horses – huge numbers of them. Britain had a million horses with the army in France by 1917. They were indispensable because they did not depend on roads; they could function in the mud and churned-up conditions of the front line. No motorised vehicle could do what a team of horses could do.

FIGHTING TRACTORS

Yet technology already existed that could mechanise the business of moving men and equipment over broken ground. In the first days of the war, a staff officer named Ernest Swinton was in France working as a war correspondent. As he watched the trench networks grow and the battle lines become fixed, he remembered a report he had read about American farm machines that ran on 'caterpillar tracks'. It was obvious to him that these tracks might have a military application; Swinton wondered whether they might be combined with armour-plating to make 'a self-propelled climbing block-house or rifle-bullet-proof cupola'.

Swinton submitted his half-formed idea to his commanding officer, who passed it to Winston Churchill, then First Lord of the Admiralty. In fact, Churchill had been looking at a similar proposal – many people were thinking along these lines. He wrote a memo to the prime minister, H.H. Asquith, recommending the experimental manufacture of 'a number of steam tractors with small armoured shelters, in which men and machine-guns could be placed'. The suggestion was forwarded to Lord Kitchener, secretary of state for war, but he was unimpressed. That could have been the end of the idea, but Churchill felt sure that the concept had potential. Under conditions of utmost secrecy, he ordered his own government department to conduct some experiments and build a prototype. In February 1915 a body called the Landships Committee was formed to oversee the work. At this stage, Churchill concealed the existence of the committee even from his own government, so that no one would try to shut it down.

MOTOR WAR-CARS

The secrecy around the new weapon extended to its name, and the precise origin of the word 'tank' is still obscure. According to one account, workers in the factories where the prototypes were being built were told that they were making water tanks for Russia. Another version has Winston Churchill presented with three possible names: the rather clumsy but descriptive 'motor war-car', or the two more obfuscatory terms 'cistern' and 'tank'. He plumped for 'tank' because it was the simplest word. Churchill himself gave his own account of the origin of the term. According to him, drawings of the early tanks were marked 'water carriers'. When it was pointed out that this would naturally abbreviate rather infelicitously to 'WCs', the headings on the pages were changed to 'water tanks'.

The expression 'landships' was used only in the weapon's early stages and just by the small group of people involved in its development. That name, an echo of Wells's 'land ironclads', acknowledged the fact that the tank idea was, thanks to Churchill's sponsorship of it, a navy project rather than an army one. The first experimental machines had none of the streamlined grace

LITTLE WILLIE *The first prototype of the tank was little more than a metal box set on caterpillar tracks. A gun turret was to have been installed on top, but a better tank design – Big Willie – went into production before this early experiment was even equipped with a gun.*

or effortless pace of a naval vessel, and the leaden monosyllable 'tank' seemed to suit the object better than 'landship'. But the names given to the various parts of the tank – hatch, hull, bow and so forth – had a distinctly naval ring to them.

THE PRODUCTION MODEL

The first manufactured tank – the ancestor of every Tiger, Sherman and T-34 – was built as a one-off by the Lincoln firm of William Foster. The man in charge of production was William Foster's managing director, a man named William Tritton. He worked alongside the Admiralty's appointee, Walter Wilson. As a result of this confluence of 'Will' names, the prototype of the tank was dubbed 'Little Willie'. It was a metal box fixed to rugged metal-plate tracks. According to the Admiralty's specifications, it had to be able to carry ten men and mount a rapid-firing 6-pounder cannon, along with two machine-guns. It was required to have a reverse gear and a top speed going forward of no less than 4mph (6.5km/h) – about walking pace. It needed to be able to span a trench 8ft (2.5m) wide, and climb an earthwork 5ft (1.5m) high.

Little Willie fulfilled these conditions, but even as it was being trialled, a new version, Big Willie, was under construction in the same factory. Big Willie, later known as Mother, looked rather different from its predecessor. The hull was sandwiched between two much larger tracks that ran all round the edge of rhomboid frames on either side of the hull – giving the tank its distinctive lozenge shape. The upward-sloping leading edge made Big Willie much better at climbing slopes than Little Willie, with its boxy front end. To keep Big Willie's profile low and so make it a harder target, the guns were set inside protruding 'sponsons' on the sides of the frames. According to one witness of the early trials, these looked rather like bay windows on a Georgian house.

Mother underwent rigorous trials in February 1916. The prime minister, the chancellor of the exchequer and King George V all saw it put through its paces. The impression the tank made was good enough for the army to place an order for 150 of them, though Lord Kitchener – even after seeing Mother in action – still thought it was a 'pretty mechanical toy'.

The British High Command wanted to preserve the valued 'element of surprise'.

The army had originally wanted the tanks for the opening of the Somme offensive in July 1916, but they were not ready in time for that vast and tragic action. Instead they were brought to France in August to inject new life into an offensive that had ground to a halt despite the unprecedented scale of the infantry attack. It was hoped that the tanks would punch a decisive hole in the German line. A total of 50 Mark 1s – Mother's first offspring – were brought up to the line. Security was tight: the British High Command wanted to preserve the much-valued 'element of surprise', and were determined that the Germans would not know what was about to hit them.

The first tank attack in history took place on the Somme battlefield ten weeks after the start of the campaign. But they were thrown into the fray in too much of a hurry. No thought had been given to coordinating the tanks' advance with that of the walking infantry, and many of the tank crews had not had enough battle training. The machines themselves had unresolved mechanical problems: of the 50 tanks, barely 30 were in a fit state to take part in the attack. Seven failed to start on the day. Of the 25 or so that managed to engage the enemy, several broke down or were disabled by German shelling before they could reach the German trenches. It was a low-key curtain-raiser for an altogether new kind of warfare.

Lieutenant-Colonel Swinton and other champions of the tank were dismayed that the generals in the field had not waited until more tanks were ready before sending them into battle. The tank specialists had believed all along that the way to make them effective was to unleash hundreds of machines, unexpectedly, on the broadest possible front. Winston Churchill agreed that a golden opportunity had been squandered. 'My poor land battleships have been let off prematurely on a petty scale,' he said.

But almost everyone outside the circle of military engineers and politicians involved in creating the new weapon saw immediately that its battlefield debut was a sensational event. The newspapers were full of wildly exaggerated stories about the effect of the new invention. It was variously reported that every tank carried 400 soldiers, instead of the eight very cramped and uncomfortable crew; that they sported huge 12in naval cannons, rather than modest 6-pounder guns and a couple of machine-guns; that they sped across no-man's land at 30mph (50km/h), when, in fact, they moved at a very slow

crawl – and had to come to a complete stop in order to change direction. Some of the stories were sheer invention. It was said that they had been built in Japan by teams of Swedes, and that the commanding officer of each tank was a former airman who had lost his nerve for flying. And some of the expressions coined to describe the tanks were equally fantastical: 'Motor-Monster', 'Old Ichthyosaurus', 'Jabberwock with Eyes of Flame', 'Travelling Turret', 'Touring Fort' and the quite nonsensical 'Boojum'. A German correspondent who saw the demoralising effect the tanks had on his own troops dubbed them the 'devil's chariots', which would have gratified the tank's inventors had they got to hear of it.

TANKS AND THE NEXT WAR

Tanks were finally used en masse at the Battle of Cambrai in 1917. On this occasion they succeeded in smashing the German line and driving deep into enemy territory, as their supporters had always intended. But battlefield tactics had still not caught up, and British forces failed to consolidate the gains that the tanks made.

It was not until after the war that serious thought was given to the best use of tanks. Visionaries such as Basil Liddell Hart understood in real-world terms what H.G. Wells had explored imaginatively: that the tank would become the key to land warfare. Liddell Hart's insights were ignored in Britain, but his views were closely studied in Germany by General Heinz Guderian. As the architect of the *Blitzkrieg* tactics of the Second World War, Guderian was the true heir of Swinton and his fellow tank men. In the rapid German onslaught of 1940 and 1941, Guderian showed how far the tank had evolved in its first 25 years and what a truly devastating weapon it could be.

The invisible spy in the sky

In 1960 a CIA spy plane was shot down over the USSR and its pilot captured. To the embarrassment of the US government, a hitherto secret aircraft – the U-2 – now became global news. It soon emerged that the plane and its surveillance role were not quite as secret as the CIA believed them to be.

On May 1, 1960, a public holiday in the Soviet Union, an American U-2 spy plane set off from a CIA base in Pakistan. Its mission was to overfly the USSR, photograph missile bases in the Ural mountains, then land undetected in Norway. Such missions were almost routine: the U-2 had passed over Soviet territory dozens of times without incident. The pilot that day, Gary Powers, had flown many such missions. The Americans knew that the U-2 operated outside the range of Soviet fighters, missiles and detection systems. They were sure that it had never been spotted.

They were wrong. The Russians had known for years that the Americans were flying over their territory, but dared not object because speaking out would have made it obvious to the world that the Soviet air force was incapable of striking back. So instead the Soviet military worked on developing a ground-to-air missile capable of bringing the U-2 down. This was the day that they fired their missile and winged the U-2.

From a political point of view, a partial hit was better than blowing the plane out of the sky. The plane crashed, the pilot bailed out and was captured alive. His trial and conviction on espionage charges was a huge propaganda coup for the Soviets.

As for the secret plane, parts of it were put on display in Moscow as a kind of cold-war trophy. It later transpired that the U-2 was equipped with a camera so technologically advanced it was itself a kind of weapon of war. Its resolution was at least four times greater than that of any aerial camera available at the time. From a height of 18km (11 miles), it could take pictures so sharp it was possible to make out individual sentries on the perimeter of missile bases and even identify what sort of rifle they were carrying.

Powers was interrogated for months by the KGB, then sentenced to ten years' imprisonment. Two years later, he was traded for a Russian spy and brought home. The episode looked like a victory for the USSR. Soviet premier Nikita Khrushchev drummed this home by rebuking US president Dwight Eisenhower: 'Don't you fly into the Soviet Union! Respect our sovereignty and know your limits! If you don't know your limits, we will strike!' In fact, the U-2 programme had already gathered much invaluable information. Earlier missions gave the USA a clear idea of Soviet missile strength, so the government could negotiate with the USSR from a position of knowledge, thanks to the U-2 and pilots such as the unfortunate Gary Powers.

Sinking the rainbow

Rainbow Warrior, *Greenpeace's flagship, was sunk* by limpet mines in Auckland harbour in 1985. Clearly, someone badly wanted to halt the group's anti-nuclear protests in the Pacific Ocean, and investigations traced the conspiracy to the very highest levels of the French state.

An unusual vessel was moored in Auckland harbour in the summer of 1985. It was a trawler that had seen long service with Britain's Ministry of Food and Fisheries. In 1977 it had been sold to the environmental group Greenpeace, and renamed *Rainbow Warrior*. Under that name, it had played a crucial part in Greenpeace campaigns against seal hunting and whaling. It was now in New Zealand, preparing to protest against, and if possible prevent, nuclear tests in the Pacific Ocean.

The French military had scheduled a programme of nuclear tests for that July. A series of controlled explosions was due to take place at Mururoa Atoll, an uninhabited islet in French Polynesia, some 4,200km (2,600 miles) east of New Zealand. *Rainbow Warrior*'s mission was to lead a flotilla of yachts to Mururoa with the aim of disrupting the tests.

In France, President François Mitterand was troubled by Greenpeace's intentions. There was a history of clashes between the eco-warriors and the French government. In 1972 French commandoes had attacked a yacht piloted by Greenpeace's future chairman as it sought to disrupt an

earlier series of tests. Public outrage at the incident had played a part in France's decision to call a halt to its atmospheric testing of nuclear warheads.

Greenpeace was making no secret of its goal this time round. The organisation knew that worldwide publicity helped its cause, and *Rainbow Warrior* was part of its media-savvy campaign. It became something of a tourist attraction in Auckland, and its crew was cheerfully welcoming visitors on board. What they did not know was that some of their guests were operatives of France's foreign-intelligence agency, the DGSE. One French agent had even become a volunteer in Greenpeace's Auckland office.

MINES ON THE HULL

Before long, the French task force in New Zealand had all the information it needed to set in motion a plan to sink the ship. The plot was codenamed 'Opération Satanique', and the attack was set for the night of July 10. The plan was to fix two limpet mines to *Rainbow Warrior*'s hull, primed to detonate a few minutes apart. The first explosion would disable the vessel, allowing time for the crew to abandon ship. The second blast would then complete the sinking. That, at least, was what was supposed to happen, but events turned out very differently.

The two bombs exploded one after the other, as planned, shortly before midnight. Most of the crew, who earlier that evening had been celebrating a birthday party aboard, did indeed manage to get off the ship. But one crew member, 35-year-old Fernando Pereira, was still below deck when the second explosion went off. It is thought that Pereira, a photographer, may have been trying to go back and rescue his expensive equipment. He was trapped by the second blast and drowned.

The sinking of the ship came as a terrible shock to Greenpeace. Elaine Shaw, the organisation's director in New Zealand, was given the news by a reporter who called her in the middle of the night. 'You can't sink a rainbow!' she exclaimed. At first, Greenpeace officials thought the explosion must have been an engine blow-out, but inspection of the damage soon showed that the metal of the hull had been blown inwards, indicating an external attack. Suspicion at once turned to France, whose nuclear activities were

STRICKEN WARRIOR *The sinking of* Rainbow Warrior *achieved the opposite of what was intended. The world was appalled by the French attack and by the death of Fernando Pereira. Greenpeace, meanwhile, garnered much attention for its mission to bring an end to nuclear testing.*

the immediate target of the Greenpeace campaign. But it seemed inconceivable that a democratic power would have ordered such a blatant attack on an internationally accredited organisation in the territorial waters of a friendly nation.

SIGN OF THE ZODIAC

The first hint of the truth about the sinking emerged through the vigilance of a group of boating enthusiasts. In response to a recent wave of thefts on the waterfront, they had organised patrols in the harbour area. The two men on duty on the night of July 10 had noted some unusual activity earlier in the evening.

This is what they saw. A grey Zodiac inflatable dinghy had made its way into the inner harbour, where it drew up alongside the embankment. A figure got out of the dinghy and looked urgently down the road. A camper van parked nearby then flashed its lights and drove up to the waterside steps. The driver and the occupant of the boat transferred some boxes from the dinghy to the van, then drove off together, leaving the Zodiac behind. It was still moored at the harbour wall when the sinking took place.

Thinking that they may have spotted the thieves they were seeking, the two amateur vigilantes made a note of the van's registration and passed it to the police. It was traced within 36 hours. The van had been rented by a married couple with Swiss passports, apparently in New Zealand for a camping holiday. It did not take long, though, to establish that the Swiss documents were fake. The true identities of the pair were revealed to be Major Alain Mafart and Captain Dominique Prieur, operatives of the French secret service. They were arrested by New Zealand police two weeks after the sinking.

It soon became clear that Mafart and Prieur were not the prime movers of the plot; their role had been to provide logistical support for the divers who planted the mines. Seeking other leads, police turned their attention to a yacht, the *Ouvéa*, whose French crew had aroused the suspicions of a local customs official even before the bombing: three of the four men on board the yacht had freshly issued passports; one claimed to be a professional photographer, but he had no camera equipment of any kind. By this time the yacht was gone from Auckland,

Who planted the bombs?

Though two French secret-service agents were put on trial for the killing of Fernando Pereira, they were always believed to have been part of the support team and not directly responsible for planting the limpet mines that sank the Greenpeace ship. The identity of the diver or divers remained a mystery. Then, in 2006, Antoine Royal, a brother of Socialist presidential candidate Ségolène Royal, claimed in a newspaper interview that another brother, Gérard, had admitted responsibility. 'He told me it was he who planted the bomb on the Greenpeace ship,' Antoine was quoted as saying. 'He took a small craft with a second person to approach the boat.' Gérard, who was employed at the time as an assault diver with the DGSE intelligence agency, subsequently refused to confirm or deny his brother's claim. His companion on the boat that night has never been named.

but it was subsequently traced to Norfolk Island, an Australian possession. Three of its crew members were questioned there, but had to be released before evidence could be marshalled to bring charges. The yacht subsequently disappeared for good, apparently scuttled by the crew, who are thought to have returned to France either by military aircraft or submarine.

THE TRAIL LEADS TO PARIS

In the aftermath of the bombing, the French government issued a statement denying any knowledge of the affair, but that position quickly unravelled and press speculation forced ministers to set up an inquiry. It concluded that agents had indeed been despatched to New Zealand, but had not been authorised to carry out the bombing. That line too proved untenable, and France's prime minister, Laurent Fabius, eventually had to release a statement admitting that the *Rainbow Warrior* had been sunk by secret-service operatives acting under orders. 'The truth is cruel,' he remarked.

The sequel was unsatisfactory for all concerned. Mafart and Prieur were put on trial for their part in the death of Pereira. They chose to plead guilty to manslaughter, for which they were given ten years' imprisonment. But the French authorities, outraged by the severity of the sentences, put pressure on New Zealand's government to revise the court's decision. A deal was struck whereby the agents were transferred to a French military base in the Pacific to serve three years' detention. In return, France agreed to apologise for the attack and pay an indemnity of 13 million New Zealand dollars. In the event, the pair spent less than two years on the island before returning to a heroes' welcome in Paris. No other agent was ever prosecuted.

New Zealand's relations with France remained frosty for some time. The uproar caused by the sinking did lead to a moratorium on nuclear testing at Mururoa, though France controversially carried out a final series of blasts there ten years later, just before the international Nuclear Test Ban Treaty came into force.

Twenty years after the bombing, the French newspaper *Le Monde* revealed that President François Mitterand had personally authorised the operation to sink the ship. Admiral Pierre Lacoste, head of the DGSE at the time of the anniversary, took the opportunity to express his personal regret for the death of Fernando Pereira. As for the *Rainbow Warrior*, it was raised, forensically

> *France's prime minister had to admit that the ship had been sunk by secret-service operatives.*

examined, then scuttled in New Zealand waters to serve as an artificial reef. It was replaced by *Rainbow Warrior II*, a refitted deep-sea fishing boat, in 1989. This second ship was retired in 2011, shortly before the inauguration of a purpose-built third *Rainbow Warrior*.

Elaine Shaw's exclamation that 'you can't sink a rainbow' was widely recalled as the new ship set sail. Her words have become an expression of ecological optimism, a kind of unofficial motto for the Greenpeace organisation.

Chapter 4
CRIME AND CORRUPTION

Downright lies and half-truths can serve to obscure all manner of crimes – from mass murder to commercial espionage. But despite criminal threats and political cover-ups, the facts have a tendency to seep out sooner or later.

THE FIRST MONUMENT *The communist-era monument to Babii Yar (below), erected in Kiev in 1976, portrays the massacre as a war crime perpetrated on a defiant Soviet population, not the genocide of defenceless Jews.*

In search of Babii Yar

In 1941 Nazi forces murdered more than 33,000 Jews at Babii Yar, a ravine on the outskirts of Kiev. It was one of the worst acts of genocide of the Second World War, yet for decades official Soviet accounts obscured the facts about who carried it out, who the victims were and where exactly it took place.

The statue at Dorohozhichi metro station in suburban Kiev is in many ways a typically grandiose Soviet war memorial. The composition, which stands in a grassy hollow just south of the station exit, consists of a number of larger-than-life figures on a granite plinth. Chief among them is a grim, powerfully wrought man in a long greatcoat. He and a second figure, who might be a soldier or a sailor, seem to be shielding an anguished mass of people, some of whom are tumbling forward and sideways. Close behind those two strong men is a young woman in a simple shift, her arms covering her face as if in pain or recoiling from some horror. The Russian inscription, written when the monument was constructed in the 1970s, reads: 'Here, in 1941–1943 the German-Fascist invaders shot more than 100,000 prisoners-of-war and citizens of Kiev.'

That inscription is true, but it is only one version of the truth. Of those 100,000, citizens of Kiev and elsewhere, 90 per cent were Jewish. And though mass executions continued sporadically for the two years mentioned in the inscription, a third of the Jews who died here (or near here) were

COMPLEX MEMORIALS *In 1991, after the fall of communism, the new Ukrainian government erected this monument in the form of a Jewish menorah (above) close to the site of the Babii Yar massacre. The sad and troubling 'children's memorial' (right) was unveiled in 2001.*

shot over the course of two days. More subtly, the ensemble of figures in the statue misleadingly implies that the massacres were resisted in some way. But when the first killings took place here at the end of September 1941, nobody – no heroic civilian nor musclebound soldier – was on hand to try to shield the victims. Quite the reverse, in fact.

The pitiful truth of what happened at Babii Yar is as follows. On September 28, 1941, just days after German forces had

occupied Kiev, a proclamation was pasted all over the city saying that 'all Yids' were to come to certain assembly points the next day. They were ordered to bring with them warm clothing and money, and told that any who did not comply would be shot. Many of the able-bodied Jewish men and women of Kiev were with the Red Army at the time, either at the front or retreating from the German onslaught, so most of those still in the city were elderly people taking care of their grandchildren.

Babii Yar. This deep gully had been sealed off with barbed wire, and there were cordons of sentries all around. The outer cordon consisted of pro-Nazi Ukrainian police; the innermost cordon was made up entirely of German troops. Once inside the wire, each group of Jews was made to leave their luggage behind and strip naked. They were then forced to run a gauntlet of soldiers who beat them with truncheons and set dogs at their heels. At the end of this punishing corridor, they were herded onto a narrow ledge at the lip of the ravine.

Machine-gunners on the far side fired along the row of people, so that as they were hit they toppled into the chasm. This gruesome process was repeated time after time until Babii Yar was filled to the brim with corpses. A dusting of earth was shovelled onto each layer of the dead, but it was said that the ground shifted and heaved for a week after the killing ended.

Many more people would die at Babii Yar during the German occupation of the Ukraine. The Nazis continued to use the ravine as a convenient killing ground for the remainder of Kiev's Jews, as well as for card-carrying communists, gypsies and others. The Syrets concentration camp was set up nearby. Before they retreated from Kiev in 1943 the Germans forced prisoners to exhume many of the bodies from the ravine and burn them – though plenty of evidence remained in the ground.

The assembly points were all near the railway lines. This fact and the deceptive detail about warm clothing led some to believe, despite the offensive wording of the proclamation, that they were merely to be deported – to Germany, perhaps, or maybe to Palestine. This seems naive, but nothing of the Nazi treatment of Jews had been reported in the Soviet press since the Nazi-Soviet non-aggression pact had been signed two years earlier.

The Germans expected four or five thousand people to comply with the order; in fact, more than 30,000 turned up. Some even came early to be sure of a good seat on the train. Groups of people were taken from the waiting crowds, and marched under armed guard to the ravine known as

So the Soviet authorities knew what had happened at Babii Yar even before the war ended. But as early as 1944 they began to play down the overwhelmingly Jewish ethnicity of the victims. A report by the State Commission for the Investigation of Nazi Atrocities referred to the dead of Babii Yar as 'peaceful Soviet citizens' and did not mention that most had been Jews. This was to be typical of Soviet pronouncements for most of the next four decades.

THE DOCTORS' PLOT

The fact was that the Soviet state looked on its own Jewish population with deep suspicion – especially in the cold-war years. The creation of the state of Israel in 1948 was a triumph for Zionist Jews, but the beginning of a dark time for Soviet ones. For Stalin, increasingly paranoid in his old age, the existence of Israel meant that any Soviet Jew might bear a secret allegiance to a state other than the USSR – one that was allied to the USA. In the years after the Second World War, nearly all of the Soviet members of the wartime Jewish Anti-Fascist Committee disappeared into the gulag. In 1952 Stalin prepared the ground for a massive purge of Jews, signalled by the trumped-up 'Doctors' Plot'. Several prominent Jewish physicians were accused of having murdered leading figures in the Soviet government. Widespread persecution of Jews – 'rootless cosmopolitans' in the coded language of the Soviet press – was planned. The anti-Semitic purge had just begun when Stalin died in March 1953.

The new leadership under Nikita Khrushchev swiftly called a halt to the arrests and sackings of Jewish doctors and intellectuals. There followed a more hopeful time, when limited criticism of the Soviet system was tolerated and artists were permitted a small measure of freedom. Among the people to benefit from the 'thaw' were two young writers: the novelist Anatoly Kuznetsov and Yevgeny Yevtushenko, a daring and rebellious poet.

Kuznetsov had grown up in Kiev during the war and lived close enough to Babii Yar to hear the shooting in September 1941. Ever since, he had been collecting testimonies and scraps of information about the massacre. In 1961 Kuznetsov took Yevtushenko to visit Babii Yar. For some years the authorities had been planning to build a sports stadium and amusement park on the site, and work was already underway to obliterate the ravine. Yevtushenko responded by swiftly writing a poem entitled simply

> *By 1961 work was already underway to obliterate the ravine of Babii Yar.*

'Babii Yar', which begins with the lines: 'There is no monument at Babii Yar / Just a sheer drop, steep like a rough-hewn headstone. / It scares me. Today I feel as old / As the Jewish people itself ...' The poem goes on to evoke the Jewish victims of a 19th-century pogrom, a nail-pierced Christ, Anne Frank dreaming of love and springtime. Yevtushenko concludes that anti-Semitism is unworthy of the Russian people: 'I'm loathed by the Jew-haters, and that makes me a true Russian.'

Yevtushenko's poem caused a sensation. He was praised by some but criticised by others for implying that Babii Yar was somehow the fault of the Russians, not

German Nazis. Yevtushenko's point was that there was in the USSR an indifference to Jewish suffering that amounted to passive anti-Semitism. The failure to erect a monument to the victims of Babii Yar, in a country bristling with war memorials, was a symptom of that insensitivity.

In 1966 Anatoly Kuznetsov published his 'documentary novel' *Babii Yar,* and this too sparked massive controversy. Kuznetsov stated that, though it was written in the form of a novel, everything described in his book had really happened. But two factors made the published work less truthful than Kuznetsov claimed. First, he used more poetic licence than he chose to admit, conflating episodes and people so as to make a stronger narrative. Second, the censor made heavy cuts and changes to the text. All references to the Ukrainian police, for example, were deleted, since the very idea that any Soviet citizens had collaborated with the Nazis – and in particular that some were complicit in the Holocaust – was by now utterly taboo.

THE FIRST MONUMENT

One outcome of these literary scandals was that the authorities decided at last to erect a monument at Babii Yar: the bombastic socialist-style sculpture by the metro station. But the half-truths and obfuscation persisted after its unveiling in 1976. When foreign delegations were taken there, the scripted story told by their official guide always stressed the 100,000 Soviet dead, not the 33,000 Jews killed here in two days. In fact, it was underlined that the victims of Babii Yar were 'not only Jews'. And it was strictly forbidden to stray from the path around the statue into the sunken area, as this was deemed a sacred war grave.

Visitors to the monument who had read Yevtushenko or Kuznetsov were often baffled by the site, which seemed too small for the enormity of the crime committed here. It does not resemble Yevtushenko's 'sheer drop' nor Kuznetsov's description of the ravine as 'deep and wide as a mountain gorge. Words shouted from one side of the ravine could hardly be heard on the other side.' Had it been allowed, you could have walked across this space in a trice.

This site seemed too small for the enormity of the crime.

The odd truth is that the monument stands some considerable distance from the ravine. The killings took place not here, as implied, but about a mile to the north, on the far side of the station. The official version and the placing of the monument in this insignificant dip, away from the site of the first shootings, turned Babii Yar into a smaller place, and so a lesser tragedy, than it really was. It also stripped the mass murders of their genocidal character.

To find Babii Yar today, you turn the other way out of the station, into an urban park. You pass the little monument to the children killed at Babii Yar and come eventually to a tall menorah, the seven-armed Jewish candelabra, on which is etched an endless queue of faceless people shuffling to their deaths. Behind that monument is a deep gash in the earth, like an unhealed wound. This is where the massacre happened, a place in which, according to Yevtushenko, 'the trees look ominous as judges ... where all is silent screams ... and, baring my head, I feel myself slowly turning grey.'

The secret of Katyn Forest

When the Red Army invaded eastern Poland in 1939, all captured Polish officers were detained in Soviet prison camps. As far as anyone knew, they were still there two years later, when Germany invaded the USSR.

With the Nazi attack on the USSR in 1941, Poland became Russia's ally. Representatives of the Polish government-in-exile went to Moscow to ask that their officers be released, so that they could join the fight against Nazism. Stalin was evasive, telling the Polish officials that all the officers had already been released. When he was presented with a list of thousands of names of officers known to have been in Soviet custody in 1939, Stalin said that they must have escaped, 'perhaps to Manchuria'. It was almost two more years before the truth, or part of it, came out. In February 1943 the German occupying force discovered a mass grave within the Katyn Forest, near Smolensk. Scraps of uniform and other remains made it clear that the dead were Polish army officers.

The Germans announced their find to the world, but few chose to believe them. Winston Churchill, aware of the need for Stalin's military support, thought 'the less said about Katyn, the better'. The Soviets, when they recaptured the area, launched an investigation which concluded that the Poles had been shot by the Germans in 1941. They pointed out that all the bullets found in the grave were from German-made weapons.

The fact was that the Polish officer corps had been liquidated in 1940 by the Soviet secret police, the NKVD. This was proved beyond reasonable doubt in the West, but in the Soviet Union it continued to be denied, which caused further anguish and deep resentment in Poland. In the 1970s and 1980s, Soviet propaganda made much of a Nazi atrocity committed in the similar-sounding Belorussian village of Khatyn, thereby confusing and conflating the two massacres, and creating the false impression that Nazis were always the perpetrators, Russians the victims.

In 1990 Soviet president Mikhail Gorbachev conceded that the Katyn massacre had indeed been carried out by Russians. It seems that Mausers had been used not to implicate the Nazis but because the German guns had a lighter recoil than Russian ones, and so made the job of shooting one man after another easier on the executioners.

OPENED GRAVE *More than 4,000 Polish officers died at Katyn. They had all been despatched with a single bullet to the back of the neck. About 18,000 more Poles were executed in other Soviet camps and prisons.*

Operation Neptune Spear

The operation to kill Osama Bin Laden was ten years in the planning, but took less than 40 minutes to carry out. Through a process of meticulous intelligence-gathering and surveillance, the leader of Al Qaeda was tracked to a purpose-built compound in the Pakistani city of Abbottabad. In the early hours of May 2, 2011, a unit of US Navy SEALs went in.

GLOBAL TERROR *Osama Bin Laden inspects a map of Afghanistan, while hiding in that country in 1998. The 9/11 attacks were still in the future, but Bin Laden was already a wanted man. He was suspected of masterminding bombings of US embassies in Kenya and Tanzania.*

The fleet of helicopters swept in over the foothills of the Himalayas. Flying low, hugging the ground, and equipped with stealth technology that made them invisible to radar, they were not spotted when they passed out of Afghanistan into Pakistani airspace. They were headed for a walled house in the suburb of Bilal Town in Abbottabad, a short walk from the elite Pakistan Military Academy. As they passed over the city, they rattled the windows of the houses in this middle-class part of town. An accountant, working late, was so startled by the noise that he spilled coffee on his keyboard. Another resident tweeted jokingly: 'Go away helicopter, before I take out my giant swatter.'

The American helicopters were not going away – not just yet. One Black Hawk came to a stop at low altitude, hovering just above a house at the end of a dirt track. The house was three storeys high, much larger than all the other houses

> *They saw a man peer down the stairs from the top landing. It was Bin Laden.*

in the neighbourhood, and its wedge-shaped grounds were hidden behind high walls topped with barbed wire. Inside the helicopter, a dozen or so Navy SEALs were making ready to fast-rope into the yard of the compound – but something went wrong. The helicopter stalled, and as the pilot tried to make a controlled landing its tail clipped the compound wall. It landed heavily on its nose, and the soldiers inside, instead of sliding down to the ground on a rope, had to pile out of the door into the courtyard. They were joined by the occupants of a second helicopter, who had landed outside the compound and scaled the wall. Together this team – perhaps 25 men in all – made their way to the main house. Along the way, an armed man emerged from a separate guesthouse, brandishing a Kalashnikov rifle. A woman stood in the doorway behind him. Both were shot dead before the armed man could fire his weapon.

ENEMY KILLED IN ACTION

Inside the house, the SEALs spread out. One team made its way up the stairs. Despite the late hour, there were clusters of wakeful children on every landing. On the first floor a second man and woman were spotted. They were unarmed, but the man looked to be about to lunge for a gun; the SEALs opened fire and killed both. A third man – now known to have been a son of Osama Bin Laden – descended the stairs, and he too was shot dead. The SEALs then saw a man peer down the stairs from the top landing of the house. It was Bin Laden himself. A SEAL fired a shot, but missed.

Bin Laden retreated into a bedroom, pursued by the assault team. Inside they found two women, wives of Bin Laden, one of whom called out his name. They were bundled out of the way, and the lead SEAL found himself facing Osama Bin Laden, architect of the 9/11 attacks on New York City. He fired two shots; the first struck Bin Laden in the chest, the second hit him in the left eye, killing him instantly. Through his headset the SEAL spoke the codeword that meant the mission had achieved its objective. 'Geronimo, Geronimo,' he said, 'EKIA [enemy killed in action].' US President

Barack Obama and his advisers, who had been following the whole operation from the Situation Room at the White House, heard that pronouncement. 'We got him,' Obama said.

PINPOINTING BIN LADEN

Ever since the Al Qaeda attacks on New York in September 2001, it had been a priority of the US government to find Osama Bin Laden and mete out justice to him. But he had proved extraordinarily elusive. In the first months after 9/11 he was believed to be in the mountains of Tora Bora in Afghanistan. As soon as the 'war against terror' got underway, the US Air Force bombed Al Qaeda's strongholds there, but Bin Laden, if he was in the mountains at all, managed to slip away. In the years that followed there were various sightings of him and reports of his activities. It was speculated that he was in Iran, indulging his passion for falconry; that he was sheltering with tribal peoples in the borderlands of Afghanistan and Pakistan; that he had died in an earthquake in Kashmir or succumbed to chronic kidney disease; most outlandishly, that he had shaved off his greying beard and was living incognito in Indonesia or the Philippines.

Nobody knows for sure where he was in the three or four years after 9/11, but by 2005 he was planning to move into the house then being built in Abbottabad. Around this time American Intelligence got the first glimmer of a lead that would eventually pinpoint him. Among the mass of information gleaned from inmates at the Guantanamo Bay detention centre was a snippet about a man known by the pseudonym Abu Ahmed al-Kuwaiti. Detainees said that he might be a courier for Bin Laden. The American authorities were keenly interested in Bin Laden's couriers. The Al Qaeda leader never used phones or any electronic form of communication, since their signals are traceable. Instead he relied on individuals to carry his messages and orders by hand. If they could track down an active courier, they would be just one step away from Bin Laden himself.

> *The Americans heard al-Kuwaiti say, 'I am back with the people I was with before.'*

By means that have not been revealed, US operatives discovered the real name of al-Kuwaiti, traced him to northern Pakistan, and managed to tap the phone calls that he received. On one occasion, while the Americans were listening in, he received a call from an old associate who asked him where he was and what he was up to. 'I am back with the people I was with before,' replied al-Kuwaiti. This portentously vague formulation was enough to alert the Bin Laden hunters, and in August 2010 US agents on the ground in Pakistan began observing the comings and goings of al-Kuwaiti. More than once he went to the prisonlike compound in Abbottabad. When he left, he would drive for 90 minutes before putting a battery into his phone and making calls.

American attention now turned to the compound itself. No phone cables went in; the balcony on the top floor of the house was screened by a wall more than 2m (6½ft) high, and the windows on the

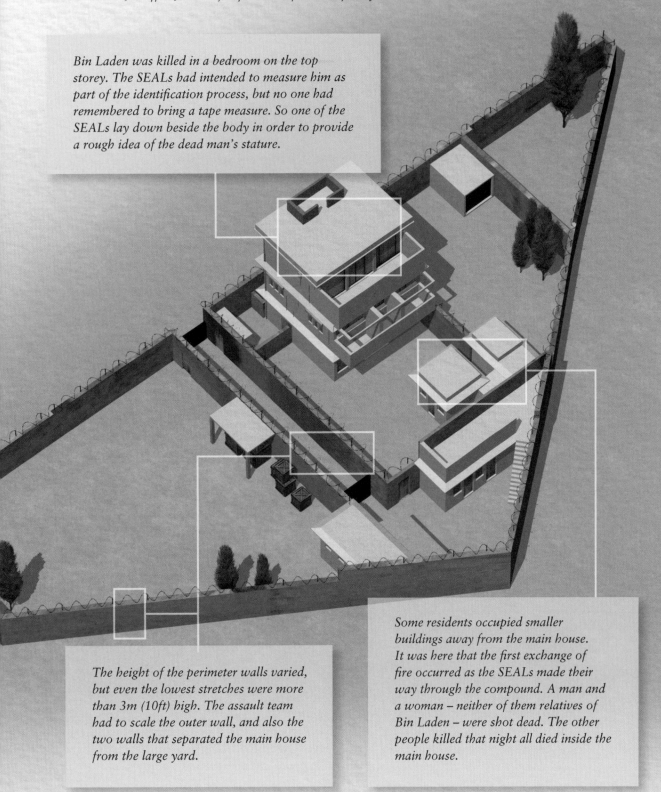

WALLED IN *The compound in Abbottabad was by far the largest house in the neighbourhood. But living conditions within were spartan, almost squalid. Bin Laden had, in effect, built a jail for himself and his family.*

Bin Laden was killed in a bedroom on the top storey. The SEALs had intended to measure him as part of the identification process, but no one had remembered to bring a tape measure. So one of the SEALs lay down beside the body in order to provide a rough idea of the dead man's stature.

The height of the perimeter walls varied, but even the lowest stretches were more than 3m (10ft) high. The assault team had to scale the outer wall, and also the two walls that separated the main house from the large yard.

Some residents occupied smaller buildings away from the main house. It was here that the first exchange of fire occurred as the SEALs made their way through the compound. A man and a woman – neither of them relatives of Bin Laden – were shot dead. The other people killed that night all died inside the main house.

northern side of the house were made of opaque glass. Whoever occupied that room did not want to be seen by anyone outside the compound. But he was not alone in there: the household comprised several women and well over a dozen children; some of the older ones sometimes emerged to buy food at the shops. The household rubbish was never put out on the street; it was burned inside the compound. This much could be ascertained by teams of watchers armed with binoculars. But the

Neptune Spear was a reference to the trident on the SEALs' insignia.

compound was also being scrutinised from the clouds. Pictures taken by a spy drone showed that the compound was home to a bearded man who never left, but who regularly went for walks in the yard. The men examining the footage back in the USA called him 'the pacer'. They couldn't be sure that he was Bin Laden, but analysis of his gait suggested that the pacer was unusually tall (Bin Laden was over 1.9m/6ft 4in), and even on the grainy spy-in-the-sky video it looked very much like him.

Taken together, the various strands of intelligence on the building and its occupants were enough to justify a military operation against the Abbottabad compound: it seemed highly likely that this was Bin Laden's hideout. At first the US authorities considered attacking the building with a missile strike, but this was ruled out: bombs and missiles, however closely targeted and clinically executed, would be bound to kill the women and children in the compound, and possibly some people outside it. Also, there would be no way of checking that a bombing raid had succeeded, and the vital proof of success – Bin Laden's corpse – would be missing or unobtainable.

The best option, therefore, was to send in a team to kill or capture him. President Obama approved that plan, and also took the decision not to inform the government of Pakistan – a US ally in the war on terror – that his special forces were about to make an incursion into their sovereign territory. The fact that Bin Laden was living so close to the country's military academy raised the possibility that some people inside the government knew he was there – or were even actively protecting him. The Pakistani government were sure to be affronted and humiliated by the American intrusion, but maintaining the security of the operation was more important than any diplomatic fall-out.

ABBOTTABAD AND AFTER

The Navy SEALs trained for months in a mock-up of the compound, constructed at a secret site in Afghanistan. The codename assigned to the raid was Operation Neptune Spear, a reference to the trident that is part of the SEALs' insignia. When they were ready, President Obama gave his authorisation for them to go in on the next moonless night. The SEALs made their final preparations, and the attack took place three nights later. The shots that killed Bin Laden were fired shortly after 1am, local time.

But that was not quite the end of the operation. There had, after all, been no positive identification of Bin Laden.

In the moments after the man in the bedroom was shot, one of the SEALs lay down next to the body to assess his height (at this moment in Washington, President Obama is said to have asked if the budget for the operation could not have stretched to a tape measure). The SEALs took DNA samples from the body, and they made digital photographs of its shattered features. The pictures were then transmitted to CIA headquarters in Virginia, where they were analysed with face-recognition software. It was swiftly confirmed, with a certainly above 90 per cent, that the man lying dead in the upstairs bedroom was Osama Bin Laden.

The SEALs had some chores to do before leaving. They tied up all the occupants and left them for the Pakistani authorities to find. Then they gathered together all the computers, disks, memory

The simple Islamic funeral rites were performed aboard a US supercarrier.

sticks, flash drives and paper documents that they could find – a massive haul of intelligence for the continuing fight against Al Qaeda. Bin Laden's corpse was put in a body bag and carried to a waiting Chinook helicopter. Finally, they placed explosive charges in the stricken Black Hawk where it lay in the courtyard. As they left, a great plume of fire lit the sky above Abbottabad.

Bin Laden's body was flown back to the Bagram airbase in Afghanistan, the country where he had lived and fought and

formulated his violent philosophy. From there it was flown with fighter escort to the USS *Carl Vinson*, a supercarrier operating in the Indian Ocean. The simple Islamic funeral rites were performed on board this ship: the body was washed and wrapped in a white sheet; religious remarks were read out by a naval officer and translated into Arabic. Then the remains of Osama Bin Laden were committed to the sea.

NO GRAVE FOR BIN LADEN

The day after the raid, when President Obama announced to the American people that Bin Laden was dead, there was jubilation on the streets of many American cities. A crowd formed outside the White House in Washington DC to chant and cheer, while there was a more muted gathering at Ground Zero in New York. When it emerged that Bin Laden had been buried at sea, some Muslim scholars voiced their concern that this was a contravention of Islamic custom. But their voices were drowned out by those who asked whether the victims of 9/11, lost in the rubble of the Twin Towers, could be said to have received a decent burial.

The US government's chief aim in disposing of the body at sea seems to have been to prevent Bin Laden's grave from becoming a shrine. Something similar may have prompted the Pakistani authorities, in February 2012, to demolish the compound in Abbottabad. Certainly, the buildings were an embarrassment: while the Pakistani army had been scouring its borderlands for Bin Laden, he had for years been living in a conspicuous house that stood almost literally in the army's back yard. At any rate, the hunt for Bin Laden ended as it began a decade before – with the breaching of solid walls, and the sound of masonry falling to the ground.

Oblivion for sale

Over the past century the trade in mind-altering substances *has become a billion-dollar business. Yet the huge drug-supply industry exists entirely in the shadows – an invisible network of clandestine corporations, untraceable revenue and a vast anonymous workforce. How did this strange and dangerous sector of the unofficial global economy arise and take shape?*

Imagine that you could travel back in time to the first years of the 20th century, and go to an ordinary pharmacy in London, Berlin or New York. In these and other Western cities, the pharmacist's polished shelves would be filled with bottled tonics and packs of brightly coloured pills. Among the medicaments on sale you would find a beautifully packaged pick-me-up called 'vin des Incas', which consisted of sweet burgundy infused with the leaves of the Peruvian coca plant. Close by you might see a rival product, Savar's Coca Wine, with a label stating that it was 'manufactured in our own laboratories [and] standardised to contain a half-grain pure cocaine per fluid ounce'.

A century ago, cocaine was sold as a cure for catarrh and hay fever, among other things. A new morphine-derived medicine, marketed under the trade name Heroin, was available over the counter to ease a troubling cough or a headache. Customers worried about the addictive side effects of opiate-based pain relief might opt for the safer alternative, a barbiturate called Veronal. For insomnia,

muscle spasms or postnatal discomfort, the pharmacist might recommend a tincture containing extract of cannabis.

All of these preparations were lawful and entirely unremarkable, yet within a couple of decades the active ingredients in them all had been outlawed across many parts of the world. People did not stop using the drugs in question, but now they had to be obtained through illegal black-market channels. At the same time, the prohibited drugs came to be re-invented as an illicit source of pleasure.

FROM MEDICINE TO VICE

It was in the 1890s that some doctors and moralists began to speak out against the free availability of drugs. In Britain a doctor named Thomas Clouston pointed out that the longer cocaine users partook of the drug, the bigger and more frequent the doses they seemed to need. In America the same point was made by Dr Jansen Mattison, one of the first to advance the idea that one drug leads to another, harder drug. On the subject of cocaine, he wrote: 'I think it for many, notably the large

COCAIN

mondaine u. demimondaine

Skizzen von

W.KOEBNER

number of opium and alcohol habitués, the most fascinating, seductive, dangerous and destructive drug extant, and [I] insist on the great danger of self-injecting, a course almost certain to entail added ill.'

Addicts were assumed to be the victims of overeager prescribing by medical professionals, which is why Mattison addressed his remarks to fellow doctors. But within a decade or so, the view took hold that users were responsible for their own addiction, that it was the result of their own greed or misjudgment. Drug use began to be seen as a vice, and that opinion became a cliché of the popular press.

In the USA, it was reported that some pharmacists sold practically nothing but cocaine, and there were clusters of such retail outlets in cities across the country. Tunnel Street in Pittsburgh was known locally as 'Cocaine Street' because the drug was so widely available there. It was also noted that in certain US towns more than half the women arrested for prostitution were cocaine addicts. Papers carried lurid accounts of depraved drug users resorting to sexual crimes, or of sexual criminals indulging in drugs – it hardly mattered which came first. In the American South, the stories regularly had a racist element: it was often implied that normally docile and law-abiding black men became violent and predatory when high on cocaine.

The legal drug trade had become a political issue, a scandal in various nations where drug use was rife, and governments decided to act. A number of international conferences on drugs were held in the years before the First World War. Governments of many Western nations sent delegations to these meetings. The agenda was always to restrict and control the global trade in addictive drugs, which were given

RAVE ON *Ecstasy was a young person's drug, widely used at raves to enhance the experience of dancing. Governments insisted it was dangerous and banned it. But medical experts pointed out that taking ecstasy was statistically far safer in terms of harmful outcomes than, for example, horse riding.*

the handy but scientifically inaccurate label 'narcotics' (a narcotic is technically something that induces sleep). The Shanghai Conference of 1909 established the principle of cross-border cooperation for controlling the movement of drugs, and agreed that opiates were a 'grave danger'. Three years later, in The Hague, delegates agreed to pass anti-opium legislation in their respective countries.

By 1920 most American states had outlawed narcotics, while the US federal government went so far as to ban all alcoholic drinks in the disastrous episode known as Prohibition (*see* page 167). In the UK, access to popular drugs was restricted by the wartime Defence of the Realm Act, and afterwards by the Dangerous Drugs Act of 1920. Around the same time, medical experts in Europe suggested that cocaine led to, or somehow unleashed, what was then seen as the unnatural and illegal vice of homosexuality. For the sake of the moral health of their citizens, governments in one country after another passed bills

similar to Britain's, prohibiting the use and possession of all narcotics, not just opium.

Partly as a result of such measures, the contention that drugs and criminality went hand in hand became a self-asserting truth: to acquire drugs required breaking the law. Suppliers of narcotics were pursued by law-enforcement agencies set up for the purpose, such as the Federal Bureau of Narcotics, established in the USA in 1930. The cash proceeds from selling drugs could no longer be openly declared, so the money now had to be 'laundered'. This brought drug traffickers and dealers into the orbit of organised crime, since career criminals had the necessary know-how and infrastructure to process tainted cash – and to buy off politicians and policemen.

By the 1930s everything about the production and consumption of drugs had become murky, tainted by corruption and exploitation. The hidden narco-economy was beginning to grow. One of the problems with legislating against drugs was that new laws had specifically to name the drugs in question. This created the possibility of loopholes: if someone could invent an entirely new drug, then it would be legal by default – and was very likely to be profitable.

Amphetamines, invented in the 1920s, represented one such instance. Like opium and cocaine before them, amphetamines were marketed at first as harmless but effective medicines. Under the trade name Benzedrine, amphetamines were sold as a treatment for nasal congestion, seasickness, obesity – even as a means of controlling hyperactivity in children. They were also widely used by pilots during the Second World War to help them stay awake while on missions. By the late 1940s they had been adopted as a recreational drug, often slipped into drinks at parties. Bohemian types liked to use them to stimulate their creativity – the beat writer Jack Kerouac was particularly fond of 'bennies', as he called them.

> *Leary advised all young people to 'Turn on, tune in, drop out'.*

In the 1950s legislators in the USA and elsewhere began banning amphetamines, citing the now-familiar argument that habitual users tended to end up engaging in criminal activity. Something similar occurred a generation later with MDMA, a drug legally distributed in discos and nightclubs in the early 1980s. It induced feelings of euphoria and fellow-feeling – so much so that it was marketed under

the name 'empathy'. Only later, as it became an integral part of rave culture did it acquire the name by which it is now known: 'ecstasy'. Once ecstasy became widespread, the authorities moved quickly to ban it. It was outlawed in the USA in 1985. In the UK, where it was always technically illegal, ecstasy was classified as a dangerous Class A drug, despite the fact that the government's own medical advisers recommended it should be in the lower-risk Class B category.

THE HIPPY REVOLUTION

The illegal status of ecstasy, the fact that the authorities disapproved of it, was part of its cachet for young users. The same had been true of marijuana in the 1960s, when drug use became a central part of the new youth culture. For many, smoking marijuana was a reasoned and legitimate act of protest, and the fact that the government disapproved of drugs just went to show how out of touch and wrong-headed the politicians could be. The moralists' link between drug use and sex ceased to be an effective argument against narcotics and became instead an integral part of their appeal. The new age was going to be all about peace and love: weed provided the peace, and the love was free.

The 1960s saw the rise in popularity of hallucinogenic or psychotropic drugs, such as lysergic acid (LSD) and mescaline. These were seen as an important part of the counterculture, because they seemed to provide a path to mind expansion and spiritual enlightenment. In the early 1950s the writer Aldous Huxley had quietly experimented with mescaline, and wondered whether the revelatory experience it provided was akin to the visionary state achieved by mystics such as the poet William Blake. In the 1960s the populist commentator and writer Dr Timothy Leary was more strident and certain. Stressing the social and political value of drug use, he advised all young people to 'Tune in, turn on, drop out' – that is to say, make use of drugs, then channel the experience into a rejection of the hidebound norms of society, and so achieve a kind of freedom.

For a generation of hippies, and the wider contingent that was sympathetic to hippy ideals, the ban on drugs was as absurd as, say, the war in Vietnam. To the youth of the 1960s it seemed obvious that only people who had not experienced the liberating effect of drugs could object to them. But mescaline was banned in the USA in 1970; the following year, LSD was outlawed worldwide by the UN Convention of Psychotropic Substances. By this time, US president Richard Nixon had declared a 'war on drugs', asserting that drug abuse was 'a national emergency' and 'public enemy No. 1'.

FIGHTING THE DRUGS WAR

There followed an attempt to disrupt the global trade in narcotics, in particular the flow of cocaine into the USA. Demand had continued to grow, and it was met largely by cartels in Colombia where, along with Peru and Bolivia, almost all of the world's coca leaves grew. By 1986 cocaine was Colombia's largest source of foreign exchange, bringing in more cash than the legitimate trade in coffee. Vast quantities of cocaine were shipped invisibly, as if it did not exist at all. Well-paid individuals did the risky work of smuggling drugs through airports, hidden in their luggage or about their person. The European supply lines ran mostly through Madrid, while the American hub was Miami. The US government estimated in 1980 that

cocaine worth $7 billion passed unnoticed through Florida each year. And that was not even the main route: more than half the cocaine that came into the USA arrived via Mexico.

Tougher law enforcement in the 1990s closed part of the cocaine business, but there was still heroin. The opium poppy, from which heroin is derived, grows in two main regions: the 'golden crescent' (Afghanistan, Iran and Pakistan) and the 'golden triangle' (Thailand, Myanmar and Laos). Between the 1930s and the 1960s, export from these zones was monopolised by Turkish entrepreneurs, while refinement and distribution was handled in Marseilles. In the 1970s, when the police smashed the 'French connection', the business migrated to Italy, where it was controlled by the Sicilian mafia. When the Sicilians in turn came under pressure, responsibility for heroin distribution devolved partly to gangs in China and Japan.

The drugs trade had become thoroughly criminal and totally global. The collapse of communism provided new markets, and new organisations eager for a slice of the action. The internet, meanwhile, furnished new ways to manage the trade, under the noses of the authorities. As long as people crave the highs that drugs (temporarily) provide, the drugs trade looks set to go on – that is its irresistible economic logic. The market has no moral dimension, which leaves it blind to the misery and chaos that drugs cause in the lives of individuals, communities and entire nations.

A UN report in 2011 stated that opiate consumption worldwide had increased by 34.5 per cent in the two decades to 2009, cocaine use by 25 per cent. Today drugs are the third biggest industry in the world, after oil and arms, estimated to be worth more than $300 billion a year.

THE HARD STUFF *US customs officials with bottles of booze seized from a speakeasy. Confiscated whisky and beer was often publicly poured down the drains.*

The brief heyday of the speakeasy

In 1920 the US government banned the production, sale and consumption of alcohol. The aim was to make America sober; instead, a huge black market opened up in liquor, sold through a network of hidden bars.

'Prohibition', as America's alcohol ban was termed, had some unexpected effects. One consequence was to turn drinkers away from beer and towards spirits such as gin, which were easier to produce and, because of the higher alcohol content, a more efficient way to fulfil the consumer's desire for a drink. Prohibition also made traditional saloons extinct; they were replaced in the cities by 'speakeasies', so called because customers were asked to keep their voices down to avoid attracting the police. These bars – unlike saloons – were welcoming to women, since a female presence encouraged men to buy drinks, and so boosted profits. Many American women who had never drunk before were introduced to alcohol during the Prohibition years; the interdiction, as with other drugs before and since, added a sheen of glamour to alcohol consumption.

To make strong-tasting drinks such as whisky and gin palatable to inexperienced female drinkers, they were mixed with fruit juices, sodas and other sweet ingredients. 'Cocktails' were not an invention of the Prohibition era, but they flourished as a result of it. The same is true, in a darker sense, of organised crime in America. Mafia families in cities such as Chicago were well placed to sell alcohol illegally, and fortunes were made during the years it was banned. They lost that revenue source as soon as the law was repealed, but as a result of the boost they received from Prohibition, they remained powerful for decades afterwards.

The 'noble experiment' came to an end in 1933, when President F.D. Roosevelt signed the 21st amendment to the Constitution that made drinking legal again. As he put pen to paper he remarked: 'I think this would be a good time for a beer.'

Inside the underworld

There have always been thieves, bandits and murderers,
but organised crime – the world of the Mafia, Yakuza, Chinese Triads – is a
different matter. For insiders, it is a way of life governed by strict hierarchical
rules, re-inforced by codes of honour and secrecy, underpinned by a system of
protection, obligation, extortion – and the threat of extreme violence.

In the St Valentine's Day Massacre of 1929, five Chicago hoodlums allegedly hired by Al Capone's South Side gang went with machine-guns to a garage and mowed down seven members of the rival Irish North Side gang. It was a brazen display of force, designed to show who was boss in the criminal underworld of Chicago. But Capone, protected by bonds of secrecy, loyalty and the fear of retribution, could declare his innocence. When he was eventually arrested in 1931, it was not for murder but for income-tax evasion.

And yet it was violence that made Capone powerful and credible as an underworld boss. He was the commander-in-chief of an illicit army of enforcers and thugs. The very word 'thug', in the sense of a foot soldier of criminal violence, has its root in organised gangs – not in Chicago, but in India.

THE THUGGEE CULT

The original thugs were professional thieves and assassins in India, notorious for their ruthlessness. Typically, they would infiltrate caravans of travellers, wait until the caravan reached a remote spot, then kill everyone in order to steal their possessions. Their preferred method of assassination was strangulation with a scarf called a *rumal*.

The ritualistic aspects of these crimes gave rise to the idea that the Thugs belonged to an ancient, secretive Thuggee cult connected to Kali, the Hindu deity associated with darkness and death. Membership was believed to be chiefly hereditary, and Thug fathers were said to introduce their sons to the cult in their early teens via a gruesome initiation that involved watching a victim being strangled. The most notorious Thug, a man named Thug Behram, claimed personally to have strangled 125 victims.

In the 1830s the Thugs were targeted in a concerted British campaign led by a Colonel William Sleeman. This initiative resulted in 400 executions and 3,000 convictions, effectively ending the curse of the Thugs. But the fear of an unfathomable undercurrent of violence haunted the British in India. Throughout the 19th century, highly coloured tales of the Thugs

FAMILY AFFAIRS *Organised crime is often based primarily on blood relationships. Mafias such as Al Capone's (above, seated in the centre) were bound by blood ties. And bands of Indian thugs (right) were made up of extended family units working together.*

appeared in popular magazines. It has been suggested that the British saw the campaign against the Thugs as a victory of Western law and order over the dark, unreasonable forces of an evil native cult, and so encouraged the sensational tales. Like all organised crime, the exploits of the Indian Thugs caught the public imagination. Very soon, violent louts in Britain were being referred to as 'thugs'.

LAW AND DISORDER

As the actions of Colonel Sleeman demonstrate, organised crime operates in a vacuum of law and order. When citizens lack the protection of central authorities, or distrust them, others may take the opportunity to step in, often shielding

their activities with codes of strict secrecy. The Chinese Triads, for example, began as social organisations, set up to support the citizenry of imperial China (the term 'triad' comes from the Chinese concept of the three linked powers of Heaven, Earth and Humankind). To the Manchu authorities, the Triads looked subversive, and they were forced underground. But to ordinary people the Triads appeared an honourable and altruistic organisation.

In the 19th century, tens of thousands of Chinese emigrated to the USA to pan for gold or build railways – and they carried the Triad ideal with them. Here, even more than in China, some kind of support network was required. The local state authorities were happy to delegate the

administration of Chinese communities to the Triads – which in the USA were known as Tongs, from the Cantonese word for a hall or gathering place.

The Tongs could offer welfare assistance, policing and protection. But protection brought its own obligations. If a shopkeeper needed to discourage thieves and vandals, a Tong could help, in return for payment. It was only a short step from here to a protection racket: if a shopkeeper refused to pay for protection, then the Tong might arrange a demonstration of how vulnerable the shop was to attack, or simply persuade customers to stay away.

The natural result of such arrangements was that the Tongs controlled the high streets – who did business there, who did not – and took a cut, a kind of informal tax, at every turn. In this way, a socially useful service degenerated into extortion

that had to be enforced – otherwise it was unfair to those who paid up. Violence was often also meted out to rival Tongs: bloody street battles called the Tong Wars raged in the Chinatowns of North American cities in the 1890s and early 20th century.

Throughout the 20th century, the Triads spread to Chinese communities around the world. Today they operate in property, industry and finance, as well as the trafficking of drugs and people. Within China itself, the Triad story has been somewhat different. During the uprising that led to the fall of the last emperor in 1912, the republicans co-opted the Triads as fellow anti-Manchu activists. In the Second World War, however, some Triads collaborated with the Japanese occupiers, offering to help them police the people. As a result, after the war, the communists under Mao Zedong ruthlessly suppressed them. They survived in the colonial outposts of Macau and Hong Kong where, in the 1950s, turf wars led to a spate of gruesome murders.

THE YAKUZA OF JAPAN

The protection racket is at the heart of most organised crime. This is particularly true of the Yakuza in Japan. Unlike the Triads, the Yakuza are not secret societies. They have publicly labelled office fronts, and it is fully understood that many businesses, both large and small, have Yakuza connections.

The close-knit, hierarchical structure of the Yakuza dates back to the 17th century. At the bottom are the henchmen, often drawn from minority groups, such as ethnic Koreans, who may harbour resentment for the social discrimination that they suffer. Becoming a member of a Yakuza clan gives them status, respect and protection. This is earned through unquestioning obedience, and instilled through lengthy initiation ceremonies. The traditional penance for misdemeanours is to cut off part of one's own finger.

The Yakuza call themselves *ninkyo dantai*, 'chivalrous organisations', and they do publicly acknowledged good works. The largest Yakuza organisation is the Yamaguchi-gumi, based in the city of Kobe. After the Kobe earthquake of 1995, it was the Yakuza who were first on the scene with rescue assistance and aid. As with the Tongs, the distinction between the philanthropic and criminal activity is not always clear-cut.

THE SICILIAN MAFIA

The reputation of the Yakuza has been glamorised in films, comic books and video games. But the criminal organisation that has received the most attention from the media, and excited the most public fascination, is the Mafia.

Like the Triads and the Yakuza, the original purpose of the Mafia was to protect local people. It emerged after the unification of Italy in 1861, when the island of Sicily found itself without an effective central authority. Local clans organised themselves to provide law and order, and these improvised groups naturally assimilated Sicilian traditions of resistance to centralised authority.

The word 'mafia' emerged at this time, but its origins remain obscure. It derived perhaps from the Arabic for 'bragging', and in the Sicilian dialect connoted manly bravado and banditry. Mafia members themselves have always used a different term, *cosa nostra*, meaning 'our thing'.

The omertà code

One of the Mafia's most effective defence mechanisms is its code of silence, called *omertà*. Loyal Mafiosi will never assist the police in the investigation of a crime, even if they are being wrongly accused or punished for a crime, or were themselves the victims. The penalty for breaking the code of silence is death. A man (and Mafiosi are primarily men) loses his honour if he cooperates with the authorities. Instead, if he has been wronged, he should rely on his own resources to avenge himself – or find a patron who will do so on his behalf.

The Mafia, again like the Triads, followed their people into emigration and soon established a presence in the Italian areas of New York. The parallel organisation from Naples, the Comorra, installed itself in many US cities. During the 1880s the Mafia was noted for an extortion racket known as the Black Hand (La Mano Nera), in which victims received written threats of kidnap, arson or murder. By the start of the 20th century Italian-American gangs were deeply entrenched, and when rivalries between clans erupted into gunfights the press was filled with shocking stories of tortured bodies stuffed into barrels, assassinations on courthouse steps or at restaurant tables, and the tongues of 'talkers' being slit in two.

Between the wars, the Mafia sidled up to the entertainment business. Clubs, brothels, gambling dens and the nascent film industry all needed protection and could be manipulated through extortion, bribery, blackmail and corruption. Mafia clans also infiltrated industrial enterprises, trade unions and politics. They competed with each other, and with equally ruthless Irish or Jewish gangster outfits.

In the 1930s the Italian-American Mafia, under bosses such as Charles 'Lucky' Luciano, Joe 'Joe Bananas' Bonanno and Carmine 'The Cigar' Galante, set up the so-called 'Commission', a loose affiliation of leading families designed to reduce clan rivalries. For years the Mafia operated almost unmolested. FBI chief J. Edgar Hoover claimed to have been unaware of the power and reach of the Mafia for most of his term of office (1935–72), protesting that he was more directly concerned with the fight against communism.

In 1957 about 100 Mafia bosses gathered for a conference at the home of mobster Joe 'The Barber' Barbara in the village of Apalachin, New York. A local police office noticed that something unusual and possibly nefarious was going on at the house. He called for back-up, and in the ensuing raid the conference broke up in panic, with many of the Mafiosi fleeing

> *In 1963 one of Luciano's 'soldiers' betrayed the code of silence.*

on foot into the woods. This event revealed publicly the extent of the Mafia crime network in the USA, a situation confirmed in 1963 when Joe Valachi – one of Lucky Luciano's 'soldiers' – betrayed the *omertà* code of silence and spilled the beans on the Mafia before a US Senate Committee.

Since then the power of the Mafia in the USA has been curtailed, but it is still present – as it is around the world. In Sicily itself, courageous magistrates such as Giovanni Falcone and Paolo Borsellino had some success in clipping its wings before an upsurge of retaliatory violence was unleashed across Italy in the 1990s; both Falcone and Borsellino were killed by car bombs in 1992. Meanwhile, independent southern Italian criminal associations, such as the 'Ndrangheta in Calabria and the Sacra Corona Unita in Apulia, have risen to become feared players across a range of activities, from drug trafficking to bid-rigging for municipal rubbish collection.

RUSSIA'S MAFIA GANGS

Following the collapse of the Soviet Union and Soviet-dominated Eastern Europe in 1989–91, new and especially aggressive mafias emerged. They exploited the precarious political situation to get involved in heavy industry, fuel trading, prostitution, gambling, weapon smuggling, drug trafficking and money-laundering. Called *bratvas* (brotherhoods), the gangs often employed former KGB agents and soldiers with first-hand combat experience in Afghanistan and Chechnya. Before long, Russian mafias, such as the Tambov Gang from St Petersburg, were found to be operating in Spain, Germany and Australia. They also entered into cybercrime, a new mafia speciality, recruiting low-paid maths and computer-science graduates to turn their skills to hacking, and – according to the FBI – stealing millions of credit card details.

So one unforeseen effect of the digital revolution has been to internationalise and impersonalise organised crime. Someone sitting at home in Cardiff or Buffalo can become the victim of a criminal group operating out of Prague or Belgrade. Organised crime, always hidden away in the shadows, has become as ethereal and invisible as fresh air.

The secret languages of crime

All professions have their jargon, and criminals are no exception. But the dialogue of career lawbreakers is more than just the talk of the trade. They use words and language to conceal their meaning from outsiders, confound the police and bond with their fellow outlaws.

Do you know what a 'prigger of cacklers' or a 'rum-dubber' is? If not, you're in good company. Few English speakers would recognise the first as a chicken-stealer or the second as an expert picker of locks. Equally, most people would take at face value the apparently innocuous 'uncle' and 'family man', but both are old criminal terms for a receiver of stolen goods.

In centuries gone by, such secret language was known as 'thieves' cant', a cant being a kind of jargon used deliberately to exclude outsiders. Many words commonly used in modern English may be derived from the cants of the 17th and 18th centuries, and many relate to the facts of criminal life: 'fleece', for example, in the sense of rob or plunder; 'pinch' (steal); 'fence' (the modern word for a receiver of stolen goods); and 'nab' (arrest).

Thieves' cants seem to be a universal phenomenon that develops wherever there is a criminal underclass. *Fenya* is a historic Russian thieves' cant, containing elements of Greek and Yiddish. Elements of *fenya* were adopted by the prison population of the gulag in the Stalin era and after. Many of the terms used in the Russian gulag and on the streets of Russian cities have the same wry wit as, say, Cockney rhyming slang – which is also, at root, a form of cant. In Russian criminal slang a *skripach* (violinist) was someone who steals from women's handbags – because of the in-and-out movement of the arm; a *stekolshchik* (glazier) was a burglar who gets in by breaking a window; a *kukushka* (cuckoo) was a lookout man; and a *desantnik* (parachutist) was a thief who purloins food from unguarded delivery vans.

The criminal cant of southern Germany was known as *Rotwelsch*, also sometimes referred to as *Gaunersprache*, which means 'language of swindlers'. Here too there is more than a sprinkling of Yiddish: *bei jom* means 'in daylight', *bei leile*, 'by night' – from the standard Hebrew *yom* and *layla*, 'day' and 'night'. The Dutch equivalent of *Rotwelsch* was called *Bargoens*, and – unlike the standard versions of German and Dutch – may have been mutually intelligible, a cross-border cant.

UNSPOKEN LANGUAGES

Many criminal communities have developed hand signals as a covert form of communication – a kind of wordless cant. The Chinese Triads used signs to express their rank in the hierarchy. The notorious street gangs of California, such as the Crips and the Bloods, can identify each other at a distance with hand signs: the Crips, for instance, 'throw up' crossed downturned palms with the thumbs and first fingers shaping the letter 'C', while the Bloods spell out the word 'blood' using upturned thumbs for the 'b' and 'd', a raised middle finger, for the 'l' and the other fingers curved into two 'o' shapes. There is colour coding too: the Bloods use the colour red, the Cribs blue. This can extend widely across neighbourhoods: people wearing red baseball caps and T-shirts, for example, may be signalling their loyalties. Graffiti can be a form of signing – or at least a significant message, a territorial marker like a flag on a pole. Rival gangs may then try to delete graffiti or write over it – or they may use it as a way of triumphantly signalling the elimination of an enemy.

Death of a revolutionary

In 1965 Che Guevara was an international icon, revered as a hero of the revolution in his adopted homeland of Cuba. Two years later he was dead, his body thrown into an unmarked grave. But the final chapter in Che's life, and his inglorious death, only burnished the man's legend.

In the spring of 1965 odd rumours began to circulate concerning the whereabouts of Che Guevara. The Argentinian Marxist had played a central role in the downfall of Fulgencio Batista's regime in Cuba. He had then gone on to become Fidel Castro's chief lieutenant in the revolutionary government. But he had not been seen in public since March. Some claimed that he had been killed fighting US Marines in the Dominican Republic, others that he had been kidnapped by anti-Castro Cubans or captured by Russian agents and sent to Siberia for his opposition to Soviet-style socialism. Some said that he was recovering from a nervous breakdown in a Cuban sanatorium, or had gone mad and was undergoing treatment in Mexico.

The truth was, in fact, quite as unlikely as the rumours. Che was in Africa, seeking to export his brand of permanent revolution to an entirely new quarter of the world. For the past six years, ever since he and his comrades had made a triumphant entry into the Cuban capital of Havana in January 1959, the guerrilla fighter had chafed under the administrative responsibilities of government. He had served as finance minister, as minister of

industry and as head of the National Bank – where he had horrified traditionalists by signing Cuba's banknotes with a casual 'Che'. But he had grown bored and increasingly disillusioned. He told the poet Heberto Padilla, 'I live like someone torn in two, 24 hours a day, completely torn in two.' So now, at the age of 36, he had decided it was time to give up the life of a bureaucrat, and go out and rediscover the sense of purpose and the camaraderie he had known as a guerrilla warrior. He was seeking new fields to conquer in the name of socialist revolution.

FIASCO IN THE CONGO

Che scanned the world's trouble spots carefully before settling on the Congo, a country in ferment both before and since it had won independence from Belgium in 1960. Che's intention was to hook up with independence fighters in the east of the country, with a view to sparking a war of liberation that would inspire anti-colonial struggles across the world.

Che and a force of Cuban guerrillas travelled secretly to Africa and established a base near Lake Tanganyika's Congolese shore. He hoped to liaise with Laurent

A rebellious life

Che Guevara was born into a well-to-do Argentinian family in 1928. His father was a supporter of the Republican cause in the Spanish Civil War, and Che grew up with strong ideals of social justice. But it was his own travels through the impoverished countries of Central and South America that convinced him of the need to overthrow capitalism through violent revolution. He joined the Cuban revolutionary movement in 1955, and was a commander in the guerrilla war that brought Castro to power in 1959. He then became a government minister and a roving ambassador for the Cuban regime. When he was killed in Bolivia on October 9, 1967, he was still only 39 years old.

Kabila, the leader of the rebels, but Kabila was spending much of his time living the high life outside the country. The rebels that Che did meet resented his presence and showed little enthusiasm for fighting. The intended guerilla campaign never got off the ground, and Guevara had to flee when his territory was attacked by mercenaries. The mission ended in farce. Che's own account of the misadventure began: 'This is the story of a failure.'

The ignominious retreat from the Congo left Che with a dilemma. He could not return to Cuba, where barely a month earlier the authorities had released the idealistic, self-confident farewell letter he had addressed to Fidel Castro before leaving for Africa. 'Other nations of the world call for my modest efforts,' Che had written. 'I carry to new battlegrounds the faith that you taught me, the revolutionary spirit of my people, the feeling of fulfilling the most sacred of duties: to fight against imperialism.' To go back now would have been not just a personal humiliation but

also a devastating setback for the anti-imperialist cause. So Che continued to live under cover, first in Tanzania and then in Prague, while he considered his options.

In the summer of 1966 Che returned to Cuba, briefly and in secret, to make the final arrangements for a new expedition to foment revolution. He was once more a soldier leaving for the front, and he took the opportunity to leave messages for his loved ones. To his five children he wrote: 'Try always to be able to feel deeply any injustice committed against any person in any part of the world; it is the most beautiful quality of a revolutionary.'

BOUND FOR BOLIVIA

That October, travelling incognito, Che caught a flight from Havana to Moscow, the first leg of a roundabout journey that would take him to Bolivia via Europe and Brazil. He was wearing a fake set of teeth and had plucked out the hair from his forehead to allow him to pass for a paunchy, balding businessman with a Uruguayan passport in the name of Adolfo Mena González.

He arrived in Bolivia in November. He had chosen this country as the cradle of his new revolution because it was economically underdeveloped and under military rule. But Bolivia's ruling general had, in fact, recently called an election in which he had been supported by a large majority of the population. The peasant farmers in the remote region where Che made his base showed no enthusiasm for his revolutionary cause. Like a man trying to build a fire with damp twigs, Che set about trying to ignite an insurgency. But he found himself in the embarrassing position of having more Cuban fighters than Bolivian ones. His global revolution was starting to look like a personal joyride.

Other things were going wrong, too. The Cuban contingent had expected help from the Bolivian Communist Party, but the Party leaders in La Paz refused to commit themselves to the uprising. And there were small practical problems as well as large political issues. The maps that the guerrillas carried proved inadequate, and as a result a two-week training exercise in the forest turned into a seven-week ordeal. Two Bolivian recruits drowned, and the rest of Che's troops survived

The paunchy, balding businessman with the Uruguayan passport was Che.

only by eating monkeys and parrots. The exhausted rebels returned from their trek to find the Bolivian army scouting in the area of their base. In March 1967 they ambushed an army patrol, killing seven soldiers. This skirmish led to the outbreak of official hostilities between the Bolivian government and the left-wing rebels.

Soon afterwards it was announced that the US government was sending military advisers to Bolivia. Che was now a hunted man, being pursued through the jungle by the Bolivian army and its American allies. The rebels split into two groups, so as to move faster and avoid detection. There were never more than 50 men in Che's band, almost half of them from outside Bolivia. They were strangers in hostile territory, and their numbers dwindled as men fell ill or were wounded in fighting. Crucially, Che's group received almost no

support from local people, who feared retribution from the Bolivian army. Che himself was sick with dysentery and chronic asthma. As supplies ran low, his men were reduced to eating their own horses and mules. Then came the news that the second column had fallen into an ambush and been wiped out. Che headed north with the 20 men still loyal to his command.

By now it was just a matter of time before the Bolivian army caught up with him. The endgame played out near the hamlet of La Higuera, 1,950m (6,400ft) up in the cordillera. Late in September, three guerrillas on reconnaissance outside the village were ambushed and killed. Twelve days later, on October 8, the remaining 17 men were caught in a firefight in a ravine barely 50m (160ft) wide. Che himself was disarmed when a bullet hit the barrel of his rifle, then he was shot in the calf. A Bolivian comrade tried to drag him to safety, but the two were quickly taken. Most of Che's colleagues were also captured or killed but, against all odds, five of them – three Cuban, two Bolivian – escaped, eventually making their way over the border into Chile.

CHE'S LAST DAY

As for Che, he was taken back to La Higuera as a prisoner. Bound hand and foot, he spent the night on the dirt floor of the mud-walled schoolhouse in the village, with the corpses of two comrades for company. He was questioned by the military officers who had tracked him down. While he refused to divulge any information about his fellow fighters, he was willing to talk in general terms about his mission. Asked whether he was Cuban or Argentinian, he replied 'I am Cuban, Argentine, Bolivian, Peruvian,

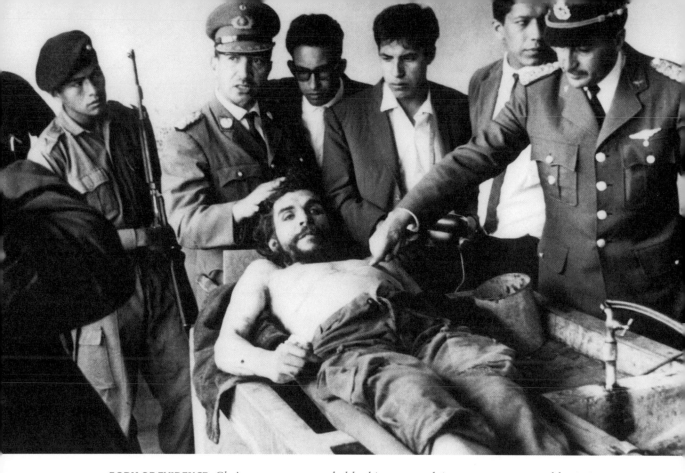

BODY OF EVIDENCE *Che's corpse, surrounded by his captors, lying atop a stone washbasin in the hospital laundry at Vallegrande in Bolivia. His body was buried soon after this picture was taken. The laundry room subsequently became a place of pilgrimage.*

Ecuadorian … You understand?' Asked why he had chosen Bolivia as his base of operations, he said, 'Can't you see the conditions in which the peasants live? They are almost like savages, living in a state of poverty that depresses the heart.'

The following morning a CIA agent, accompanied by a senior Bolivian officer, arrived to check that it was indeed Che who had been captured. Both men spent time with him, and again he willingly discussed his political goals. Shortly after noon, an order came through from La Paz, reportedly from the Bolivian president himself, for Guevara's immediate execution. None of the officers who had spoken with him had the heart to carry out the deed, so a volunteer was requested

from among the soldiers. A sergeant named Mario Terán offered his services. The CIA man instructed him not to shoot Guevara in the face, thinking it more appropriate to make it look as though he had been killed in combat.

Guevara's last words as his executioner entered the schoolroom were, 'I know you've come to kill me. Shoot, coward, you are only going to kill a man.' Then a burst of semi-automatic rifle fire cut him down. He had already written his own epitaph in the message he left for his children: 'Your father has been a man who acted according to his beliefs and has surely remained faithful to his convictions.' He signed off with the words: 'A really big kiss and a hug from Papa.'

What became of Che's body?

Guevara's body disappeared, and for almost three decades the secret of its whereabouts was known to only a handful of people. The truth about what happened to the corpse did not emerge until 30 years later, and even now some of the details remain obscure and controversial.

Following Che's death, the Bolivian military needed to convince the world that they had indeed killed the famous guerrilla warrior. His corpse was strapped to a helicopter's landing skids and flown to the provincial capital, Vallegrande, where it was exhibited in the laundry room of the local hospital. There it lay for a day. Curious visitors were able to troop through the room and view the dead Che, lying unceremoniously in state.

To stave off decay, a doctor had injected the body with formaldehyde. The chemical had the unexpected effect of opening Che's eyes, making him look almost alive. Seeing his long hair and beard, some local people saw a similarity with images of the dead Christ, and began surreptitiously snipping off locks of hair to keep as mementoes.

Meanwhile, the Bolivian authorities, fearing that a marked grave might become a rallying point for resistance, had determined to deny Che and his men a public burial. Yet the authorities also needed incontrovertible proof that the corpse was Che's. A proposal to cut off and retain his head was rejected as too barbaric. Instead, they decided to amputate his hands, so that experts from Buenos Aires could match the fingerprints with samples kept on police files in his Argentinian homeland. The rest of the body was buried secretly that night in an unmarked grave, alongside six of his fellow guerrillas.

A relative who arrived to reclaim Che's corpse for burial was told that he had been cremated. The true story came out only in 1997, when a Cuban team located a mass grave near Vallegrande's dirt airstrip. In it were seven bodies, one of them with the hands cut off at the wrists. Further investigation revealed that the teeth of the skull matched a plaster cast of Che's dentition preserved in Havana. Also found, in the pocket of a jacket buried next to the corpse, was a tobacco pouch. It was known that one of Che's captors had provided him with just such a pouch shortly before his death.

> *Cutting off Che's head was rejected as too barbaric, so they amputated his hands.*

The remains were officially declared to be Che's and were returned with full state honours to Cuba, to be buried there in a purpose-built mausoleum. Even so, there were questions that remained unanswered. For example, a CIA operative who had worked with the Bolivians insisted that Che had been interred alongside only two other guerrillas. Could this point to the remains being someone else's, not Che's? There were also inconsistencies between the remains discovered and the state of the body as described in a 1967 autopsy. So the mortal remains of Che Guevara in their grandiose tomb are an uncertain relic, a slightly dubious object of secular homage, like the bones of many a Christian martyr in times past.

Ransom on the high seas

Until recently, pirates were a thing of the past, like the galleons they once sailed in. Then, in the 1990s, piracy re-appeared. This time round the pirate gangs were armed with rocket-propelled grenades, their targets huge oil tankers. How did this extinct form of banditry re-emerge – and why?

The narrow Strait of Malacca, separating Malaysia and Singapore from Indonesia, is one of the world's busiest shipping lanes, a bottleneck through which at least 50,000 ships pass every year. But it is flanked by coastlines pockmarked with mangrove islands, channels and inlets – ideal hideaways for seafaring criminals. This is where, in the 1990s, the modern resurgence of piracy first came to notice. In 2005, at the height of pirate activities in the Strait of Malacca, there were 79 reported attacks. In reality, there were probably far more incidents, but shipping operators often failed to report them because they were bad publicity, caused delay and resulted in increased insurance premiums. It was easier to absorb the costs. All the same, the shipping insurers at Lloyd's of London declared the straits a war zone.

ARMED AND DANGEROUS *A pirate with a high-calibre weapon on the Somali coast at Hobyo, a village where stolen ships were sometimes anchored.*

The pirates of Malacca followed a modus operandi that earned them the nickname 'jumping squirrels'. Under cover of darkness, fast motorboats would steal up behind a moving cargo ship or tanker and hook a long bamboo pole to the stern. Then a raiding party, faces hidden beneath ski masks and with machetes strapped to their backs, would shin squirrel-like up the pole. The machetes were usually enough to cow an unarmed crew; within minutes the pirates would be on the bridge and in control of the vessel.

Some of the attacks were little more than a kind of maritime highway robbery. The pirates' aim was to steal valuables and cash – ships often carried large amounts of money in their safes to pay for salaries, supplies and port charges. In the more ambitious raids, the pirates took control of the ship, sailed it to a rendezvous point at sea where they transferred the cargo to another vessel, then simply abandoned the hijacked ship. The pirates often depended on an insider, who would supply details of the target ship's course, speed and position in text messages. In the most complex operations, the ship itself was part of the booty; its crew would be offloaded into boats or abandoned on some remote island. Once the cargo had been removed, the ship could be repainted at sea – like a stolen car being resprayed and given false plates – then, with a fresh name and a different identity, it would be handed over to a new owner.

For crews, a pirate raid can be traumatic. Modern cargo ships have few personnel, perhaps just 25 people on an oil tanker the length of three soccer pitches. They are easy prey for pirates prepared to use violence. In general, crew members are rarely harmed, not out of any scruples on the part of the pirates but because the poorly paid crew

has little to gain by resisting. Yet in one infamous case in the South China Sea, Chinese pirates posing as customs officials boarded a cargo ship, the MV *Chang Sheng*, and killed all 23 crew members and dumped their bodies in the sea.

The *Chang Sheng* pirates were captured by the Chinese authorities, who executed them using machine-gun. They sang as they went to their deaths, exhibiting all the devil-may-care bravado of the pirates of old. The same swagger was characteristic of the pirates in the Strait of Malacca. After a successful raid, they would head back to their lawless bases on the Indonesian coast to spend their loot on drink, drugs, gambling, tattoos and women.

But the days of the Malacca pirates were numbered. In 2004 Malaysia, Indonesia and Singapore formed a joint coastal patrol force, and soon afterwards pirate attacks began to diminish. The force was later strengthened by assistance from the navies of India and Thailand. In 2011 the reported number of attacks in the Strait of Malacca was close to zero.

OFF THE HORN OF AFRICA

But by now the world centre of piracy had shifted to another ocean bottleneck: the shipping lanes that lead in and out of the Suez Canal and the Arabian Gulf. Piracy operates only where coasts are not properly policed and the rules of maritime law are not enforced. This has long been true of the waters off Somalia, a country that has been in a state of political turmoil since the early 1990s. For years there was no central authority in the country, let alone a coast guard or navy.

One of earliest reported incidences of piracy in this region took place in 1994, when MV *Bonsella*, carrying a cargo of medicine, was raided by 26 Somali pirates on a dhow. From then on the attacks began to increase in ambition, sophistication and number. In 2008 alone, 111 attacks were reported, of which 42 were successful. The most daring and notorious of these took place in November 2008, when pirates seized the Liberian-flagged MV *Sirius Star*. One of the world's largest oil tankers, operated by the Saudi Arabian Oil Company, the ship itself was estimated to be worth $150 million, and it was carrying a full load of crude oil valued at $100 million. After seven weeks, the pirates released the ship on payment of a ransom of $3 million.

Now no ship or boat of any size was safe in this region. In 2009, in an act of old-fashioned kidnap, Paul and Rachel Chandler, a British couple on a round-the-world sailing trip, were taken from their 11.5m (38ft) yacht. They were held in the desert scrubland of eastern Somalia for over a year before they too were released when a ransom was paid – reported to be in the region of $800,000.

BRIGANDS WITH ROCKETS

In the early days, the pirates targeted only ships close to the Somali coast. Later, attacks were reported out in to the Indian Ocean, more than 2,000km (1,250 miles) from Somalia. To operate so far from home, the pirates used 'mother ships' – stolen trawlers and cargo vessels from which they launched their speedboats. These pirates were not armed with mere machetes: they had an armoury of modern military weapons, including machine-guns and rocket-propelled grenades, to help them capture ship and crew.

Some Somali pirates became immensely rich, especially in the context of one of the world's poorest nations. Some of their money went on more sophisticated weaponry and equipment, and some was spent – in the manner of Robin Hood – in their homes and in their villages. So the pirates were often supported and even encouraged by their communities.

Many of the Somali pirates claimed that they were simply fishermen, forced by circumstances to turn to piracy. With the collapse of central government in Somalia, the coastal waters were left with no protection. Foreign trawlers fished illegally, and large ships dumped toxic and

How could poor Somali fishermen be holding the whole world to ransom?

nuclear waste off the coast. Both activities caused a dramatic reduction in fish stocks. So the pirates could claim to be acting in defence of their home waters and their own livelihoods, and, as if to underline that contention, they adopted names such as the National Volunteer Coast Guard. Some even argued that their activities were a legitimate way of exacting compensation from the international community.

By 2010 estimates of the cost of Somali piracy to the global economy ranged from $7 billion to $12 billion a year – this included not just lost cargo and ransom money, but also increased insurance premiums and the added costs of security. The international community came under increasing pressure to act – because how was it that poor fishermen from an impoverished failed state were holding the whole world to ransom in this way?

In 2011 several countries, including the USA and the UK, set out proposals to permit merchant ships to carry detachments of armed guards. Meanwhile, shipping companies were encouraged to improve their defences – by fitting alarm systems and detectors, ringing the decks with razorwire, reinforcing the bridge, and installing non-lethal means to discourage and incapacitate attackers, such as slippery foam dispensers, powerful water-hoses, sonic devices and so-called 'dazer lasers'.

BATTLING THE PIRATES

The international community ratcheted up its response to piracy in general. Beginning in 2006, the USA, the European Union, India, Russia, South Korea, Japan and Australia all increased their naval presence in the Arabian Gulf. They acted in concert to protect vessels of their own nations, but were less willing to intervene for ships sailing under flags of convenience, such as those of Panama or Liberia. Nevertheless, in 2008 an international flotilla cornered and recovered the pirated MV *Faina*, a Belize-flagged Ukrainian ship carrying arms and tanks to Kenya.

Over the next few years the response grew tougher and more uncompromising, and pirates were dealt with like seagoing terrorists. In 2009 the US Navy rescued the crew of the MV *Maersk Alabama*, which had been hijacked by just four pirates; Navy SEALs killed three of the pirates as they tried to flee in a lifeboat with the ship's captain as hostage. The Indian navy scored a number of successes in 2011, capturing mother ships, arresting pirates and releasing hostages. In 2011 South Korean commandos stormed the pirated MV *Samho Jewelry*, released the crew, killed eight pirates and captured five more. But such operations were risky. And pirates could always try to persuade rescuers to back off by putting a gun to a hostage's head. In 2011 four Americans were killed when US forces attempted to rescue them from a hijacked yacht. International law was another inhibiting factor. When pirates were captured, it was far from clear what should be done with them. Suspects were taken to the USA and to European countries, but the difficulty of assembling evidence tended to make trials impossible. Some accused pirates even managed to claim political asylum.

Such anomalies led to calls for a place of jurisdiction where all pirates could be tried. Kenya agreed to take on this role in 2009. But the lack of legal and political clarity was not just a shield for the pirates, it was also a weapon to be used against them. In recent years there have been signs that covert operations against pirate strongholds may have taken place. Operations to retake ships generally have

Some pirates may even have been made to walk the plank.

no witnesses, and in some cases summary justice may have been applied: pirates may have been made to walk the plank, or its modern equivalent.

'We will have to act as our forefathers did when they encountered pirates,' said President Dmitry Medvedev of Russia, speaking after commandos retook the tanker MV *Moscow University* in the Gulf of Aden. Ten captured pirates were reportedly set adrift in an inflatable boat some 560km (350 miles) from the Somali coast. They were never seen again.

The silk robbers

For thousands of years the secret of silk production belonged *to China alone. From around 200* BC *the precious fabric was exported across Asia along the Silk Road, eventually reaching the Mediterranean world. But in the 6th century* AD *China's monopoly was breached, and the long-guarded mystery of silk manufacture unravelled in imperial Constantinople.*

Silk is a textile beyond compare: soft, light, lustrous and strong. Chinese legend says that the magical properties of silk were discovered by Empress Leizu, wife of Huangdi, the Yellow Emperor, in about 2640 BC. While looking at the cocoons that had colonised the mulberry trees in the palace garden, she accidentally dropped one into a cup of hot tea. The cocoon unravelled, and the empress realised that it was made of a single fine thread.

The legend is an indication of the great age of China's silk industry, and of its close link with imperial power. Silk weaving and embroidery developed into a highly sophisticated craft: Chinese tombs of the 2nd century BC have been found to contain silk textiles of exquisite delicacy, and the prominence given to them is an indication of just how much silk was treasured as a symbol of high status and wealth. It was used not just for clothing, but also as a surface for painting and calligraphy.

Silk is the product of a specialised, labour-intensive industry. It is made from the cocoons of the silkmoth, *Bombyx mori*. Blind and flightless, this moth has become utterly dependent on human cultivation. It is the caterpillars – called silkworms – that spin the cocoons. After hatching from eggs, the silkworms are carefully mollycoddled and fed copiously on the fresh leaves of the white mulberry tree. During this feeding frenzy they grow rapidly. After about four weeks they stop eating and begin to extrude sticky filaments that combine into a single thread to form the cocoon. One cocoon contains a thread up to 900m (3,000ft) long. For this thread to be harvested intact, the developing moth inside has to be killed, which is done by heating or steaming. Some moths are allowed to mature, however, so the females can produce eggs, and the whole process can begin again – as happens anywhere from six weeks to a year later. Each female produces 300 to 500 eggs, and it takes about 800 silkworm cocoons to make a single blouse.

ON THE SILK ROAD

The complexity of silk production made the fabric costly in China, but it was many times more expensive once it had made

its journey down the Silk Road, changing hands for a greater price at each stage along the way. By the time it reached the Mediterranean it was worth more than its weight in gold. The Greeks and the Romans had some notion that this extraordinary fabric came from moth cocoons, but only the Chinese knew how to exploit the silkmoth – and they knew the importance of maintaining their monopoly. For anyone caught trying to export their secrets of silk production, the penalty was death.

But this law needed little enforcement: it was in the interests of everyone involved in the trade to preserve the secret. In practice, too, it was always going to be hard to replicate Chinese silk elsewhere, as both the cultivated silkmoth and the white mulberry tree were found only in China. Nevertheless, sericulture – the cultivation of the moths and trees – did leak beyond

China's borders. Chinese emigrants took the secret to Korea as early as 200 BC, and from there it reached Japan in around AD 300. In about AD 50 it arrived in the Buddhist kingdom of Khotan on the Silk Road (though legend has it arriving several centuries earlier with a Chinese princess who travelled to Khotan to be married and smuggled out silkmoth eggs in her hair). By AD 300 sericulture was known in India, and by AD 600 the oasis cities of Kashgar and Samarkand had their own production. The output of these local industries remained small, however. Most fine silk still came from China, and the Chinese monopoly was not seriously threatened by the inferior competition.

In the 4th century, after the Roman Empire moved its centre east to Constantinople, silk became even more highly prized. In the courts of Byzantium, as Constantinople was also known, silk was reserved for the emperor and his entourage, and for the high dignitaries of the Christian Church.

By now, silk thread and silkworm cocoons, as well as finished textiles, were reaching the West. The ports of Beirut and Tyre in Syria, and Alexandria in Egypt had become the Mediterranean specialists in silk processing. All these cities fell within the Byzantine orbit, but the raw materials still had to reach them. The vital silkmoth cocoons came through the Byzantines' great rival in the Middle East, the Persian Empire of the Sassanians. But then, in AD 532, the Persians conquered Syria and the eastern Mediterranean, cutting off the commercial link to Byzantium.

This interruption in the westward flow of silk occurred during the reign of Emperor Justinian I (AD 527–65). The main chronicler of his era was Procopius, an official born in Palestine. Procopius wrote eight books about the wars that Justinian fought to preserve and expand his empire. In the seventh of these, on the war against the Goths in Italy, Procopius tells briefly how the key secret of Chinese silkmaking was stolen for Justinian some time around AD 552.

RECEIVING STOLEN SECRETS

According to Procopius, two monks from India came to Justinian and persuaded him that he should not buy silk from his enemies the Persians. They told him that they could bring him silkmoth eggs and the knowledge of how to use them, and so create a home-grown silk industry. Justinian accepted the offer and sent them on their mission to 'Serinda', the 'land of silk' – meaning Central Asia. In due course the monks returned with the eggs, which were nurtured on mulberry leaves – initially, it seems, on the native black mulberry before white mulberry trees were procured.

Modern-day industrial espionage

The smuggling of silkworms out of China is an early example of industrial espionage – the theft of information or technology from a rival in order to gain, or destroy, a commercial advantage. 'Corporate espionage', as it now more usually called, is alive and well. In fact, the advent of the internet age gave it a massive fillip. Digital information became easy to steal once huge amounts of data could be carried out of a building on a pocketable floppy disc (or, nowadays, an even smaller memory stick). In such instances of info-theft, the 'spy' is often a disgruntled employee. In 2004, for example, an IT engineer working for the internet service provider AOL was convicted of stealing the company's entire customer list – 92 million email addresses – and selling them to a spammer for thousands of dollars.

But this kind of espionage is not just a loner's game. In 2001 Procter and Gamble, producer of well-known brands such as Fairy Liquid, was found to have hired a specialist 'corporate intelligence' firm to uncover information about products in development by its rival Unilever. The company used a technique borrowed from tabloid journalism: they went through Unilever's rubbish, looking for unshredded documents containing commercial secrets. Phone-hacking is another part of the corporate spy's dubious armoury, as are hi-tech devices such as laser microphones and fibre-optic 'snake-cams'. In today's world, no secret – personal, corporate or state – is ever entirely secure.

A different account of this key act of industrial espionage is given by the historian Theophanes of Byzantium, writing later in the 6th century. He stated that a Persian smuggled the eggs from 'Seres' (that is, China) in a hollowed-out cane. But whatever the details of the trickery and deception, Constantinople became the first European centre of silk production – a palace industry overseen by the imperial court.

That is almost all we know – almost, but not quite. Procopius, the laudatory historian of Justinian, is also known for his 'Secret History', a scurrilous account of Justinian's reign that was discovered in the Vatican Library more than a thousand years after it was written. In this revisionist work, Procopius provides ribald details of the scandals, perversions and corruption of Justinian and his wife Theodora, deliberately demolishing the reputation he had so carefully promoted in his official histories. Procopius also presents a rather different picture of the silk episode,

accusing Justinian of manipulating the silk market for his own personal profit, and blithely destroying the livelihood of silk workers within the empire.

Whatever Justinian's motives, silk production was now firmly established in Europe. From Constantinople it went to Sicily and from there, in the 13th century, to mainland Italy. Lucca, Florence, Genoa and Venice became famous centres of silk manufacture. The French kings brought silkmakers to France in the 15th and 16th centuries to reduce their nation's huge expenditure on Italian silk; by the following century it was a major industry in many cities across Europe – the source of the exquisite clothing of the rich.

The Asian silk trade collapsed with the spread of Islam, which did not approve of such finery. China lost its monopoly, but the fabric itself lost none of its allure. Four thousand years after the Empress Leizu's fabled and accidental discovery, silk remains a byword for luxury, a queen among textiles.

In the murder hotel

The Chicago World's Fair of 1893 attracted visitors in their millions from across the USA. But some unsuspecting guests who chose to stay at the wrong boarding house would never see home again. They joined a growing list of victims of one of America's first and worst serial killers.

In the hot summer of 1886 a young man called Dr Henry Howard Holmes arrived in Chicago. The name that he used was a pseudonym – he was born Herman Mudgett – but the title was genuine, for Holmes had graduated from medical school two years earlier. He had come to America's most exciting, fastest-growing city to make money for himself. He also had ambitious plans for murder.

Even before his move to Chicago, Holmes had flirted with crime. He had dabbled in insurance fraud, and he was, at the age of 25, a bigamist, having left two wives, each with a young child, behind him in his home state of New Hampshire. In Chicago, Holmes took a job as assistant manager of a drugstore whose owner was dying of cancer. When, in due course, his boss died, Holmes offered to buy the store from the man's grieving widow, promising that she could continue to occupy the flat upstairs. Soon after the store had been transferred into Holmes's name, the widow disappeared. Holmes told customers that she had decided to move to California.

Holmes expanded the pharmacy business by selling mail-order cures for hair loss and alcoholism. He also had an eye for real-estate opportunities, and somehow found the money to buy an entire block of undeveloped land directly across the street from the pharmacy. Construction on the plot was already underway when news came through that the site of the 1893 World's Fair would be Jackson Park, on the shore of Lake Michigan, due east of Holmes's property.

Holmes had his building constructed to a unique plan of his own devising, and he employed many different builders, often finding trivial reasons to replace workmen. As a result, few questions were asked

DOCTOR DEATH
Henry Holmes, like many a sociopath, was charming and very persuasive. He talked some victims into taking out insurance policies on which he could collect, so his compulsion to kill also became financially rewarding.

HOUSE OF HORRORS *The unremarkable façade of the Castle, Holmes's purpose-built boarding house, concealed an interior built for committing murder – and for disposing of the evidence.*

at the time about the structure's odder features: the windowless, iron-walled chamber next to his office, for example, which was fed by a gas jet controlled from Holmes's closet; or the coffin-sized furnace that he installed in the spacious basement.

WITH MURDER IN MIND

The finished building, known locally as 'the Castle', had a row of street-level commercial properties that Holmes leased out, keeping one for his own pharmacy. The two upper storeys, packed with small rooms, were intended to function as a boarding house. Millions of visitors were expected at the World's Fair, and they would need a cheap place to stay.

Holmes had a specific clientele in mind: single women, especially those from distant parts without friends or relatives in the city. For by that time the young man was already indulging his penchant for seduction and murder, using his personal charm to lure his victims. One unfortunate woman was Julia Conner, the wife of one of his employees. Holmes gave Julia a job too, and provided the family with a flat in the Castle. Julia fell for her benefactor, and divorced her husband to be with him. But not long afterwards, she and her eight-year-old daughter disappeared, never to be seen again. When people made inquiries, Holmes said that Julia had decided to return to the family home in Iowa. He told a similar tale about his secretary, an attractive 24-year-old named Emeline Cigrand. When she vanished, Holmes said that she had left town to get married.

The disappearances began to raise suspicions, but Chicago in the 1890s was

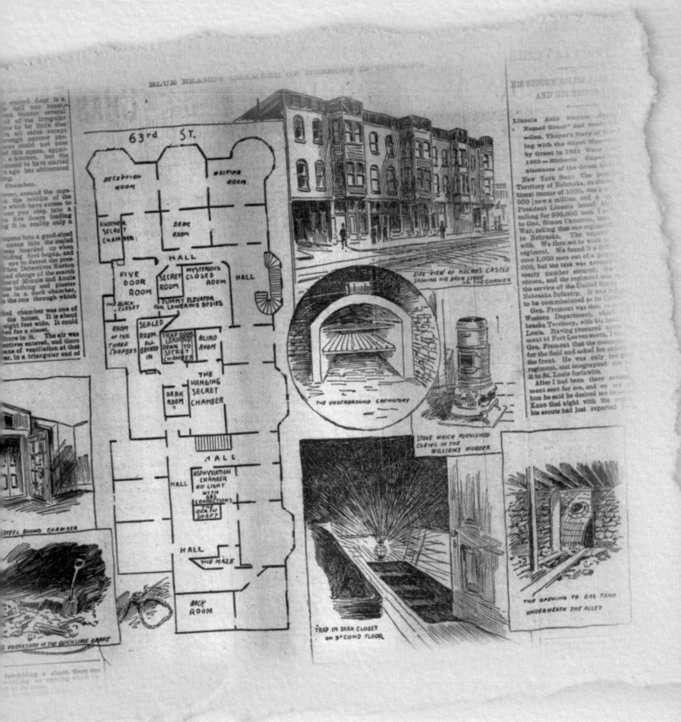

MURDER MAZE *An article in the* Chicago Tribune, *published on August 18, 1895, tried to make sense of the bizarre internal layout of the house that Holmes had built. At the core of the building was a hidden nest of windowless rooms where his victims were incarcerated and killed. Shafts led from some of the rooms to the 'operating room' in the basement. Some of the cells functioned as tiny gas chambers, while others had trap doors, hinged walls or false partitions. The rooms were accessed via twisted corridors and concealed lift shafts.*

a place where people were constantly on the move and it seemed unlikely that the personable young doctor was up to any harm. People might have been more alarmed if they had known of Holmes's more sinister entrepreneurial activities. One involved supplying corpses to an 'articulator', who stripped the flesh off dead bodies. Holmes then sold the skeletons to medical schools, no questions asked.

THE TRUTH COMES OUT

Late in 1893 Holmes made a spurious insurance claim following a fire in the Castle's upper storey. The investigator assigned to the case quickly discovered a host of unpaid creditors: suddenly Holmes was not looking quite so much the pillar of the community. And he had made another error. One of the people who disappeared after associating with Holmes was Minnie Williams, a young woman of good family. Before she vanished, she had transferred land in Texas to Holmes. The girl's guardians despatched a private detective to investigate. Holmes, feeling the heat, decided to get out of Chicago.

For the next year he was on the road in eastern USA and Canada. He took with him a man named Benjamin Pitezel, who had originally been hired to work on the construction of the Castle. Holmes talked Pitezel into a dubious money-making scheme. Pitezel would take out a life-insurance policy with his wife and five children as beneficiaries. Holmes would then fake Pitezel's death, using the practised ruse of a disfigured corpse to fool the investigators, and they would split the money. But Holmes modified the plan and killed Pitezel so he could take the money.

This time the authorities were not fooled. Holmes went on the run, taking three of Pitezel's children with him.

News of the father's murder reached the newspapers, and the hunt for the children became a media sensation. Holmes was eventually tracked down in Boston – without the children. Further investigation turned up the corpses of two girls in Toronto, buried in the cellar of a rented house. The third, a boy, had been killed earlier, his body incinerated.

Holmes was put on trial for the killings. While in prison he published a memoir insisting that the girls were alive when last he saw them: 'I hurriedly left them – felt the innocent child's kiss so timidly given and heard again their earnest words of farewell.' He was more honest in a final confession, composed after he had been sentenced to hang. 'I was born with the devil in me,' he wrote. 'I could not help the fact that I was a murderer, no more than the poet can help the inspiration to sing.'

The Castle mysteriously burned down shortly after the girls' bodies were found. The police had had time to make only a cursory investigation, but what they had found in the basement gave some idea of the horrific crimes committed within its walls. They had found surgical tools, a bloodstained dissection table and a vat of acid containing eight rib bones and part of a skull. Elsewhere were cavities containing quicklime and further human remains.

No one will ever know how many people died in the Castle. Holmes went to his grave charged only with the Pitezel murders. In his unreliable memoir he confessed to 27 killings. The real number could have been higher. Holmes's career had been made possible by the social mobility of railway-age America, a rootless time when it was easy for people to go missing. This he exploited with dreadful cunning, combined with a psychopathic disregard for the value of other people's lives.

Finding the disappeared

When the military took over Argentina in 1976 they made it their job to rid the nation of 'subversive elements'. In what became known as the 'Dirty War', people were snatched off the streets or taken from their homes. The story of what happened to them would emerge only in fragments.

Argentina in the early 1970s was a country in crisis. Thirty years earlier, it had ranked as the eighth wealthiest nation in the world, but its economy had since crumbled. Politically, it was bitterly divided. Radical left-wing factions had taken up arms and were waging guerrilla war against the state. Matters came to a head in 1973 when the charismatic but divisive Juan Perón, who had ruled the nation from 1946 to 1955, returned from 18 years' exile to reclaim the presidency. In his earlier spell in power Perón had combined populism and nationalism to attract both left- and right-wing support. Now, though, the two wings of the Peronist movement split amid a wave of kidnappings and executions.

When the 78-year-old president died, the nation was left in the hands of his third wife, Isabel. Political violence increased, and the new government responded by authorising the military to 'annihilate' the terrorists. Death squads targeted not just active guerrillas but also union leaders and political activists. The situation continued to deteriorate until 1976, when Isabel Perón was removed in a military coup. For

LOST RELATIVES *After the fall of Argentina's military junta in 1983, public displays of the faces of the 'disappeared' became familiar on the Plaza de Mayo in Buenos Aires. They were both an appeal for information and a memorial of sorts for those known to have been killed.*

the next seven years Argentina would be ruled by a series of unelected juntas made up of leaders of the armed forces – the first was headed by General Jorge Videla.

THE START OF THE TERROR

At first most Argentinians welcomed the coup, hoping for stability. 'Now we are governed by gentlemen,' proclaimed the writer Jorge Luis Borges (who later retracted his support). The junta began by declaring a 'national re-organisation process', with the restoration of order the key aim. Strikes were banned and employment protection laws rescinded in the name of reviving the struggling economy: Argentina had a billion-dollar deficit, and inflation was running at 30 per cent a month.

But Argentina's new rulers had more than economic goals in mind. As General Videla had made clear some

months earlier: 'As many people must die in Argentina as is necessary for the country to be secure again.' Sure enough, the weeks after the coup saw a new and terrifying form of public control. Unsuspecting people from many walks of life began to be grabbed from their homes by snatch squads. Others were bundled off the streets into Ford Falcons without number plates – the cars became symbols of the repression.

Most of those who were taken had no link to guerrilla activity, but were simply suspected of holding left-wing views. Journalists, lawyers, lecturers, teachers and social workers were all targeted, as were trades unionists and farm workers' organisers. When anguished relatives tried to find out what had happened to them, they ran up against a wall of silence. No one knew where they were or what

had become of them. Rumours began to circulate that the *desaparecidos*, the 'disappeared ones', were being killed.

The truth was, if possible, even worse. Detainees were taken to detention centres, mostly located in police stations or military bases. They were stripped naked and subjected to intimate body searches before being clamped in chains that quickly opened sores on the skin. Some were forced to wear hoods or blindfolds.

Accommodation varied from centre to centre, but 'tubes' were typical – tiny cells too low for the prisoners to stand upright and sometimes too short for them to stretch out. From here detainees selected for interrogation were taken to torture chambers known chillingly as 'operating theatres'. In many cases the torturers themselves lived in barracks on the premises, and this lent a weird

intimacy to their relationship with their victims. Surviving detainees have described how some guards would visit the cells for company in the evenings, removing prisoners' hoods so they could play cards or chess together.

In the first months after the coup, desperate relatives seeking to trace their loved ones took out writs of habeas corpus at a rate of 800 a week. By law, anyone detained who was named in such a writ should have been brought before a judge or court, but the writs produced no results. In some cases, parents of detainees from wealthy families were confronted with ransom demands in return for the captives' release; some who paid up later found that their children had been killed anyway.

The grim truth was that detainees were of no further use to their captors once there was no more information to be had from them. Given the junta's stated aim of eradicating 'subversives', there was no question of releasing them back into society. Some with practical skills were assigned jobs within the detention camps. A few were 'turned', bribed by threats against

Some were thrown to their deaths from aeroplanes.

themselves or their families to become torturers themselves. But the constant influx of new prisoners meant that space was at a premium. So, by an implacable process of logic, the majority were permanently 'disappeared'. Many were shot and buried in mass graves. Some were drugged then thrown to their deaths from aeroplanes circling over the sea. This bizarre and terrible practice meant their bodies were almost certain never to be found.

THE SEARCH FOR TRUTH

Mothers of *desaparecidos* were among the first to demand to know what had become of prisoners held incommunicado. They organised a demonstration in Buenos Aires's main square, the Plaza de Mayo, in April 1977, and in December took out a newspaper advertisement naming their disappeared children. The leader of the movement, Azucena Villaflor, was snatched from her home that same evening.

Meanwhile, international pressure was growing, for a few of the disappeared were foreign nationals. The case of two French nuns, 61-year-old Léonie Duquet and 40-year-old Alice Domon, attracted particular attention. But it was only in 1983, after military rule came to an end, that definite facts began to emerge. In that year Argentina's new civilian president, Raúl Alfonsín, set up a commission, known by its Spanish acronym as CONADEP, to investigate the disappearances. It managed to document nearly 9,000 cases, including those of some 200 children under the age of 15. Roughly 30 per cent of the victims it identified were women.

CONADEP's final report was presented to President Alfonsín in September 1984, opening the way for the prosecution of junta members. In 1985 General Videla was sentenced to life imprisonment. But then, unwilling to alienate the military even more, the government passed the so-called *Punto Final* ('Full Stop') law, which put an end to further investigation. In 1990 President Carlos Menem went further. He pardoned Videla and his junta colleagues and, to be even-handed, some former guerrilla leaders too.

Operation Condor

Argentina was not the only South American country to be terrorised by its own rulers in the 1970s. Military dictatorships held sway over many of the other nations. They even cooperated with each other to crush political dissent throughout the continent. In 1975 intelligence officers from Bolivia, Argentina, Chile, Paraguay and Uruguay met in the Chilean capital Santiago to coordinate the kidnapping and assassination of left-wing activists in each other's countries. The plan was named Operation Condor, and it was a kind of murderous, multilateral, underhand extradition treaty. Its activities continued until the fall of the Argentinian regime in 1983, by which time perhaps 60,000 people had been killed in Condor's operations.

In 1995 a retired naval captain named Adolfo Scilingo made a public confession on national television, in which he revealed that as a young officer he had assisted in 'death flights'. He said that he had personally despatched 30 people, including a 65-year-old man and a 16-year-old boy. A decade later the remains of Azucena Villaflor were identified. The injuries on her body were consistent with having been dropped from an aeroplane.

The total number of *desaparecidos* is disputed. It may be as many as 30,000, but no full list has ever been published. For the most part the perpetrators have gone unpunished, though the Punto Final law was rescinded in 2003, re-opening the way for prosecutions. Some of the detainees who survived have had the unnerving experience of encountering their torturers in the street. As for the relatives of the *desaparecidos*, most – even those who discovered the fate of their loved ones – have been unable to bury their dead.

NAT TATE

AN AMERICAN ARTIST: 1928 – 1960

HITL

ILLIAM BOYD

Chapter 5

DARK SCIENCE, HIDDEN ARTS

Much creative work – both scientific and artistic – goes on behind closed doors. Some experimenters and inventors, like some painters and writers, have secrets they must keep. And some creators or their works bring mystery in their wake.

The Gioconda smile

The Mona Lisa *is the most famous painting in the world, and it evokes the strangest reactions. Some people want to worship it, others to decode it, possess it or even destroy it. What is the peculiar power of Leonardo da Vinci's mesmerising portrait, and what secrets does it hide?*

On August 21, 1911, a 30-year-old Italian man named Vincenzo Peruggia entered the Louvre in Paris, where he had been employed as a painter-decorator. A few minutes later he walked out with the *Mona Lisa* concealed under his workman's smock. No one realised anything was awry until the next day; everyone who noticed that the picture was missing assumed it had been removed for routine cleaning.

Once it was established that a theft had taken place, the picture became a global sensation. Crowds who had never been to see the portrait flocked to the Louvre to stare at the empty space where it had hung. Police questioned the Cubist painter Pablo Picasso and the surrealist poet Guillaume Apollinaire, thinking – hoping – that one or both of them had taken the picture as some kind of avant-garde joke.

Though the original had disappeared, the image of the *Mona Lisa* was everywhere: newspapers reproduced it in reports of the police investigation, while cartoonists depicted a liberated Lisa enjoying the sights of Paris. Leonardo da Vinci's early 16th-century portrait of a young Florentine lady had become an international celebrity. It was now one of the most widely known and instantly recognisable faces in the world.

The *Mona Lisa* was recovered in Florence more than two years later, when Peruggia tried to sell it. After his arrest, he claimed he was merely trying to return the picture to the land from which – he wrongly believed – Napoleon had stolen it. Peruggia had intended to steal a different Italian masterpiece, Mantegna's *Parnassus* (also known as *Mars and Venus*), but it was too big to hide under his clothes so he opted for Leonardo's smaller work instead. That circumstance, the whim of an opportunist thief, did more to popularise the *Mona Lisa* than all Leonardo's genius could achieve. When she was returned to France in 1914, she was greeted like a homecoming heroine.

WHO WAS MONA LISA?

Most experts agree that the *Mona Lisa* is a portrait of Lisa Gherardini del Giocondo, wife of a Florentine silk merchant named Francesco del Giocondo (hence the name by which she is known in Italy and France, *La Gioconda*, or *La Joconde*). When she first

THE PRODIGAL PICTURE *The* Mona Lisa *under police guard in 1914, during her triumphal journey back to France from Italy. Once re-installed in the Louvre, her fame was assured forever more. From now on, she would be constantly mobbed by admirers.*

sat for Leonardo, in around 1503, she was about 24 years old. Her *contrapposto* pose – the body angled away from the viewer, head turned forward – was widely admired and copied by Leonardo's contemporaries. And his *sfumato* technique, whereby sharp edges are blurred and shaded to create an uncannily lifelike effect, was seen as a brilliant technical innovation, very unlike the slightly frozen human figures of earlier, lesser painters.

Leonardo worked on the painting for four years, and possibly at intervals after that. Strangely, he always took it with him when he travelled, and he never signed or dated it. The picture went with him when, towards the end of his life, he moved to France. It was sold to his last patron, King François I, and remained out of sight in the royal collection for almost 200 years. In 1799 Napoleon, then first consul of

France, came across the painting and commandeered it for his bedroom.

It was only in 1804 that the *Mona Lisa* went on public display – in the newly founded Louvre museum. At that time, and for decades afterwards, it was not seen as particularly interesting, but in the middle of the 19th century Leonardo's stock as an artist slowly rose. He came to be seen as the equal of the two acknowledged Renaissance greats, Michelangelo and Raphael.

This new-found interest in Leonardo as a painter drew attention to his few known works. The *Mona Lisa*, easily accessible in the Louvre, became an object of interest to critics and aesthetes at just the time that a new and deeply sensual attitude to art was emerging in France. One of the high priests of the new aesthetic cult was the poet Théophile Gautier, who happened to have written a popular guide to the paintings in the Louvre. On the subject of the *Mona Lisa* he had this to say: 'I have seen her frequently ... this adorable Joconde. She is always there, smiling with sensuality, mocking her numerous lovers ... she will remain beautiful for ever ...'

The 'numerous lovers' could be read as a reference to the many people who came to admire the picture. But Gautier's ambiguous critique introduced the novel idea that the lady in the painting was disturbingly sexy, possibly promiscuous – a courtesan or a dangerous *femme fatale*. This was a theme that Gautier explored at length: 'The expression, wise, deep, velvety, full of promise, attracts you irresistibly and intoxicates you, while the sinuous, serpentine mouth, turned up at the corners, in violet shadows, mocks you with so much gentleness, grace and superiority, that you feel suddenly intimidated, like a schoolboy before a duchess.'

Was she a courtesan or a dangerous femme fatale?

For Théophile Gautier, the power of the *Mona Lisa* lay in how she made him feel, how she moved or even aroused him. A similarly subjective approach was taken by Walter Pater, an English critic who wrote one of the most ecstatic passages ever dedicated to the lady. 'She is older than the rocks among which she sits,' he wrote. 'Like the vampire, she has been dead many times, and learned the secrets of the grave; and has been a diver in deep seas, and keeps their fallen day about her; and trafficked for strange webs with Eastern merchants: and, as Leda, was the mother of Helen of Troy, and, as Saint Anne, the mother of Mary; and all this has been to her but as the sound of lyres and flutes, and lives only in the delicacy with which it has moulded the changing lineaments, and tinged the eyelids and the hands.'

THE SEARCH FOR SECRETS

Pater's commentary, published in 1869, was learned like a poem by a generation of English intellectuals. His characterisation of the portrait as a mystery, an enigma as broad and unfathomable as life itself, was so influential that it became the default view. After Pater, everyone who looked at the picture felt sure that La Gioconda was keeping some profound secret, that her smile, whatever else it meant, said, 'I know something, but I'm not saying what.' In the hundred years since her kidnapping from the Louvre placed the *Mona Lisa* permanently in the spotlight, millions of words have been written in an attempt to unlock her riddles, to make her speak.

One of the first things that was asked of her was that she state her name. For 400 years, no one had doubted that she was Lisa, wife of the wealthy Giocondo, but suddenly her identity became a matter of doubt. Over the past century, it has been proposed that she was a noblewoman – Isabella d'Este, marquise of Mantua, or Costanza d'Avalos, duchess of Francavilla. Others have stared at that unsettling visage and seen the face of a man – Leonardo himself, or the man who was for 20 years his assistant (and perhaps his lover), Gian Giacomo Caprotti. There is even a theory that the picture may have started out as a portrait from life but, over the years that Leonardo worked on it, evolved into an abstract vision of the feminine ideal. That would constitute a very empty,

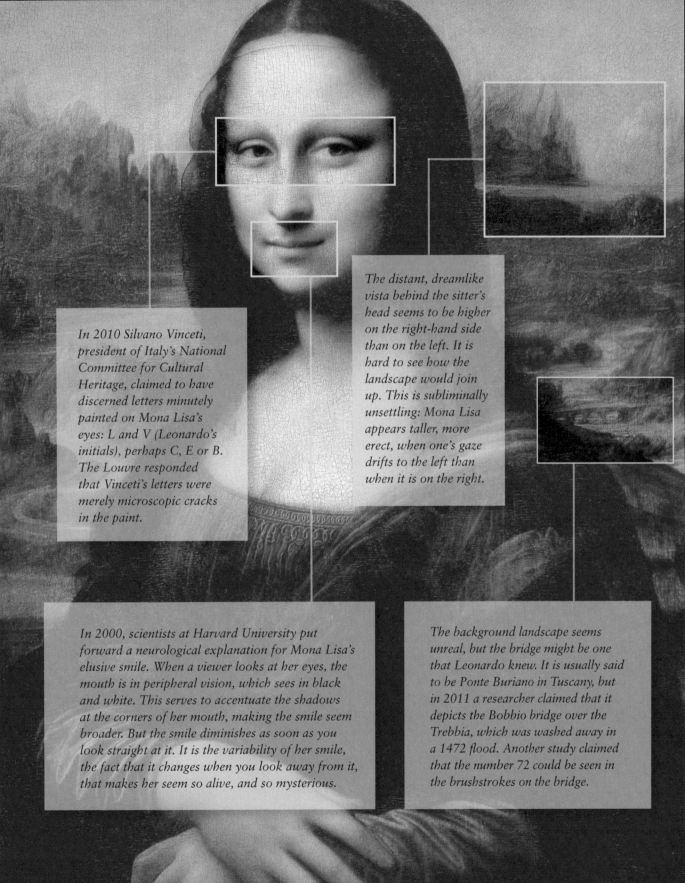

In 2010 Silvano Vinceti, president of Italy's National Committee for Cultural Heritage, claimed to have discerned letters minutely painted on Mona Lisa's eyes: L and V (Leonardo's initials), perhaps C, E or B. The Louvre responded that Vinceti's letters were merely microscopic cracks in the paint.

The distant, dreamlike vista behind the sitter's head seems to be higher on the right-hand side than on the left. It is hard to see how the landscape would join up. This is subliminally unsettling: Mona Lisa appears taller, more erect, when one's gaze drifts to the left than when it is on the right.

In 2000, scientists at Harvard University put forward a neurological explanation for Mona Lisa's elusive smile. When a viewer looks at her eyes, the mouth is in peripheral vision, which sees in black and white. This serves to accentuate the shadows at the corners of her mouth, making the smile seem broader. But the smile diminishes as soon as you look straight at it. It is the variability of her smile, the fact that it changes when you look away from it, that makes her seem so alive, and so mysterious.

The background landscape seems unreal, but the bridge might be one that Leonardo knew. It is usually said to be Ponte Buriano in Tuscany, but in 2011 a researcher claimed that it depicts the Bobbio bridge over the Trebbia, which was washed away in a 1472 flood. Another study claimed that the number 72 could be seen in the brushstrokes on the bridge.

postmodern answer to the question 'Who is Mona Lisa?' It would make her a fictional character, no more a flesh-and-blood person than, say, Minnie Mouse.

LISA'S MANY AILMENTS

And yet in many ways the lady is painfully real. She has often been scrutinised by medical men, and she turns out to be a fascinating patient. In 2010 an Italian doctor looked at the apparent swelling around her eyes and diagnosed excess cholesterol in her diet. Other conditions ascribed to her include facial paralysis, deafness, even syphilis. More happily, it has been suggested that the inscrutable look of contentment on her face, as well as the coy placement of her hands, indicate that she is pregnant.

Dentists have also had their say. It has been posited that her expression suggests bruxism, compulsive grinding of the teeth; or that the line of her top lip suggests that her front teeth are missing – which, along with the faintest hint of a scar on her lip, raises the troubling possibility that she was a victim of domestic violence. Sigmund Freud, the founder of psychoanalysis, looked at her face and glimpsed the unconscious mind of its creator: 'Leonardo was fascinated by Mona Lisa's smile because it awoke something which had long lain dormant,' wrote Freud. 'It was his mother who possessed the mysterious smile, the smile that he had lost …' To Freud, Mona Lisa was the very image of the mother fixation, the Oedipus complex. Jungians, meanwhile, have seen her as an accomplished representation of the anima, the female archetype that resides in each one of us.

It seems that almost any condition can be read into that puzzling face, and that some of the diagnoses, such as poor diet and dysfunctional marriage, are reflections of contemporary preoccupations. Just as the poet Gautier saw his own stormily romantic vision of womanhood in the *Mona Lisa*, so modern viewers see their own obsessions reflected in her dark, unreadable eyes.

This is especially true when it comes to 'giocondology', the search for some hidden code within the frame or features of the *Mona Lisa*. Researchers looking for a message from Leonardo to future generations have claimed to have found unexplained numbers and letters, so small that they are visible only under a microscope, minutely inscribed in the pupils of Mona Lisa's eyes. Others have said that the top lip, when turned sideways and magnified, turns out to be an erotic representation of a man's arched back – Leonardo's cryptic admission of his own homosexuality. It has been said that by placing a mirror at La Gioconda's shoulder, it is possible to generate a reflection that is the awe-inspiring countenance of Jehovah.

All this and much more has been read into a portrait of a plainly dressed woman, painted in oils on a warping piece of poplar just 77cm (30in) high and 53cm (21in) wide. But why this painting? Leonardo painted other women who (most would agree) are just as expressive, and rather more alluring, too. Perhaps the strangest thing about the *Mona Lisa* is the accident of her fame, the series of coincidences and occurrences that led to her becoming the most famous work of art in the history of humanity. It is now impossible to view her simply as a portrait. She has become a symbol, an icon in the ancient sense of an object of worship and in the modern sense of a universal point of cultural reference. Her mystery is this: we can all claim to know her intimately, but in the end, none of us knows her at all.

The garden-shed forgeries

One of the most successful art forgers in history created his works in the back garden of a small, rented house. Completely self-taught, Shaun Greenhalgh was, in his way, a talented artist in his own right.

There was something undeniably impressive about Shaun Greenhalgh's versatility as an artist and the scope of his ambition. He created convincing Roman and Egyptian artefacts, and also works by 20th-century masters such as Man Ray, L.S. Lowry, Thomas Moran, Henry Moore and Otto Dix. He worked in metal, glass, stone and ceramics; he could sculpt, draw and paint. Sometimes he had very little reference material to go on: he produced a fine terracotta goose purporting to be by Barbara Hepworth, having seen just one picture in a book.

NEFERTITI'S DAUGHTER

Greenhalgh's career as a forger spanned 17 years, from 1989 to 2006. He forged not just artworks but the documents that proved their provenance. His Lowrys, for example, came with letters that looked to have been written in the artist's own hand. He was careful to forge works that were known to have existed but had since been lost – such as the Hepworth goose – or that were mentioned or hinted at in historical documents but had never been seen.

The whole Greenhalgh family was involved in the scam. Shaun's elderly parents did the selling, posing as naive individuals with interesting heirlooms that they would like to have valued. Shaun's brother George handled the money – though none of the family made much use of their earnings. All the time the forgeries were going on, they lived in a small house in Bolton, northern England, with Shaun creating fake art in his bedroom or the garden shed.

In financial terms, Greenhalgh's most successful work was a beautiful Egyptian statuette of one of the daughters of Akhenaten and Nefertiti. The Greenhalghs claimed, when they sold it for £440,000, that it was a piece mentioned in an

NOT A GAUGUIN *Paul Gauguin considered sculpting a faun, but there is no evidence that he ever did so. Greenhalgh did it for him: this fake Gauguin sold for £20,700 in 1994.*

old auction catalogue. They cooked up a plausible story about how the piece found its way from the auction rooms to their suburban attic.

Shaun's downfall came from a tiny error. In 2005 he created a set of Assyrian reliefs, which his father showed to the British Museum. A diacritic mark was missing from the cuneiform inscription – unthinkable in a piece made for a royal palace. The museum alerted the police, who found materials and unfinished works in the Greenhalgh home. The whole family was arrested and convicted. Shaun was sentenced to four years' imprisonment.

The imagined artist

On the eve of April Fool's Day, 1998, leading figures of the New York art world attended a launch party for a book about a neglected abstract painter named Nat Tate. David Bowie read extracts from the manuscript. None of the critics, artists and journalists who went along that night knew that they were the victims of an elaborate hoax, a clever practical joke.

The invitation to the book launch, to be held in the studio of the fashionable painter Jeff Koons, went to all the right people in New York's avant-garde art scene. The leading critics were invited, as were the writers Paul Auster, Jay McInerney and Bill Buford, the painter Frank Stella and the artist/filmmaker Julian Schnabel. They were attracted by the pedigree of those behind the event: Karen Wright, editor of the prestigious journal *Modern Painters*; the Scottish novelist William Boyd, author of the book that was to be showcased; and the singer David Bowie.

The book in question was entitled *Nat Tate: An American Artist 1928–1960.* It was a slim but beautifully produced tribute (just 66 pages long) to a neglected painter of the abstract expressionist school. It came with a blurb written by David Bowie and with a cover commendation penned by the author and political commentator Gore Vidal, who was also quoted in the text. Vidal's assessment of the man was cool, sharp and damning. He described Tate as 'an essentially dignified drunk with nothing to say'.

Tate's life as told in the book made sad reading. He was born in New Jersey shortly before the Wall Street Crash, and orphaned as an infant. He was brought up by a timber magnate named Peter Barkasian, who sent him to art school and encouraged him in his ambition to be a painter. Tate built something of a reputation in the buzzing New York art world of the 1950s, but he was also a heavy drinker, prone to bouts of depression.

He burned almost all of his paintings over a single weekend.

On a trip to Europe, Tate met Picasso and Georges Braque, and his encounter with these modern masters made him question the value of everything he had ever done. Returning to the USA, he burned almost all of his paintings over a single weekend, then threw himself from the Staten Island Ferry. He was just 31. His body was never found.

NAT TATE

AN AMERICAN ARTIST: 1928–1960

WILLIAM BOYD

COVER STORY *William Boyd's false monograph looked convincing, but there were clues for the wary. The artist's very name was a jesting conflation of two art museums, the National Gallery and the Tate Gallery, both in London. As to the identity of the grainy man with the piercing eyes, no one – not even Boyd himself – knows who he is.*

Only, Tate had never existed – as Vidal, Bowie and the other people in on the joke knew very well. He was an entirely fictional figure, a character cooked up in the mind of novelist William Boyd. The book, and the party organised to launch it, were both elaborate deceptions.

The idea was born at an editorial meeting of *Modern Painters*, when Karen Wright had innocently suggested that it might be good to add some fiction to the magazine's content mix. On the spur of the moment, Boyd suggested that he

invent a painter. He had some previous experience in blurring the line between fact and fiction: 11 years earlier he had published a novel, *The New Confessions*, that presented itself as the autobiography of a non-existent filmmaker. When he made the suggestion, Boyd had in mind a short story along similar lines, but he soon found that his invented character, Nat Tate, took on a life of his own. As the character became more alive to Boyd, the short story grew into a fake monograph, the story of Tate's life and work. For extra authenticity, Boyd illustrated the book

Fake tales of Formosa

In 1704, a book entitled *An Historical and Geographical Description of Formosa* was published in London. Its author, George Psalmanazar, claimed to be a native of the island – modern-day Taiwan – abducted in his youth by missionaries. According to him, Formosans were cannibals who lived underground in the summer to preserve their fair complexions, hunted snakes for food and sacrificed the hearts of small boys to their gods. To lend a scholarly gloss to the book, Psalmanazar included a detailed account of Formosa's language.

The book was a great success, and was reprinted more than once. Plenty of people believed every fantastical word of it. By 1706, though, so many doubts had been raised about his account that Psalmanazar was forced to admit the hoax. He was not Formosan, but French. He had adopted a false name and nationality as a teenage runaway, originally claiming to be Irish, then Japanese, before finally settling on Formosa – because the island was so little known that his claims about his origins were unlikely to be challenged. His book tested that idea to the very limit, and in the process exposed the gullibility of the general public.

with 1950s photographs purporting to represent Tate and his circle. They were in fact shots of anonymous individuals that Boyd had bought in junk shops over the years. The book also contained reproductions of the handful of paintings said to have escaped destruction; these were Boyd's own works.

As Boyd tells the story, he viewed the invention of Tate largely as a game, but his co-conspirators quickly saw an opportunity to play a prank on the New York art world – so the invitations went out, and the guests turned up to celebrate the life of someone none of them could have known, or ever even heard of.

The following week *The Independent* newspaper in Britain published a piece claiming that 'some of the biggest names in the art world have been the victims of a literary hoax'. Its author described how no one he had spoken to at the gathering had admitted to never having heard of Tate (though equally none claimed to have known him well).

WHO LAUGHS LAST

Unsurprisingly, the revelations caused some ill feeling, not least because the sophisticated individuals on the guest list for the party did not take kindly to the suggestion they had been fooled. The perpetrators were quick to point out that their intentions were not malicious, though Karen Wright commented that, 'we were very amused that people kept saying: yes, I've heard of him. There is a willingness not to appear foolish. Critics are too proud for that.' Boyd insisted that the idea was primarily a literary conceit. But he did add, 'It's a little fable ... particularly relevant now when, almost overnight, people are becoming art celebrities.' A fable – or perhaps a fairytale, a modern take on the emperor's new clothes.

Even if the Tate hoax was a mere joke, it was a good one – retold in three separate TV documentaries over the next decade. The best joke of all, though, came in 2011 when a work purportedly by Tate, *Bridge No. 114*, was sold at auction for £7,250 (the proceeds went to the Artists' General Benevolent Institution). The anonymous buyer was no doubt pleased to have acquired a genuine Tate that was also a William Boyd original.

The lost masterpiece that wasn't

The most popular work of the Venetian composer Tomaso Albinoni is his Adagio in G Minor. *Everyone recognises this classic when they hear it. But the piece we know is not by the 18th-century master at all. And it is no older than Bill Haley's 'Rock Around the Clock'.*

Albinoni composed more than 40 operas as well as many cantatas, orchestral works and sonatas for solo instruments, but one piece is known above all others. His stately *Adagio in G Minor* has become one of the best-known melodies in the classical canon. Its measured tones have featured in films as diverse as *Flashdance* and *Gallipoli*.

And yet the piece was unknown until 1958. The man responsible for its publication was a musicologist named Remo Giazotto, an established Albinoni expert who had written a biography of the composer and produced a catalogue of his work. When the *Adagio* first appeared, he was working as a professor of the history of music at the University of Florence.

OUT OF THE FLAMES

The *Adagio*, it seemed, was the lucky survivor of a fire. Before the Second World War, most of Albinoni's manuscripts were held at the Saxon State Library in Dresden. When that city was destroyed by bombing in 1945, the library and all its contents were burned to ashes. A few of Albinoni's papers escaped the flames, having been sent to other locations for safe-keeping.

As Giazotto told the story, the *Adagio* was based on a manuscript fragment, saved from the Dresden archive, that was sent to him after the war. This scrap of Albinoni's work contained a few measures of the melody line plus the entire basso-continuo section of what Giazotto took to be the slow movement of a trio sonata. From this unpromising start Giazotto constructed the work

MAKING NOTES
Albinoni, with one of his manuscripts. Though he penned dozens of complete scores, he is remembered now for a piece that is, at most, an unfinished jotting.

known today, publishing it under the title '*Adagio in G Minor for Strings and Organ, on Two Thematic Ideas and on a Figured Bass by Tomaso Albinoni*'.

As the popularity of the *Adagio* grew, Giazotto changed the emphasis of his account, eventually claiming the work as his own composition. But he never produced the manuscript, and this led some critics to wonder whether it had ever existed. After his death in 1998, an independent transcription of the bass section, clearly marked with the Dresden library stamp, turned up. This lent credence to Giazotto's original story.

But the question of the authorship of the *Adagio* remains open. Perhaps Giazotto modestly declined the credit for the piece at first but wanted to be recognised for all his work on it once it became popular. Perhaps it dawned on him that his forensic reconstruction was closer to an act of original composition than he had realised at the time, that the fragment he began with was a mere seed, an inspiration. Perhaps he wanted – for once – to step out of the shadow of the prolific Albinoni, his specialist subject, and take a bow for himself.

Lenin lives!

In his will, Vladimir Lenin left strict instructions that he should be buried in a modest grave, next to his mother. Instead, his Bolshevik comrades decided to make a kind of holy relic of his body and put it on display for ever. Lenin's tomb became a shrine, the focus of a new cult.

Lenin, chief theorist of Bolshevism and architect of the Russian Revolution, suffered a massive stroke in March 1923. He was 53 years old and had been the undisputed leader of Soviet Russia for just over five years. But this stroke (he had suffered smaller ones in 1922) spelled the end of his political career, and presaged the end of his life. The right side of his body was paralysed, he was bereft of speech, and he became prone to sudden inexplicable terrors. For his own comfort, and in order to keep the severity of his condition from the people, he was moved out of his apartment in the Moscow Kremlin. He spent the last months of his life confined to a wheelchair in a heavily guarded mansion near the village of Gorki.

THE BODY IN QUESTION

When Lenin died at last, on January 21, 1924, a peculiar set of events was set in train that led to his unique posthumous fate: the modern mummification and permanent public display of his corpse. A funeral committee, chaired by Felix Dzerzhinsky, head of the Bolshevik secret police, was set up the day after Lenin's death. That same morning, Professor

Alexei Abrikosov performed an autopsy and removed Lenin's brain. Before the organ was set aside for further study, it was first weighed and found to be – at 1,340g (3lb) – unusually large. After the autopsy, Abrikosov embalmed Lenin's body in readiness for the funeral, which was scheduled to take place six days later.

Abrikosov removed Lenin's brain and had it weighed.

On January 23, Lenin's body was brought to Moscow and laid out in state in the Hall of Columns, near the Kremlin. Over the next three days, perhaps half a million people queued through day and night, in the bitter cold, to file past the body, which, despite the subzero temperature and Abrikosov's mortuarial skills, was starting to decompose.

A funeral, of sorts, was held on January 28. The body was moved to Red Square,

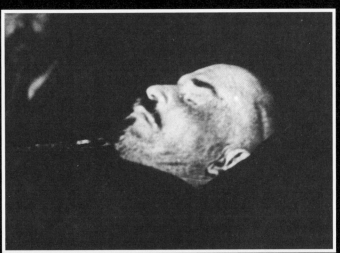

RESTING IN PEACE
Lenin in the late 1980s (above), his skin smooth, his beard trimmed, his nails polished, looked younger and in better shape than he did in the days after his death. He seemed so well preserved that there were persistent rumours that the body was a waxwork model.

BODY GUARDS *The team of scientists and politicians charged with preserving Lenin's body for all time. They claimed to have invented an entirely new method for embalming a body in the six months following Lenin's temporary funeral in January 1924.*

where a wooden crypt had been built at the foot of the Kremlin Wall. At 4pm, as factory sirens sounded across Moscow and throughout the Soviet Union, Lenin's coffin was lowered into the crypt. He had not been committed to the earth because the ground was frozen solid – digging a grave was out of the question. So for now it was still possible to visit the crypt and gaze on Lenin, and vast numbers of Soviet citizens did so. Most people – including Lenin's wife – assumed that he would be buried quite soon, perhaps after the 40 days of mourning that are the Russian Orthodox tradition.

But by now a plan had been conceived to keep Lenin's corpse on display for far longer than 40 days – for ever, in fact. Even as he lay in state, letters began to appear in the press demanding that the mortal remains be kept on view. 'Lenin's Body Must Be Preserved' declared a headline in the paper *Workers' Moscow*. 'Under no circumstances can we give to the earth such a great and intensely beloved leader as Ilyich,' wrote one worker, using Lenin's middle name, the respectful yet affectionate peasant form of address. 'We suggest his remains be embalmed and left under glass for hundreds of years.'

It is highly unlikely that such letters were the sole initiative of their authors; they would certainly have been placed by high-ranking members of the government so as to create the impression that a decision taken behind closed doors in the Kremlin actually proceeded from the wishes of the masses. Indeed, members of the Funeral Committee were already talking to Abrikosov about how to keep the body in a presentable condition indefinitely. Abrikosov told the politicians that the initial embalming, designed to last a week, had probably rendered it impossible to prevent natural decay setting in later. But, if the crypt were kept at a constant temperature, then it might be feasible to maintain the body in a viewable state for a longish time, 'three or four years at least'.

TO FREEZE OR TO EMBALM

Heaters were immediately installed in the crypt – so that the corpse didn't freeze solid in the intense Moscow cold. Meanwhile, an engineer named Leonid Krasin was commissioned to build two large refrigeration units (one of them a spare), on top of which a glass vacuum-sealed sarcophagus might sit. Krasin had no background in biology, but he was a passionate believer in Lenin and also in cryonics, the idea that science (in Krasin's view, Soviet science) would one day be able to revive the dead. So Krasin set about his task enthusiastically, certain that he was playing a vital part in the future resurrection of Vladimir Lenin.

Krasin's refrigeration units were ready by the beginning of March, but by that time the winter was coming to an end. The warmer weather was having an effect on Lenin's mortal remains. Patches of mould had begun to appear on his skin, he was becoming visibly wrinkled and his face was turning an unnatural grey. The funeral committee, which had not been disbanded, had noted this alarming new development and met in the last days of February to discuss it. One option was simply to bury him after all. But to do so would be a defeat, an admission that their Leninist faith had not been strong enough to achieve their goal. The committee members decided to persevere but changed tack. They summoned Vladimir Vorobyov, professor of anatomy at the Kharkov Medical Institute, and asked if he could reverse the decomposition of Lenin's body.

Vorobyov knew that refrigeration was hopeless, and that no technology existed for halting the decay of an already embalmed body. But he also understood that refusing the party's call was not an option. So he accepted the job, and was immediately co-opted onto the 'Commission for the Immortalisation of the Memory of V.I. Lenin', as the committee was now renamed.

> *Refusing the party's call was not an option.*

Vorobyov enlisted the help of a young biochemist named Boris Zbarsky. Together they worked frantically to invent an entirely new embalming process, one that would reverse the deterioration of the corpse, restore a lifelike colour to the skin and fix its appearance for decades or centuries to come. They experimented on many dead bodies, treating them with various fluids and chemicals. By trial and error, they came up with a cocktail containing glycerin, formalin, alcohol and other substances – the exact recipe has never been made known – which seemed to fulfil the brief: to embalm the body in a way that was chemically stable and visually lifelike. In July 1924, the Immortalisation Commission was invited to inspect the scientists' handiwork. They declared that the treatment had been a complete success, and publicly announced that a unique technological triumph had made it possible for the genius of the revolution to remain among his people.

In 1930, Lenin's body was placed in a new marble-and-granite mausoleum. On top of the tomb was a balcony where, for the next 60 years, Soviet leaders would stand to watch the military parades on Red Square. Beneath it was a secret laboratory in which the work of keeping Lenin fresh continued – for he needed constant maintenance to retain the look of someone only hours dead. The lab was secret, but it had a name – the Institute of Biological Structures – the 'biological structure' in question being Lenin's cadaver.

The immortalisation of Lenin was now a family business.

The institute was headed first by Vorobyov, afterwards by Zbarsky. Later, Zbarsky's son joined the staff: the immortalisation of Lenin had become a strange kind of family business. In 1953, the institute embalmed Stalin's body so that it could be placed alongside Lenin's (in 1961, in the dead of night, Stalin was removed from the mausoleum and buried beneath the Kremlin wall). In 1970,

members of the institute flew to Vietnam to embalm the body of Ho Chi Minh. But Lenin remained the principal client of the Institute of Biological Structures.

Its existence became public knowledge only with the collapse of the Soviet Union in 1991. At the same time, all manner of details emerged about how Lenin's body had been tended over the previous decades. Every week since his death, Lenin's face and hands were dabbed with a mild bleach to keep mould from forming. Every 18 months, the body was stripped and immersed in a vat of Vorobyov's secret fluid – or an improved version of it. After these chemical baths, Lenin would be dressed in an entirely new set of clothes.

LENIN AFTER LENINISM

Lenin's care was an expensive business, but the post-communist regime, under Boris Yeltsin, cut the supply of money to the Institute of Biological Structures. The then director, desperate to keep his post and his organisation's *raison d'être*, made it known through the press that his lab's expertise was for sale, and was not restricted to communist heads of state. Anyone with the money could now be eternalised, Lenin-style. In the meantime, the founder of the USSR was kept in pristine condition through donations from affluent admirers.

In the 1990s there were calls for the body to be buried at last. This had been Lenin's wish, after all. But devotees of the old Leninist cult still had enough political weight to quash such demands. More than 20 years have passed since the USSR sank, and its founder is still on view. He has become a tourist sight, a grotesque sleeping beauty never to be awakened. Lenin would surely be appalled by what has become of his country, his political creed, his own flesh-and-blood self.

Creating a cult

To the outside world he was a towering revolutionary and statesman, but in his homeland Lenin was far more than that. In the USSR, where the state controlled every aspect of his image and legacy, Lenin was made into a kind of secular deity, a Marxist messiah, something superhuman.

The adoration of Lenin in the Soviet Union, rooted and focused in the mausoleum where he lay, grew over subsequent decades to the point where Leninism was a kind of official state religion. The slogan 'Lenin is with us' was almost literally true, as his image was inescapable. Every factory and office had its Lenin bust or statue, and a 'red corner' where his memory was honoured. Children in kindergarten were told improving parables about 'Grandfather Lenin' that closely resembled the Bible stories heard in Sunday schools. Every book and student thesis, whatever its subject, began with a formulaic quotation from Lenin. Vast portraits of him covered the façades of buildings on political holidays. All cities had at least one Lenin statue, usually on a central plaza named Lenin Square. Towns and cities across the USSR bore his name. St Petersburg was renamed Leningrad immediately after his death, and was later joined by dozens of places named Leninabad, Leninsk, Leninavan, Leninakan, Leningori, Leninaul – or simply Lenin.

The official attitude to Lenin's political legacy was utterly reverential. The Communist Party held a monopoly on his biography, and all accounts read like the life of a saint or even like a gospel. Invented incidents from Lenin's life were used to persuade children to study hard or to avoid taking

RED GOD *A typically heroic Soviet image of Lenin. The caption reads 'Lenin lived, Lenin lives, Lenin shall live!' – a quasi-religious line from Vladimir Mayakovsky's epic poem 'Vladimir Ilyich Lenin', published in 1924.*

up smoking. His passing remarks about capitalist countries – Britain, say, where he lived for a time at the start of the 20th century, or America, which he never visited – were quoted in the cold-war years as if they were eternally valid cultural insights into those countries. The Lenin of Soviet history books was all-seeing, wise beyond ordinary human understanding. He never in his life made a political error, nor was he once surprised by events. His writings had the authority of scripture, in that they could be countered only by another quotation from Lenin. It would have been considered absurd, not to say blasphemous, to say 'Lenin was wrong about that.' He was seen as perfect, omnipotent, infallible, godlike – 'the most human of humans'.

Faces of the bard

Did Shakespeare write Shakespeare? Over the years, personalities as varied as Sigmund Freud, Mark Twain, Malcolm X and Charlie Chaplin have expressed doubts that the actor-manager from Stratford really penned the plays and poems attributed to him. But if not Shakespeare, then who? Many 'true authors' have been proposed – some of them downright bizarre.

In 1855 a long essay entitled 'William Shakespeare and his Plays: An Enquiry Concerning Them' appeared in an American journal called *Putnam's Weekly*. The article, the first published attempt to challenge the idea that Shakespeare was the author of the plays that bear his name, had been written by a gifted amateur scholar named Delia Bacon. She argued that Shakespeare's plays were actually the work of a secret committee, a group of highly educated and politically committed courtiers and aristocrats. They were using the theatre, she said, to air ideas that were too dangerous and subversive to raise in the political arena. Bacon saw her writerly cabal as a group of failed revolutionaries, a 'little clique of disappointed and defeated politicians who undertook to head and organise a popular opposition against the government'.

Miss Bacon was at first strangely coy about the identities of the men in this postulated underground movement, but she believed its leader to be her

THE USUAL SUSPECTS *Shakespeare's authorship went unquestioned by contemporaries such as the playwright Ben Jonson, who knew him personally. He wrote of Shakespeare that, 'in his writing, whatsoever he penned, he never blotted out a line'. That may or may not be true of Shakespeare's writing method, but it does establish that he was a writer. Supporters of candidates such as Bacon or Oxford say that Jonson was lying, that he was part of the cover-up.*

William Shakespeare

namesake, the philosopher Francis Bacon (to whom she claimed no relation). As for Shakespeare himself, Miss Bacon said that he was no more than a front, a decoy whose function was to draw attention from the high-born conspiracy against the despotism of Elizabeth I. Miss Bacon called him 'Will the Jester', and this is one of her kinder epithets. In the book that she wrote after her original article, she describes him as 'a pet horse-boy at Blackfriars' and a 'stupid, illiterate, third-rate play-actor'.

BUMPKIN WILL

These rather intemperate insults contain the key element of almost every theory postulating that William Shakespeare, the tradesman's son from Stratford, did not write his own plays. 'Anti-Stratfordians', whomsoever they propose as the true author, nearly always argue that Shakespeare did not have the life experience, the education or the artistic sophistication to produce works of such depth and brilliance. He was a provincial grammar-school boy who, as far as is known, never left England. Whereas the plays (say the anti-Stratfordians) could have been written only by someone equipped with a university knowledge of the Latin classics, acquainted with the mores and customs of royal courts, and widely travelled in France and Italy.

Orthodox Shakespearean scholars, meanwhile, question whether the plays truly imply that the author (whoever he was) had any of the experiences that anti-Stratfordians claim for him. It has been amply demonstrated, for example, that mentions of Roman authors in the works are limited almost entirely to those taught in Elizabethan grammar schools, and that the author often quoted not from the originals but from English translations – even reproducing printing errors, such as 'Lydia' for 'Libya' – so he need not have studied the classics at university. Equally, the knowledge of Italy displayed in the plays does not demonstrate that he knew the country – quite the reverse. The inland city of Milan, for example, is often described as a port, and *The Merchant of Venice* never once mentions that city's main distinction, its canals. The rigmarole of court life is almost entirely absent from the royal plays, and much of the background to the history plays would have been available to the author in easily accessible books.

Francis Bacon

17th Earl of Oxford

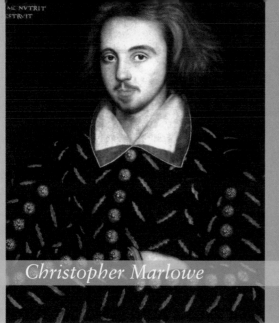
Christopher Marlowe

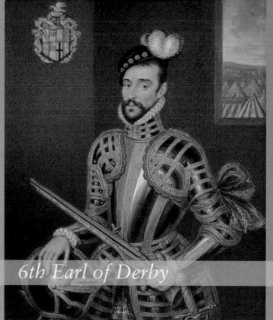
6th Earl of Derby

Books: there's the rub. The author of the plays demonstrably made great imaginative use of his research. The description of Cleopatra in her barque is a beautifully vivid example based on a prose account in a history (Thomas North's 1579 English translation of Jacques Amyot's 1559 translation of Plutarch's *Lives*). By special poetic alchemy the description there was transmuted into a wonderful word-picture. All writers of fictional tales do this, and Shakespeare did it supremely well ('The barge she sat in, like a burnished throne, / Burnt on the water. The poop was beaten gold, / Purple the sails, and so perfumed that / The winds were love-sick with them').

FROM BACON TO OXFORD

Despite the fact that design by committee rarely succeeds, Delia Bacon's thesis was widely believed. Respected literary figures such as Mark Twain accepted her reasoning, and other people built on it – for example, by uncovering encrypted messages in the plays. In 1905 a man named Isaac Hull Platt took the joke-word 'honorificabilitudinitatibus', which appears in *Love's Labour's Lost*, and re-arranged its letters into a Latin anagram that reads: *hi ludi, F. Baconis nati, tuiti orbi*, 'These plays, offspring of F. Bacon, are preserved for the world.'

Such desperate and torturous wordplay probably did more harm than good to the Baconian cause, but it did not kill off the authorship debate. For many years it was a straightforward two-horse race: if Shakespeare was not Shakespeare, then Bacon surely was. Then, in 1920, a book entitled *Shakespeare Identified* broadened the field. Its author was an English schoolteacher named John Thomas Looney, who began with the idea that the author of the plays seems to sympathise with kings and noblemen, whereas he draws the lower-class characters as villains or buffoons. Therefore, reasoned Looney, the author must be of noble birth. Support for this view came from the unlikely figure of Charlie Chaplin, by then world famous for making a hero of a downtrodden tramp. 'In the work of the greatest geniuses, humble beginnings will reveal themselves somewhere, but one cannot trace the slightest sign of them in Shakespeare,' he said. 'Whoever wrote [the plays] had an aristocratic attitude.'

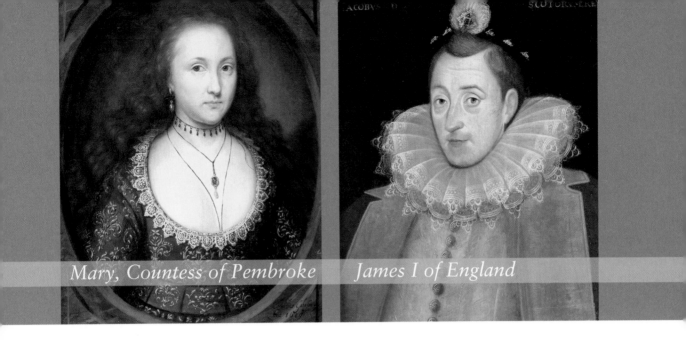

Mary, Countess of Pembroke　　*James I of England*

For Looney, it was clear that the author was an aristocratic contemporary of the bogus 'Stratford man', but who? Looney's attention lighted on the Earl of Oxford, Edward de Vere. Oxford was a charming, dissolute and handsome courtier who was also a (mediocre) poet and playwright. Looney found numerous correspondences between his biography and incidents in the plays: Oxford's mother, like Hamlet's, remarried after his father died; Oxford had three daughters, just like King Lear. Looney concluded that these and other coincidences were evidence of authorship, a palpable link between the life and the work. He went on to identify many characters in the plays as thinly veiled portraits of Oxford's contemporaries.

FREUD WADES IN

The Oxfordian theory (for obvious reasons, supporters avoid calling it the 'Looney theory') gained much currency after *Shakespeare Identified* was published. Sigmund Freud was convinced by it, and was particularly interested in the Oedipal implications of the death of Oxford's father as expressed in *Hamlet*. But late in life, after contemplating the swarthy features

WHO WAS WILL? *Fellow playwrights, nobles, even kings are among the people put forward as the author of Shakespeare's works. More than 70 candidates have been proposed, and as many as 5,000 books claim to name the true genius behind Shakespeare.*

of the Shakespeare portrait in London's National Gallery, Freud changed his mind, and decided that the author was a man of Mediterranean origin – a Frenchman named Jacques Pierre, mispronounced Shaks-Peer.

The Oxfordian theory still has currency. The 2011 film *Anonymous* was based on the idea that the Earl of Oxford wrote the plays, while Shakespeare is depicted as a sad drunkard. But there are many problems with the theory. Why, for example, are Oxford's 'Shakespearean' works so much better than the ones published under his own name? And, given that he was known to be a writer, why did he hide behind a *nom de plume* at all? But the biggest issue is biographical: the Earl of Oxford died in 1604, before many of Shakespeare's plays were written.

Undeterred, Oxfordians argue that the accepted chronology of the plays must be wrong, or that Oxford had produced a catalogue of plays that were somehow released one at a time after his death. But it is hard to explain away *The Tempest*, which most authorities date to 1611, and is without doubt based on accounts of a shipwreck that occurred in 1610, six years after Oxford's death.

The unanswerable questions around Oxford led proponents of the aristocratic author theory to scout around for other candidates. Among those who have been proposed are William Stanley, 6th Earl of Derby, who shares Shakespeare's first name and initials, thereby accounting for all the puns on the word 'will' in the sonnets, and for the poems signed W.S. A relative newcomer is Sir Henry Neville, first posited in 2005. He was a distinguished and well-travelled politician, distantly related to William Shakespeare of Stratford, so perhaps he used his country cousin as the face of his playwriting activities?

WRITERS AND ROYALS

A number of genuinely literary candidates have been proposed for the authorship of Shakespeare's works. Foremost is the poet and playwright Christopher Marlowe. The orthodox view is that Marlowe was killed in a brawl in 1593, at the age of 29. The 'Marlovian' take is that his death was faked by his friends in government (he is thought to have worked as a spy) to protect him from political enemies. Significantly, Shakespeare rose to prominence as a playwright only after Marlowe's death.

One of the few women in the long list of possible Shakespeares is Mary Sidney, Countess of Pembroke. A fine wordsmith, she was also the guiding light of a kind of literary salon. The *First Folio* (the first printed edition of Shakespeare's plays) was dedicated to her two sons – so she has a connection with the published works. Her personal symbol was the swan, and she had estates on the River Avon – which would make sense of Ben Jonson's description of Shakespeare as the 'sweet swan of Avon'. And if Mary Sidney were the author of the sonnets, that would explain away the apparently homoerotic tone of some of them (but would create a parallel issue vis-à-vis the 'dark lady' sonnets).

Two royal lines of inquiry stretch credulity to the limit. In 1995, an article in *Scientific American* proposed that the famous Dreshout engraving of Shakespeare, a portrait that appeared originally in the *First Folio*, was a disguised likeness of Queen Elizabeth I. The article made a forensic comparison of the so-called 'Armada painting' of Elizabeth and of Dreshout's Shakespeare, and claimed that the two faces were an astonishing match in the shape and distribution of the features. If so – and the methodology has been challenged – that would suggest that Elizabeth herself was the author of the plays, which she wrote while also ruling England. A corollary to this theory says that William Shakespeare was Elizabeth's illegitimate son.

The other royal name cited in the authorship debate is Elizabeth's successor, James I. According to the American civil rights activist Malcolm X, there is something fishy about his failure to employ William Shakespeare on the Authorised Version of the Bible. 'They say that King James got poets to translate, to write the Bible,' said Malcolm X. 'Well, if Shakespeare existed, he was then the top poet around. But Shakespeare is nowhere reported connected with the Bible. If he existed, why didn't King James use him?'

In fact, no one doubts that William Shakespeare existed, and for more than 200 years after his death no one had the slightest doubt that he wrote the plays. But we do not know much about his life, and that is one reason why the authorship speculation flourishes. We have a record of Shakespeare's baptism, his will, some contemporary references to his work as an actor and a theatrical impresario, a few mentions of him in legal documents – and that is all. There are no manuscripts of the plays, and only one document of the time states unambiguously that the actor William Shakespeare was also a playwright. This is why most anti-Stratfordians rely so heavily on the evidence of the texts, as if the full biography of the author must be contained somewhere within them.

ALL IN THE WORDS

If close scrutiny of the texts tell us anything about the author, it is that he was a man acquainted with the bourgeois world of manufacture, in particular, leatherwork (Shakespeare's father was a glove-maker by trade). The clues are not in the incident of the plays (which can be made up) but in the language (which is innate). The word 'cheveril', to take one example from hundreds, refers to a particularly pliant form of kidskin; Shakespeare twice uses the word as a metaphor for something elastic. 'Here's a wit of cheveril,' says Mercutio in *Romeo and Juliet*, 'that stretches from an inch narrow to an ell broad.'

So the imagery in the plays suggests that the writer hailed from the commercial middle class. There are also figures of speech and turns of phrase that point to an upbringing in the county of Warwickshire. Actors like to tell of a Shakespearean thespian, out for a walk in the Stratford countryside, who got talking to two hedge-cutters about their work. 'I rough-hews them,' said one of the workmen of a hedge,

'and he shapes their ends,' – unconsciously echoing a famous phrase from *Hamlet*: 'There's a divinity that shapes our ends, rough-hew them how we will.' There are many similar instances. Take this rather lovely line from *Cymbeline*: 'Golden lads and girls all must / As chimney-sweepers, come to dust.' Jonathan Bate and other modern Shakespeare scholars have pointed out that only a country boy could have written those lines – and they are all the more meaningful when you know that in Warwickshire dialect a 'golden lad' was a dandelion in bloom and a 'chimney-sweeper' one that was about to scatter its seeds to the wind.

Of course, the Stratfordian arguments based on the texts are no more positive proof than the anti-Stratfordian ones. But in the end, the texts themselves are what matters: their universal scope and psychological depth, the sheer inexhaustible richness of the language. The importance of the plays lies in what they

> *In the end, the texts themselves are what matters.*

say about all of us, not what they tell us about one man, long dead. And even if we had no idea at all who wrote the plays and poems – as is the case with, say, the works attributed to Homer – that would not make them one jot less valuable as works of art or monuments of world literature. So perhaps the truest verdict on the authorship question is contained in the old joke: 'If Shakespeare did not write his works, then it was someone else of the same name.'

The strains of the flute

Mozart's Magic Flute *is one of the towering achievements in the operatic repertoire. Its fairytale plot, complete with handsome prince and separated lovers, seems straightforward if fanciful, but the tale, staging and music conceal a raft of Masonic symbolism.*

Wolfgang Amadeus Mozart was only 35 years old when he wrote *The Magic Flute*. He didn't know it, but he was already in the last year of his life. That life had been filled to the brim with music. He began composing tunes at the age of four. From the age of six he toured Europe with his father and his very talented sister. The Mozart siblings played before kings and princes from London to Munich and Paris to Prague. Wolfgang was composing mature works – symphonies, cantatas, concertos – by his late teens, and continued to do so throughout his 20s.

But after he turned 30, Mozart had difficulty making ends meet so, in 1791, he was happy to be commissioned to compose the music for an opera. The commission came from a family friend, an actor and theatrical impresario named Emanuel Schikaneder. He managed a theatre in the Vienna suburbs and was in the process of building up a repertoire of operas with fairytale themes. Mozart had already written incidental music for one of these musical fantasies, a work called *The Philosopher's Stone*. The new work was intended to continue the folklorical theme of Schikaneder's production.

Schikaneder was writing the libretto himself. He borrowed his plot from a story in a collection of Oriental tales compiled by the poet Christoph Martin Wieland. The story, *Lulu, or The Magic Flute*, was an almost frivolous piece in which a good fairy persuades a handsome young prince to rescue an enchanted sword from the castle of an evil magician, promising him the love of her beautiful daughter if he should succeed in his mission. To help him on his way, the fairy gives the prince a magic ring and a flute with the power to win all hearts. He duly completes the task, and is rewarded with the fairy princess's love.

A DIFFERENT TUNE

Schikaneder was already deeply immersed in the project when bad news reached him. Another theatre in Vienna was staging an opera drawn from the same source, and their production was more advanced than his. The rival version, called *Kaspar the Bassoon Player or The Magic Zither*, opened that June, while Mozart was still writing his score. This disappointment forced the collaborators to rethink their plot, and in the process they changed the simple folktale into something richer and

A mysterious messenger

One evening in 1791, when Mozart was still working on *The Magic Flute*, he received an unexpected visitor. The stranger brought good news for the cash-strapped composer: a commission to write a requiem mass. Even so, he hesitated when the messenger proved unwilling to reveal who his unseen patron was. Mozart started work on what would turn out to be his final, unfinished masterpiece only after a second visit and a down payment on the agreed fee. In the film *Amadeus* it is suggested that this visitor was the jealous composer Antonio Salieri. In fact, it is now generally accepted that the patron was a music-loving aristocrat, Count Franz von Walsegg, whose 20-year-old wife had died five months earlier. Walsegg, it seems, wanted to commission the *Requiem* anonymously so that he could pass it off to his friends as his own work.

more profound. Though *The Magic Flute* retained all the guileless charm of its source, the finished version became a complex allegory about the human quest for love, happiness and wisdom. And the inspiration for these themes came not from fairytales, but from the ideals of Freemasonry.

THE SPREAD OF FREEMASONRY

The Masonic movement claimed to have roots in the medieval craft guilds, but it was in the 18th century that it emerged as an organised force, an international, somewhat secretive network of men. The first Grand Lodge was founded in England in 1717, and the movement then spread swiftly across Europe. Freemasonry was forward-looking and liberal-minded, embracing the humanist ideals of the Enlightenment. In reaction to the religious wars that had riven Europe in previous centuries, it was staunchly universal in its sympathies and open to all faiths. It preached the virtues of tolerance, obliging members to commit only to 'that religion in which all men agree, leaving their particular opinions to themselves; that is, to be good men and true, or men of honour and honesty, by whatever denomination or persuasion they may be distinguished'. Masons acknowledged a Supreme Being, but He did not resemble the paternal God of mainstream Christianity; he was instead the 'Great Architect of the Universe'. The Catholic Church, naturally, deeply disapproved of Masons and their works.

Mozart's initiation into Freemasonry took place in December 1784, when he became an 'apprentice' in Vienna's Charity Lodge. He advanced to the degrees of fellow and master mason over the next four months. Vienna's musical world was at that time suffused with Masonic connections. Mozart is known to have attended the Masonic induction of his friend, the composer Josef Haydn, early in 1785. On the surface at least, Austrian Freemasonry was – despite the view of the Church – a respectable activity. The head of Mozart's own lodge was a senior diplomat in the imperial government, and the nation's new ruler, Leopold II, was himself said to be a Mason.

Yet many European rulers were suspicious of Freemasonry's clandestine rituals, and feared the political implications of its free-thinking ideals. Such concerns seemed to have been justified when Europe's old order was battered by the storm of the French Revolution. The Masons were not

Freemasonry was a respectable activity; the king of Austria was said to be a Mason.

responsible for that upheaval, but to the monarchs and autocrats of Europe they seemed to be speaking the same language of subversion as the revolutionaries. In Austria, too, the authorities came to see Freemasonry as dangerous – Leopold's successor, Francis II, closed down all the nation's lodges in 1795.

Schikaneder's libretto and Mozart's music, written two years after the French Revolution, was not a veiled piece of Masonic subversion, but it did observe the movement's commitment to secrecy and hidden meanings. Masonic preoccupations were encoded in the revised storyline, which in *The Magic Flute* takes the form of a quest. Tamino, the hero, is on a mission to find the abducted princess; this romantic pursuit represents the human yearning after wisdom and spiritual insight. Tamino's efforts are echoed in the misadventures of his companion Papageno, who comically fails all the tests that Tamino overcomes and looks only to satisfy his need for the material comforts of food, wine and a pretty woman.

In *The Magic Flute* there is a tussle between good and evil – but appearances are deceptive: the good fairy of Lulu is revealed to be the wicked Queen of the Night, and the evil magician who holds her daughter captive turns out to be the benevolent Sarastro, a model of the Masonic man of wisdom.

KEYS AND THREES

Masonic themes are even to be found in Mozart's musical score. A triple-note figure that is heard at significant points is thought to be a musical rendering of the three knocks on the door that start Masonic initiation ceremonies. The overture is in E-flat, 'the Masonic key', so called because it contains three flats. These triads are seen to be part of the Masonic fascination with three as a mystical number, with the triangle as a powerful geometric shape, and with the three-sided façade of the pyramid as an architectural form.

The entire second and final act of the opera take place in Sarastro's castle, where Tamino and Papageno are subjected to a series of tests, watched over by priests of the Egyptian gods Isis and Osiris. The trials involve remaining silent while being tempted to speak by women (the Masonic vow of secrecy), then overcoming the fear of death in ordeals by fire and water (a dramatised picture of a Masonic initiation). After winning through, Tamino is united with Pamina and is promised that he will eventually replace Sarastro as leader of his wizardly order. The Queen of the Night, who has attempted to invade Sarastro's palace and destroy its temples of Wisdom, Reason and Nature, is cast away into eternal darkness.

SEEDS FROM SETHOS

The Egyptian garb of *The Magic Flute* may have been suggested by a novel called *Sethos*, published anonymously in 1735 and widely read in Masonic circles. The book describes the ritual initiation of a young prince into the mysteries of ancient Egyptian religion. In the year of Mozart's own initiation, a Viennese Mason had cited *Sethos* in an article on 'the Egyptian mysteries' – an Egyptian veneer provided a ready-made cover that allowed Masonic concerns to be addressed. Many attempts have been made to find a pro-Masonic political agenda in *The Magic Flute*. Some people claim to see a portrait of the anti-Masonic Empress Maria Theresa of Austria in the Queen of the Night, and a more flattering image of the regal initiate Leopold II in Tamino.

If the opera was making a timely political point, then that hardly matters any more. For modern audiences, *The Magic Flute* carries an uplifting message of a twin triumph: true love conquers all obstacles, and the light of reason defeats the darkness of superstition. It is part fairytale, part Enlightenment tract – and also a complete musical masterpiece. The German poet Goethe, himself a Mason, wrote of it: 'It is enough that the crowd find pleasure in seeing the spectacle; at the same time, its high significance will not escape the initiates.'

Die Reichsregierung

Hitler's lost words

HITLER

Adolf Hitler had kept a diary – or so it
*seemed when the bound volumes of his previously
unknown journals came to light in the 1980s.
The discovery was a huge publishing sensation, the
journalistic coup of the century, but then the diaries
were exposed as laughably crude fakes.*

The greatest and most embarrassing hoax
in the history of journalism began when
a seasoned German hack chanced on the
scoop of a lifetime. Gerd Heidemann was a
51-year-old investigative reporter for West
Germany's respected news magazine *Stern*.
In 1980 he decided to sell his boat. This
was, however, no ordinary boat. It was
the *Carin II*, a motor yacht that had once
belonged to Hermann Goering, Hitler's
second-in-command. Heidemann was a
collector of Nazi memorabilia, but the
restoration of this boat was proving to be
a hobby he could not afford.

So he put out the word in the murky
world of Third Reich aficionados that
Goering's yacht was for sale. This brought
him into contact with a wealthy potential
buyer, who happened to show him a diary
he had recently acquired from a dealer.
It was, he said, one of a series of diaries
secretly penned by Hitler himself; the
one Heidemann saw dated from the first
months of 1935. This was an astonishing
find and Heidemann immediately saw
that it would make a massive news

story. The background circumstances
of the diary seemed credible enough,
based as they were on the known facts
of Operation Seraglio. In April 1945, as
the Russians closed in on Berlin, Hitler
and his entourage – now holed up in his
bunker – devised Seraglio. Hitler would fly
to his mountain retreat at Berchtesgaden
in Bavaria, where he would stage his
last stand. To this end, his personal pilot
General Hans Baur organised ten planes
to transport files, archives and personal
possessions to an airport nearby. One of
these planes crashed near Dresden. When
Hitler was told the news, as Baur later
recalled, he visibly paled and said, 'In
that plane were all my private archives
that I had intended as a testament to
posterity. It is a catastrophe.' To Gerd
Heidemann, it seemed perfectly plausible
that the personal diary had been salvaged
from this crash.

Using his journalistic contacts,
Heidemann traced the source of the diary
to a dealer in Stuttgart, a 'Dr Fischer',
who confirmed the story of its provenance.

Tantalisingly, Fischer told Heidemann that there were a further 26 volumes in the series, covering Hitler's years in power, from 1932 right up to two weeks before his suicide in April 1945.

FISCHER'S BAIT

There were complications, however. Fischer's supplier was his brother, a high-ranking military officer in East Germany. The diaries had apparently been rescued from the plane by a farmer, but had now come into the possession of Fischer's brother, who was risking his life even to smuggle the volumes to West Germany. He was prepared to take the risk in exchange for hard currency. Utmost secrecy was required. Heidemann agreed that no one else from *Stern* would contact Dr Fischer.

Heidemann was convinced, but he knew that his editors at *Stern* might be sceptical. There had been a number of fake diaries supposedly by eminent players in the war, including a 30-volume diary of Mussolini, forged by two women in 1957. But for Heidemann this was different, because the background story made such good sense. He now made the dubious decision to bypass his editors and instead approach the management at *Stern*'s parent company, Gruner & Jahr. The management knew that Heidemann was one of *Stern*'s leading journalists and decided to back him. Understanding the need for utmost secrecy, they authorised payment for the remaining diaries – at the colossal sum of 85,000 deutschmarks per volume.

Little did Heidemann know that Dr Fischer was in fact a man named Konrad Kujau, who for many years had been dealing in, and forging, Nazi memorabilia, which he supplied to eager customers. Kujau was, naturally, delighted with the offer. In fact, he was so encouraged by Heidemann's gullibility that he dared to stretch it further, telling the journalist that the haul from East Germany was not 26 volumes of diaries but 60, and that there were other riches, too: paintings, documents, even a libretto written by Hitler for an opera. Given the difficulty of getting it all out of East Germany, however, delivery would take time. It would indeed take some time – because Kujau now had to fake all the material he had promised.

He claimed there was even a libretto written by Hitler.

Kujau wrote the diaries himself, imitating Hitler's handwriting and signature. For their content, he turned to existing memoirs and documentation, primarily a known scholarly work called *Hitler: Speeches and Proclamations 1932–45*, published in the 1960s. Kujau's fake diary entries were short, mainly factual records of daily events – with just the occasional personal comment. The remarks put into the mouth of Hitler were frankly dull, but their very banality made them seem more authentic. As for the diary volumes, they were a set of old school notebooks that Kujau had originally bought to catalogue his own collection. On the outside cover he added wax seals and ribbons, and embossed Hitler's initials. He then knocked the volumes about, and tipped tea onto them to give them a distressed look that matched their

COLLECTED WORKS *Konrad Kujau holds up a volume of the Hitler diaries, which he himself had written. 'Little Dr Goebbels is up to his old tricks with women,' read one typical entry.*

supposed history. This was a breathtakingly lackadaisical approach to the act of forgery, given the money Kujau was set to earn. In all, 2 million deutschmarks (then worth about US$1.2 million) were delivered to Kujau – briefcases full of cash for one forged volume after another. Heidemann, meanwhile, was turning a nice profit by skimming millions off the money that was passing through his hands.

SEALING THE DEAL

The executives of Gruner & Jahr decided that for secrecy's sake they would expose the diaries to the scrutiny of only a very few outsiders. Three handwriting analysts were consulted, and they confirmed the authenticity of the documents – mainly,

it seems, because the samples of Hitler's writing that they were given to compare with the diaries had themselves been forged by Kujau.

Once these checks and assurances were in place, *Stern*'s editors were brought into the loop. By the first weeks of 1983, after 18 months' hard forging by Kujau, all the diaries had been delivered. In March, secret negotiations were opened for international rights to publish the diaries. *Stern* knew this was a colossal story, worth millions. They very quickly garnered the interest of Rupert Murdoch, who owned *The Times* and *The Sunday Times* of London.

Editors at *The Sunday Times* insisted that the diaries be properly authenticated. As it happened, Times Newspapers had a

Hitler expert on their board. Hugh Trevor-Roper, Lord Dacre, was a former Regius Professor of Modern History at Oxford. He had served in the Secret Intelligence Service (SIS) during the war and was later sent to Berlin to investigate the circumstances of Hitler's death. His account, *The Last Days of Hitler*, was published in 1947. It was a classic piece of investigative reporting, as well as a primary historical source.

On April 1, 1983, Lord Dacre received a telephone call from *The Sunday Times* telling him about the diaries and asking him to assess them. He was initially sceptical. There were no credible accounts of Hitler ever having kept a diary of any kind; and besides, Hitler was known not to like writing in his own hand. Nonetheless, Lord Dacre agreed to fly to Zurich, where the volumes were being held in a bank vault. In Zurich he was given assurances that the paper on which the diaries were written had been checked – which was not true. He was also told that the source was known and trusted – which was not true either. Dacre was impressed by the sheer volume of material: a forger would not give himself so many chances to slip up, surely? He made his judgment: the diaries seemed to be authentic. The next day Murdoch offered US$3 million for world rights.

Two weeks later, *The Sunday Times*, in a coordinated splash with *Stern*, broke the story to the world. *The Sunday Times'* headline claimed 'The Secrets of Hitler's War: How the diaries of the Führer were found in an East German hayloft'. *Stern's* cover featured a photograph of one of the diaries, with Hitler's initials embossed on it in gold. The Gothic capitals seemed to read 'FH', not 'AH', but no one had noticed.

Stern staged a press conference to coincide with publication. It was planned as a chance to trumpet the story of the century, but it rapidly turned into a disaster. Journalists pummelled *Stern's* editors with penetrating questions, and the lack of proper forensic investigation was immediately exposed. Lord Dacre, whose doubts were growing, chose this moment to voice them. 'I must say I regret that the normal methods of historical verification have been sacrificed to the requirements of the journalistic scoop,' he said.

THE HOAX UNRAVELS

To shore up the story, *Stern* agreed to submit the diaries to scientific tests at the Bundesarchiv, the German state archive. It took just a week for the results to come in: the diaries, purporting to date back to 1932, were written on paper that contained polyamide 6, a synthetic material not invented until 1938 and not widely used until 1943. The ink, glue, bindings and ribbons were all postwar. A new set of handwriting experts, properly briefed, later pronounced the text to be a crude imitation that failed to reproduce many of Hitler's distinctive letter shapes. The source of the content – the long-since published book of speeches – was identified.

Kujau fled to Austria, but he gave himself up a few weeks later. Heidemann was arrested. When Kujau heard that Heidemann had pocketed much of the money that was supposed to come to him, he told all in a fit of pique. Both men were tried in 1985, and each was sentenced to more than four years in prison. Lord Dacre's reputation was badly battered, and never fully recovered. The editor of *Stern* resigned, as did the editor of *The Sunday Times*. Andrew Neil took over as editor later in 1983. 'This story was so big,' he later said, 'and *The Sunday Times* so wanted it to be true, that it became almost too good to check properly.'

Hollywood Kabbalah

A highly esoteric branch of medieval Judaism has recently been rediscovered and re-invented as a fashionable lifestyle programme, much favoured by rock stars and Hollywood actors. How did the almost forgotten mystical teachings of Kabbalah re-emerge, and what do they mean?

When the pop singer Madonna first walked through the door of the Kabbalah Centre in Beverly Hills, she had not been invited or courted. She came, apparently, on the recommendation of a friend. She liked what she found. Her interest was picked up by the press, and this acted as a kind of endorsement. It seemed, for a time, that Kabbalah was the religion of choice for American celebrity women. Demi Moore, Elizabeth Taylor, Britney Spears, Roseanne Barr and Jerry Hall are just a few of the stars who became associated with the mysteries of Kabbalah.

Madonna's first visit took place in 1997. Over the next decade, the profile of the Kabbalah Centre grew ever higher, and by 2009 it was reported to be in receipt of annual revenues of $60 million. These earnings came from adherents' donations, and also through sales of merchandise such as 'red string' bracelets worn to ward off the evil eye, Kabbalah water that devotees believed could 'heal and protect', and a range of DVDs, CDs and books explaining the teachings. Quite how many followers the Kabbalah creed attracted remains obscure: estimates range from tens of thousands to several million.

This success was perhaps surprising, given that the word 'kabbalah' carries a number of negative connotations. Though in Hebrew *kabbalah* simply means 'what is received' or 'tradition', for centuries the term was associated with cult practices and dark arts, the use of secret symbols, numbers and spells in pursuit of mystical knowledge and the philosopher's stone – a history entwined with alchemy. The term 'cabal', meaning a group of intriguers, is derived from *kabbalah* and has been used in that sense since the 17th century. Even within Judaism, Kabbalah teachings were always treated with caution. The practice was restricted to married men over 40 who had a solid grounding in Jewish law, or else to selected male students judged to be reliable and of sound mind. This has been interpreted by some as respect for the power of Kabbalah, by others as an indication of its dubious value.

CENTRAL BELIEFS

Kabbalah, in its original form, is a difficult philosophy, expressed in obscure and complex texts. The central scripture is the Zohar, meaning 'splendour' or 'radiance'. It is said to have been handed down from one generation of scholars to the next for thousands of years before being written down in Aramaic either by Simeon bar Yochai in Israel in the second century AD or, more probably, by Moses de León, a Spanish-Jewish scholar who lived in the 13th century. Some suspect that Moses de León may have written the Zohar himself.

Whatever its origin, the text purports to reveal how an individual can know and come close to God. According to the Kabbalists, at the shattering cataclysm of the Creation, God or *Ein Sof* (The Infinite) entered the world as light and, through a set of ten spheres, this light was distributed among living creatures. All joy, happiness and fulfilment comes from this light. But in human beings, the self-centred ego (associated with Satan) cuts them off from it. Only by casting out the ego and reviving the desire to share will people be able to reconnect to the essence of the Creator, referred to as the 'Light', and attain fulfilment. They can do this in their own lives through prayer and meditation, and by resisting negative forces through the practice of 'Restriction' – learning how to remove the ego when reacting to events, so as to escape emotional chaos and take control of their destiny.

It is claimed that the arcane texts and symbols of the Zohar and other Kabbalist literature provide the codes for this healing process and the means to achieve a full understanding of reality. Ordinary mortals perceive just a tiny portion of reality through the five senses. By applying the techniques of the Kabbalah, adherents can access the fullness of reality, and thus attain a state of pure truth and understanding.

MODERNISING THE FAITH
These central tenets of the medieval Kabbalist tradition are embedded in obscure texts of immense complexity and mind-boggling obfuscation. The modern Kabbalah movement extracted and simplified the essential message, making it available to all-comers, regardless of gender, religion, ethnic background, age or sexual orientation. This broader, more populist version of Kabbalah is the central achievement of the Los Angeles Kabbalah Centre and its other bases around the

THE DOORS OF LIGHT *The frontispiece of a 16th-century Latin translation of a Kabbalist text. The ten spheres represent the divine emanations, which include Love, Wisdom, Majesty and Power.*

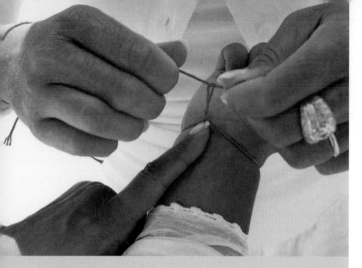

world. It is in many ways analogous to the explosion of Western interest in a simplified form of Buddhism during the 1970s.

The Kabbalah Centre was founded by Philip Berg and his second wife Karen in New York in 1973. Berg had trained as an orthodox rabbi and spent time in Israel in the 1960s studying the Kabbalah under Rabbi Yehuda Zvi Brandwein, who in turn had studied under Rav Yehuda Ashlag. Ashlag, born in 1885, was one of the first to try to bring the Kabbalah to the masses, or at least to a wider audience of Jews. He translated the Zohar from Aramaic to Hebrew and founded a Kabbalah *yeshiva* (college) in 1922.

While Berg was rooted in traditional Jewish scholarship, his young wife had sympathies for 'New Age' philosophies. She persuaded Berg of the potentially broad appeal of the Kabbalah, particularly among women. Modern Kabbalah can be seen as a kind of marriage of these two streams: a holistic, self-help programme couched in the language and practice of Judaism. The Centre requires no prior knowledge of Judaism from its followers, and insists that Kabbalah is not a religion but a 'technology of the soul', a conduit of the universal wisdom that all religions share. But this universal attitude to spirituality goes hand in hand with Jewish rites such as observance of the Sabbath and a kosher diet. Such strictures seem to be part of the appeal.

WEST-COAST WAVELENGTH

At any rate, the New York Centre was a success, and in 1984 Philip and Karen Berg opened a new centre in Los Angeles. Kabbalah bloomed in sunny California. Its promise of spiritual fulfilment attracted people who felt that their lives lacked meaning – including some rich and famous people, unsatisfied by worldly success.

The teachings of the Kabbalah Centre were designed to be accessible, modern and user-friendly, incorporating concepts such as astrology and the 'recycling of departed souls' (re-incarnation). These ideas chimed with established New Age ideas, and offered individuals ways to overcome negativity and take control of their lives. The Bergs claimed that Kabbalah reconciles spirituality with modern science, that it anticipated the Big Bang theory, DNA, string theory and nanotechnology.

By encouraging a habit of giving ('to give, the better to receive'), the Kabbalah Centre also made adherents feel good about themselves, and helped them to discharge their social responsibilities through charitable donations – including, of course, donations to the Kabbalah Centre itself. But it imposed no heavy obligations on its adherents, favouring an easygoing approach to traditional concerns of religion such as doctrine and personal morality. That made it a perfect creed for the modern age of celebrity, mass marketing and universal branding. Today there are centres in more than 40 countries worldwide, and Kabbalah continues to grow.

A priest named Ship

Many modern Jewish surnames contain the story of how Jews were subjected to petty persecution in the 17th and 18th centuries, and how they found clever and inventive ways to retain their traditions.

In the Middle Ages, Jews, like some other close-knit societies, got by without using surnames. Their communities were generally small enough that people simply used first names, perhaps supplemented with a father's name to avoid confusion: Isaac, or at most Isaac ben Abraham (son of Abraham). But in the 18th century, certain European states began to insist that Jews take surnames to facilitate taxation and military service. In many German states, the requirement to take a surname was linked to a wider policy of assimilation. Jews were not allowed to express their Jewishness through their new-minted names; no Hebrew words were allowed; the names had to sound German.

Judah was a lion, Benjamin a wolf.

Most Jews objected to the compulsory adoption of surnames and the conditions attached, but rather than resist the decree openly, they found ways to subvert the system and invest their names with hidden meanings. Sometimes it was a matter of pious word association. In the Jewish tradition, for example, the name Judah is linked to the image of a lion, because of the Biblical epithet 'the lion of Judah'. So many men named Judah simply called themselves Judah Loeb (lion), or an elaborated version such as Lowenstein. The name Benjamin is linked to the wolf, so many Benjamins took a surname such as Wolff, or Wolfberg. A Napthali might take the name Hirsch – 'hart' – because the Biblical Napthali is called 'a swift-footed hart'.

Some played more convoluted word games. A member of the priestly caste, a *kohen* in Hebrew, might adopt the German word Kahn – 'boat' – as his name: it contains the same consonants as *kohen*, and in Hebrew only the consonants are written. To hide the meaning still deeper, a *kohen* might take the name Schiff – 'ship' – because it is a close synonym of Kahn. Only a fellow Jew would know that a Ship was a man of priestly lineage.

Many a *kohen* took the name Katz – 'cat'. In this instance, the name was an acronym derived from the first letters of the Hebrew phrase **k**ohen **ts**edek, 'priest of righteousness'. Acronyms became a fruitful way of circumventing the national naming authorities. A Jew who took the name Atlas – German for 'satin' – was often invoking the Biblical phrase **a**kh **t**ov **l**yisrael **s**elah: 'may God be good to Israel'. A newly named Stamm – meaning 'tree trunk', but in a significant metaphorical sense a 'clan' or 'tribe' – might also have been thinking of his job as a **s**ofer **t**efillim **m**ezuzot, a scribe of phylacteries and mezuzah parchments.

DIAMONDS AND GOLD

Some well-off Jews managed to bribe officials to allow them to take more prestigious 'decorative' surnames such as Rosenthal ('valley of roses'), or Diamant (meaning 'diamond'). But here, too, a little subterfuge came into play. A large proportion of Goldbergs ('golden mountain'), Goldblums ('golden flower') or Goldsterns ('golden star') had in mind not the precious metal but a revered mother or family matriarch named Golda, whose memory is preserved in the surname of her descendants, though she herself is long forgotten.

Oppenheimer's boys

It was the biggest secret of the Second World War – the product of years of intense research by the USA's top scientists, corralled in a remote desert location. They were working at the pinnacle of an enterprise codenamed the Manhattan Project, which employed 130,000 people – most of whom had no idea what they were really involved in.

The most dangerous, secret and spectacular experiment in the history of science took place in the desert of New Mexico on July 16, 1945. A device known as 'The Gadget' was winched very gingerly to the top of a tower 30m (100ft) tall. It was a test version of the atom bomb. Nobody knew what would happen when it was set off, but some of the scientists who built it feared that the entire state of New Mexico might be obliterated – or worse, that the heat of the explosion might ignite the very atmosphere and burn it up like a piece of tissue thrown onto a bonfire.

The bomb was detonated at 5.30 in the morning. Its effect was utterly astounding. The desert floor erupted into a violet, green and orange fireball, sending a plume of super-heated debris 11km (7 miles) into the sky, where it formed a shape not seen before: a mushroom cloud. The noise was heard in El Paso 130km (80 miles) away. Residents there were told that a munitions dump had exploded.

As for the creators of the bomb, most were in a bunker 16km (10 miles) distant, where they watched their awesome experiment through welding goggles worn over the top of sunglasses. Chief among them was physicist Robert Oppenheimer. He was amazed by the outcome of his work, and recalled a line from the Hindu scripture: 'I am become Death, the destroyer of worlds.' One of his colleagues had similar troubling thoughts, but expressed them rather differently. 'We are all sons of bitches now,' he told Oppenheimer.

SPLITTING THE ATOM

Theoretical physicists had long known that splitting the nucleus of an atom would release massive amounts of energy. Ernest Rutherford had first demonstrated it back in 1917. There was speculation that this process might be used to generate power or fuel a bomb, though the practical difficulties seemed insurmountable. But in 1938 Otto Hahn and Fritz Strassmann, working in Nazi Germany, succeeded in splitting an atom of uranium by bombarding it with neutron. Still a weapon based on nuclear fission seemed unachievable since it would require a shipload of uranium (or so it was thought).

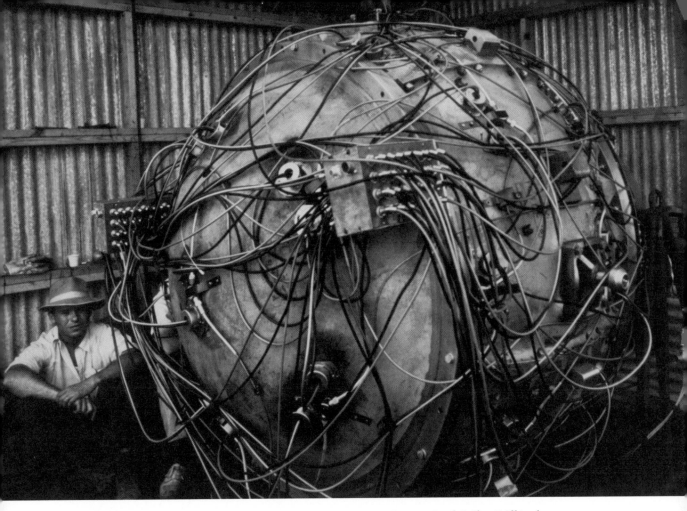

DRY RUN *'The Gadget', ready for testing in New Mexico. It contained 4.5kg (10lb) of plutonium encased in high explosive, like the yolk of an egg within the white. The plan was to detonate the explosives, compressing the plutonium. The crowded plutonium atoms would smash into each other and break apart, releasing energy in the form of a nuclear explosion.*

Nevertheless, worries grew. In 1939 Albert Einstein wrote a letter to US president Franklin D. Roosevelt, alerting him that a ship-delivered atomic bomb was at least theoretically possible, and that German scientists were likely to be working on one. (Einstein would later regret this letter and was horrified by the eventual outcome.)

A few months later, anti-Nazi German physicists working in Britain calculated that – theoretically, again – an atomic bomb could be made from just 1kg (2.2lb) of a refined isotope of natural uranium, uranium-235. So it was clear by the start of the Second World War that atom-splitting

could lead to a terrifying weapon: the side that developed it first would be able to deliver a crushing blow to its enemy.

Once the USA entered the war in 1941, top scientists from across the country were called together. They first met on Manhattan Island in New York, hence the codename of the operation that they and thousands of others would work on over the next three years: the Manhattan Project.

The Project grew rapidly in 1942 and 1943, spreading to more than 30 secret sites across the USA. It was already the most expensive scientific experiment ever. At the headquarters in Oak Ridge,

0.016 SEC.
N

100 METERS

FLASHPOINT *An official photograph taken sixteen-hundredths of a second into the nuclear age. In the act of exploding and expanding, this, the world's first atom bomb, made a strange perfectly formed dome of blast material perhaps 300m (1,000ft) across. This momentary blister is about to erupt into a vast mushroom cloud reaching up into the stratosphere.*

Tennessee, a thousand families were relocated to create an exclusion zone around the 'Clinton Engineer Works', three huge factories processing uranium. Around 51,000 people were employed at Hanford, Washington, where plutonium was separated from uranium. By the end, the Manhattan Project employed some 130,000 people, the majority of whom had no idea that its aim was to develop a new and hugely destructive kind of bomb.

At the sharp end of the project, under the cloak of absolute secrecy, the USA's leading physicists and chemists were battling to turn theory into practice. The project director, Brigadier General Leslie R. Groves, had drawn together a team of professors and their most brilliant students. They included Enrico Fermi, who carried out the first experimental artificial nuclear chain reaction in December 1942; Edward Teller,

He was committed to making the bomb before the Nazis.

who went on to develop the H-Bomb; and Nobel prize-winners past and future – Louis Alvarez, Hans Bethe, Felix Bloch, Richard Feynman, Dudley Herschbach, Edwin McMillan, Isidor Rabi, Norman Ramsey, Frederick Reines, Emilio Segrè and Owen Chamberlain. They were, Groves quipped, 'an expensive collection of loonies'.

To lead them Groves selected J. Robert Oppenheimer, a 38-year-old professor from the University of California. Oppenheimer was known for his work in quantum mechanics and astronomy, and he spoke six languages. He was a controversial choice

because of his links, through friends and his wife, with the Communist Party. But he was also a Jew of German descent, and unquestionably committed to creating a weapon to win the war – before the Nazis did. Oppenheimer turned out to be an inspired appointment. He had the ability to recruit the best minds and to keep them focused. This was essential, because his team was about to be locked into high-security seclusion in the middle of nowhere.

LIFE ON THE HILL

Oppenheimer loved New Mexico. He learned to ride horses there when he was a teenager, and he owned a ranch in the midst of its wild, sagebrush landscape. When Brigadier General Groves was looking for a suitable secret location for a centralised weapons research laboratory, Oppenheimer brought him here. They found a boys' boarding school in Los Alamos that looked fit for their purpose. It was commandeered in November 1942, surrounded by a barbed-wire fence, and renamed Site Y. The grounds around the school buildings were soon filled with trailers and prefabricated huts. Oppenheimer thought initially that just a few hundred people would work here; by 1945 there were 6,000. The Los Alamos site took on the appearance of a gold-rush boom-town, complete with a grocery store, laundries, bar, cafeteria, post office, library, hospital, all connected by unmade roads that turned to mud in rain.

Hundreds of security-vetted scientists were posted here, some travelling under false names, uncertain how long they would stay or quite what they would be doing. Many came with wives, and some with young children. They were effectively incarcerated in an army camp, surrounded with armed guards and working alongside army personnel. Army intelligence agents and the FBI – acutely aware that many of the scientists had been involved in radical politics in the 1930s – were on the alert for any leak of information to the outside world. Mail was opened and read, telephone calls monitored. (After the war, it turned out that at least three spies were operating at Los Alamos, feeding information to the Soviet Union.)

The scientists worked intensely and for long hours in the laboratories. But for the most part, the atmosphere was positive. Many were driven by a belief that their research was essential to the war effort and to the survival of civilisation itself. The majority were young, in their 20s and 30s. The company was intellectually stimulating, as they were the elite of their fields. To ward off the boredom of isolation, they filled their spare time with hobbies, music, parties, sports – baseball in summer, skiing in winter. The camp had two dance bands and its own radio station. Babies were born – including, in December 1944, a daughter to Oppenheimer and his wife Kitty.

The physicist Richard Feynman recalled the pranks. He used his spare time to learn how to pick locks and took bets that he could crack any combination. He alarmed one colleague by opening three filing cabinets where top-secret papers were stored and leaving telltale notes inside. To relieve stress, Feynman also took himself off to an isolated part of 'The Hill', as Los Alamos was nicknamed, and indulged in Native American drumming and chanting.

Many of the scientists contributed a similarly quirky personality to Los Alamos, as well as a sharp mind, but the constructive atmosphere was down to Oppenheimer himself. He took a keen interest in all departments, and was a master of every technology – physics, chemistry, metallurgy, engineering, weaponry. By establishing trust

and the free exchange of information, he was able to knit his disparate colleagues into a team and push them towards the ultimate, and still unproven goal.

The goal was achieved when that first atom bomb exploded in the New Mexico desert. The experiment was a success. The technology worked, and now it was placed at the disposal of the war effort. Germany had surrendered by this time, and the war in Europe was over. But the war against Japan continued and was proving brutal. As US forces fought their way across the Pacific, it was surmised that the millions of hardened Japanese troops would refuse to surrender, and America could face losing perhaps another 500,000 men. The new weapon looked like the most certain way to bring the war to an end.

LITTLE BOY, FAT MAN

On July 26, 1945, the USA, Britain and China issued an ultimatum to Japan: surrender unconditionally or face the consequences. They did not mention the bomb. Some argued that a second test bomb should be dropped on uninhabited ground as a kind of show of might. But what if this time it failed? The decision was taken to drop the bomb on a Japanese city.

In the air raids against Japan, several cities had deliberately been left untouched. One of those cities was Hiroshima. On the morning of August 6, 1945, the citizens of Hiroshima paid little attention to the three B-29 bombers high in the sky – normal bombing raids involved dozens of aircraft dropping scores of bombs.

A single bomb – dubbed 'Little Boy' – fell from one of the planes, the *Enola Gay*. It exploded in the air, 580m (1,900ft) above the city as the bomber turned rapidly away to evade the blast. Hiroshima was incinerated. An estimated 78,000

AFTERMATH *In September 1945 Oppenheimer (in the white hat) and Groves (in uniform) inspected the remains of the tower on which The Gadget was suspended. The desert floor was turned to green glass, which was named trinitite after the codename for the experiment: Trinity.*

people were killed immediately, perhaps a further 170,000 died later of wounds and radiation sickness. Three days later a bomb nicknamed 'Fat Man' was detonated over Nagasaki with similar devastating effect. Japan surrendered on August 15.

Back in Los Alamos, as Oppenheimer's team dispersed, feelings were mixed. There was pride in what they had achieved scientifically and in their contribution to bringing the Second World War to a close. But there was regret for the colossal loss of life and the suffering that their work had brought on Japan. There was also a deep

fear for the future in this new atomic age. Feynman, for one, felt sure that a nuclear war could not be long in coming, that he was living in the last generation of mankind.

Others were more hopeful. Haakon Chevalier, a professor at Berkeley, wrote to his friend Oppenheimer the day after the Hiroshima bomb: 'There is a weight in such a venture that few men in history have had to bear. I know that with your love of men, it is no light thing to have had a part – and a great part – in a diabolical contrivance for destroying them. But in the possibilities of death are also the possibilities of life.'

"COULD BECOME AS IMPOR...
MAGAZINE

WikiLeaks is a non-profit me...
an innovative, secure and an...
We publish material of ethica...
providing a universal way for...

WikiLeaks relies on its supp...
today. You can also read m...

nate

...hlegate: 250,000 U...

Chapter 6

BURIED TREASURE, HIDDEN TRUTH

History, or its raw data, is often to be found below ground – in caverns, bank vaults and burial chambers. But there are other ways of hiding the facts of the past, or even changing the facts entirely.

Genghis rides home

Genghis Khan forged a mighty empire, but in his homeland his achievements were forgotten or denied for most of the 20th century. His rehabilitation, a strange outcome of the collapse of communism, led Mongolians to re-assess their own history, and their place in the new world order.

Genghis Khan is everywhere in modern-day Ulaanbaatar, the Mongolian capital. His face is monumentally etched in white on a green hillside to the south of the city. On the broad streets there are advertising hoardings that show Genghis texting a friend from the saddle of his warhorse; a neon Genghis hangs above the entrance to the Great Khan Irish Pub; and outside the central Palace of Culture there are posters advertising the venue's biggest draw, a Genghis Khan rock opera. Mongolia's most famous son is loved and revered by his compatriots, his descendants. But the most surprising thing about the ubiquity of Genghis Khan, and the esteem in which he is held, is that his very name was banned in Mongolia for decades. Under the communist regime, which lasted from 1921 to 1990, his life and deeds were barely taught in schools. If he was mentioned at all it was to point out that he was a cruel oppressor, a mass murderer and an all-round disaster for civilisation (much the view that has always been held of him in the West). How did this extraordinary transformation in Genghis Khan's posthumous reputation come about? The answer is rooted in the life of Genghis Khan himself, and in the twisted path of Mongolian history.

RISE OF THE OCEANIC KING

This is what the chronicles say about the early life of Temujin, the future Genghis Khan. He was born under the Eternal Blue Sky some time around 1162. He was the head of his own clan, and used this position of authority to bring other clans under his control. Through persuasion, subjugation or the gravitational attraction of his own commanding personality, he bound the nomadic tribes together and turned them into a nation. By his early 40s he was the acknowledged leader of 'all who lived in felt tents'. In 1206 Temujin summoned a meeting of the Mongol tribes at which his overlordship was formally acknowledged. It may well have been here that he took the title Genghis Khan, rendered in Mongolian as Chingis Khaan, 'the Oceanic King'. Now began the empire-building. Genghis Khan organised the entire male population of his fiefdom into a disciplined mounted army, an invasion force. Every warrior went on campaign with two or three hardy steppeland horses. Mongol cavalrymen could ride without a break, sleeping on the hoof if necessary. They could cover ground at speeds undreamed of in the prior history of warfare – and so to their enemies they seemed to have the terrifying ability to appear out of nowhere. If food was scarce, a Mongol warrior would make a small incision in the jugular vein of his horse and drink its blood. Every soldier was equipped with a short but extremely powerful bow that he could deploy in the saddle. Mongol horsemen knew how to shoot arrows backwards over their shoulder – a technique they used to devastating effect.

In 1211 Genghis Khan unleashed his army on the Jin Empire of northern China. The Mongol cavalry crossed the Great Wall, and laid waste to Beijing. They slaughtered untold thousands of civilians and stripped the city of its wealth. Endless

STEEL HORSEMAN *This giant statue of Genghis Khan, 40m (130ft) high and made of stainless steel, stands in the Mongolian steppe, east of Ulaanbaatar. It is one of several monuments erected to commemorate the 800th anniversary of the unification of the tribes under Genghis in 1206, the event that marked the birth of the Mongol nation.*

A FACE THAT SELLS *The commercial exploitation of Genghis Khan took off after Mongolian independence. His portrait was already on the paper currency; he now became a brand name for vodka, beer, cigarettes and other goods. References to him became a cliché of marketing in Mongolia, and the use of his image was so rampant that the government considered imposing a ban on its use in advertisments.*

1161-1227

caravans of booty were despatched back across the Gobi desert to the Mongolian homeland. In 1219, having subdued the east, Genghis turned his attention to the west. The unstoppable Mongols smashed into the Persian-Muslim Empire of Khwarezm, and in the course of a ten-year campaign obliterated it completely.

By the time of his death in 1227 Genghis Khan had earned the terrifying epithet 'the scourge of God'. His empire extended right across Asia, from the Sea of Japan to the shores of the Caspian. Under his son Ogodei it continued to expand, until it became the largest land empire the world had ever seen. Russia was conquered, as were the southern reaches of China. Genghis's grandson, Batu Khan, led an army into central Europe, ravaging Poland, Hungary and the Czech lands. His Mongol army was at the gates of Vienna when word came, in 1242, that Ogodei had died. Batu abandoned the siege of Vienna and returned home with his armies to stake his claim to the succession. It was only this small chance

that saved western Europe from destruction and subjugation.

The Genghisid Empire faded away over the course of the Middle Ages. The Mongols converted to Buddhism, and the Mongolian heartland came under the influence of China's Ming emperors. It was finally absorbed into the Manchu Empire. When the Manchus fell in 1911 Mongolia briefly became independent, then descended into political turmoil. That turbulent time ended in 1921. Mongolian communists, led by a revolutionary named Sükhbaatar and aided by Russia's new Bolshevik regime, seized control.

Communist Mongolia aped the USSR to a degree that would be comical if it were not so tragic. Sükhbaatar died within a year of Lenin, was embalmed like him and put on display in a mausoleum. He was succeeded by Choibalsan, a Stalin clone who presided over disastrous experiments in collectivisation, mass purges and vicious campaigns against religion. He died a year before Stalin himself, and was followed by Tsedenbal, who, like Leonid Brezhnev in Russia, ruled a country in terminal economic decline. The ailing Tsedenbal stepped down in 1984, and when Mikhail Gorbachev came to power in Moscow the following year, the winds of *glasnost* blew across the Mongolian steppe as they did over the plains of eastern Europe. In 1989 Mongolia, like the other socialist states, broke free of Soviet control.

REVIVING THE GREAT KHAN

For most of the communist era, Genghis Khan had been regarded in Marxist terms as a reactionary feudal baron, a brake on the revolutionary process. To speak of him was deemed un-internationalist, criminally unsocialist. Mongolians were made to feel slightly ashamed of Genghis Khan and his bloodthirsty colonialism. But now that communist oppression had evaporated, the right to praise Genghis Khan became the touchstone of freedom of speech within Mongolia. Commentators began to paint a new and altogether positive portrait of Mongolia's most famous son. Genghis began to be seen in patriotic terms as a man of genius – a man of war, too, but one who brought east and west together.

It was pointed out that Genghis Khan introduced elementary primary education into the countries he conquered, that he set up an empire-wide postal system and was a law-maker. He was praised for opening up the Silk Road, facilitating trade and the exchange of ideas throughout Asia; he smashed ancient feudal systems, ending aristocratic privilege. Far from wreaking havoc wherever he set foot (it was said), Genghis facilitated a great flowering of civilisation inside his vast empire.

The domestic revival of Genghis Khan was no mere historiographical exercise. He was vital to the new political dispensation

because he was above ideology. After independence, Genghis swiftly became the symbol of the modern, forward-looking Mongolian state. Nambaryn Enkhbayar, president from 2005 to 2009, spoke of Genghis as if he were some kind of superlative management guru: 'He thought fast, acted fast and got results fast. That's what you have to do in the modern world: get an idea, then make it happen.'

Enkhbayar was in office when, in 2006, Mongolia marked the 800th anniversary of the unification of the tribes under Genghis Khan, and so the founding of the Mongolian state. The jubilee was a grand national event, in the course of which the exaltation of Genghis Khan went

> *The new statue looks like a kind of fierce Buddha.*

beyond mere political rehabilitation and came close to worship. The centrepiece of the octocentenary was the unveiling of a monument on Ulaanbaatar's main square. The mausoleum of the communist Sükhbaatar was removed and replaced by a statue of Genghis Khan 8m (26ft) high. He sits on a throne, clutching its arms as if restraining his mighty wrath. In this pose he looks for all the world like a kind of fierce Buddha. 'May the spirit of the Lord Chingis Khaan bless the Mongol people and lead Mongolia to eternal prosperity,' intoned the president at the unveiling. Ghenghis Khan, reviled in Mongolia for a lifetime, had been reborn as a national idol, a deity made in the image of a proud, resurgent Mongolian people.

Explorers in disguise

By the 19th century the blank spaces on the map of the *world were in regions that were inaccessible, dangerous or hostile to outsiders. To explore the interior of the Muslim world or the heights of Tibet, intrepid travellers were wise to go in disguise.*

Throughout the long age of Western exploration, trade and colonial possession were the main motives. Explorers were also conquerors, or brought conquerors in their wake. But by the late 18th century there was a new mood in exploration as two new driving forces emerged. On the one hand, missionary societies began to venture into unknown and difficult territory. On the other, expeditions to the unexplored corners of the world were driven by scholarly societies in search of knowledge.

TO TIMBUKTU AND BACK

The interior of Africa, for example, was still a complete mystery. This included Islamic North Africa, and the tendrils that spread southwards along trans-Saharan trade routes that had been used for centuries by Arab merchants. West Africa was a rich source of gold, ivory and slaves, and the unexplored interior became the object of fascination – especially the legendary city of Timbuktu, said to be roofed in gold. But getting there was a hazardous business. In 1795 the London-based Association for Promoting the Discovery of Interior Parts of Africa (also known as the African Association) sent an expedition led by the young Scottish doctor Mungo Park, who reached the River Niger, on the banks of which Timbuktu was believed to stand. He was captured by Arabs and imprisoned for four months. He returned to Africa in 1805, only to be killed in what is now Nigeria while most of the other members of his expedition died of diseases. West Africa became known as the White Man's Grave.

In 1824 the Geographical Society of Paris offered a prize of 10,000 francs to anyone who could reach Timbuktu – and return alive. In 1826 a Scottish officer of the British army, Alexander Gordon Laing, rode south from Tripoli at the head of a small camel caravan. He made little secret of his origins and was attacked, wounded and robbed by Tuareg bandits, but he did manage to reach Timbuktu. Here, however, he was killed and decapitated. More rigorous subterfuge was clearly required.

The following year, 1827, a French explorer named René Caillié took the precaution of disguising himself convincingly as an Egyptian Muslim. He accounted for his imperfect knowledge

Exploring in disguise required a highly disciplined attention to detail. The smallest slip of the tongue or error in social etiquette could draw suspicion. The Swiss orientalist and traveller Johann Burckhardt was one of the most methodical. His dream was to cross the Sahara from east to west with an Arab caravan, but he knew that to achieve this he would have to be able to play the role of a native Arab convincingly. He learned Arabic in London before sailing for Aleppo, in Syria, in 1809. As he disembarked, he took on his new persona: Sheikh Ibrahim Ibn Abd Allah, a 'reduced Egyptian gentleman'.

Starting from Damascus, Burckhardt travelled south with a caravan of pilgrims on their way to Mecca. Near the Dead Sea he heard enticing rumours of ruins. For the price of two horseshoes he hired a local guide under the pretext that he wanted to make a sacrifice at the nearby altar of Aaron, an Islamic patriarch. The guide led him down a narrow canyon, and suddenly Burckhardt was in the lost city of Petra. All around him lay the ruins of temples and tombs carved into the cliff-faces of a narrow valley. This was the ancient capital of the Nabataeans – a nation of merchants operating at the western end of the trans-Asian Silk Road during Roman times.

If Burckhardt had shown his excitement, he would have invited suspicion: it was a pre-Islamic ruin, so of little interest to

of Arabic by saying that he had been captured by the French as a child and brought up in West Africa. Travelling inland from Senegal, he reached Timbuktu, which turned out, disappointingly, to be nothing more than an impoverished town of mudbrick. Caillié then travelled north with a caravan heading for Fez. Here his disguise proved too convincing for his own good: though he was weak, ill and impoverished, the French consuls refused to help him, and he had to stagger on to Tangiers to find a crossing back to France.

faithful Muslims. Instead, he studied the site as if indifferent to it, surreptitiously making notes. In the same guise, Burckhardt travelled to Cairo and on into the Arabian Peninsula, joining the pilgrimage to Mecca, where he stayed for four months. On his return to Cairo he contracted dysentery. He died in 1817, aged 32, but his discovery would be recalled by the English poet John Burgon, who described Petra as 'a rose-red city – half as old as time'.

ARABIA DESERTA
The dashing and unashamedly self-promoting Richard Burton followed Burckhardt to Mecca in 1853. While still a lieutenant in the British Indian army, and with the backing of the Royal Geographical Society, he undertook the journey in various disguises, including that of a Pashtun Muslim from northern India.

His preparation was meticulous – he even had himself circumcised in the Muslim manner. Following much the same route as Burckhardt, he duly reached Mecca and Medina. His detailed and – unlike Burckhardt's – very readable report was published in 1855. It was filled with highly coloured descriptions of his derring-do, and it made him an instant celebrity.

Disguise and discovery now seemed to go hand in hand. When, for example, William Gifford Palgrave crossed the Arabian Peninsula in 1862, he pretended to be a Syrian doctor called Mahmoud el-Eys. His motives for being in Arabia were complex: he was reconnoitring for the British but was also working for Louis-Napoleon of France. And as a Jesuit priest he was surveying the Middle East for its potential for conversion.

DESERT SON *Harry Philby (in the foreground) made his name in the Nejd, the central uplands of Arabia. It was his deep local knowledge, as much as his dress, that enabled him to blend in.*

While Burckhardt, Burton and Palgrave prided themselves on their ability to melt into the Arab background, Charles Doughty demonstrated emphatically how it should not be done. More a poet than an explorer, he adopted Arabic dress and learned rudimentary Arabic in Damascus as a prelude to venturing alone into the Arabian peninsula in 1876. But he would not countenance deception and categorically refused to disguise his Christianity, so travelled openly as a Nasrani (a Christian infidel).

Doughty joined a pilgrimage caravan on its way to Mecca, then split off to travel with Bedouin nomads. They showed him remarkable kindness, but he exasperated them by exploiting their traditions of hospitality, and by his persistent refusal to observe or respect their Islamic customs. He also aroused suspicion by constantly making notes, which seemed to his hosts to be mystical symbols; any misfortune was blamed on him. For two years he roamed the deserts and oases of the Hejaz, a region normally barred to non-Muslims. He repeatedly ran into trouble: Doughty was abandoned by guides, robbed, stoned, imprisoned, attacked with a knife, stripped and humiliated – and he was lucky not to be killed. Eventually, sick and almost blind, he staggered to the Red Sea coast and made his way back to England. He then spent ten years writing *Travels in Arabia Deserta* in strange Chaucerian English.

Through the efforts of these brave or foolhardy men, the blanks in the map of Arabia were gradually being filled in. The last unknown was the Rub al'Khali, the Empty Quarter, a vast ocean of sand crossed only by hardened Bedouin traders. It became the unconquered Everest of Arabist explorers. One of these was the British intelligence officer Harry St John

Philby, who in the 1920s travelled widely in Arabia dressed as an Arab, with the blessing of the emerging local power, the House of Saud. In the course of these expeditions he immersed himself in the life of the desert Arabs. No one ever suspected that he was not a born son of the desert, and by the time he ventured into the Empty Quarter in 1932, with 32 camels and three months' provisions, he was, in a sense, not in disguise at all. He converted to Islam in 1930, and kissed the Kaaba in Mecca (something 19th-century Western explorers had never done). Philby had become as much an Arab as it was possible for an Englishman to be.

INSIDE CENTRAL ASIA

Arabia was not the only unexplored region of interest to the British government. In the course of the 19th century, Britain consolidated its control over India, but the area to the north – the Himalayas and Tibet – remained unknown and uncharted. Their great height and remoteness meant that the mountains provided an excellent natural defence and buffer zone, but as the century progressed, the rapid southward expansion of the Russian Empire to the north unsettled the British. So began the 'Great Game' of cat-and-mouse gambits, a complex international contest involving spies, secret treaties, skirmishes and assassinations – all played out against the backdrop of one of the most inhospitable and savagely beautiful parts of the world.

The old Islamic trading cities of Bukhara, Khiva and Samarkand in central Asia formed part of this frontier zone between the two empires. Lieutenant Alexander Burnes – an officer in the Indian army and a classic player in the Great Game – reached Bukhara disguised in Afghan dress in 1832. 'Bokhara Burnes' was instrumental in British meddling in Afghanistan, which led to the First Afghan War of 1839–42. He was assassinated during an insurrection in Kabul in 1841.

During the 1860s Arminius Vámbéry, a Hungarian of Jewish extraction and a gifted linguist who worked for the Ottoman court, travelled around Persia dressed as a Sunni dervish, reaching the slave-trading city of Khiva in 1863. Here he was twice interviewed by the khan, a monster of cruelty and suspicion, without betraying himself. If his true identity had been guessed, he would certainly have been executed on the spot or made a slave. When Vámbéry returned from Asia he went to London, where he was given a hero's reception. It later transpired that he was not just a double agent, collecting information for both the Ottomans and Budapest, but was also in the service of the British Foreign Office, feeding back information on Russian activity.

THE ROOF OF THE WORLD

The last great blank on the Western map of Asia was Tibet itself – high, remote, impoverished and the mystical domain of a god-king, the 13th Dalai Lama. Tibet enforced a strict rule that no foreigners were allowed in. But it was not totally unknown for one to turn up: the British scholar of Chinese, Thomas Manning, had reached the capital Lhasa, undisguised, in 1811; and the French missionaries Abbé Huc and Joseph Gabet did the same in 1846, disguised as lamas (Buddhist monks), but were expelled after six weeks.

In 1878, the British heard that Nikolai Przhevalsky, Russia's most experienced explorer, had come within 260km (160 miles) of Lhasa before being turned back. A race was now on between Britain and Russia, with the Tibetan capital Lhasa as

the finish line. In 1903–4 Colonel Francis Younghusband led a military expedition into Tibet and forced his way to Lhasa. The Dalai Lama fled, and the British negotiated trade agreements with his regent.

The Anglo-Tibetan treaty enshrined the continued exclusion of foreigners, with the exception of the British and the Chinese. This infuriated the female French orientalist Alexandra David-Néel, who had made a special study of the Tibetan language and its arcane form of Buddhism.

She dressed as a Buddhist nun to journey in Tibet.

After concluding her work in neighbouring Sikkim, and visiting the exiled Dalai Lama in India, in 1912 she began a series of clandestine journeys in Tibet.

David-Néel dressed as a Buddhist nun and was accompanied by a young monk named Aphur Yongden. Though repeatedly expelled by the British, they doggedly resumed their secret pilgrimages, staying in monasteries, the caves of hermits and village hovels. David-Néel qualified as a lama and was permitted to wear the revered yellow silk, but the pair also travelled as poor pilgrims and beggars, or as a young lama accompanied by his mother. In 1924 David-Néel became the first European woman to reach Lhasa. Climbing to the roof of the Potala Palace to witness the New Year celebrations, she was stopped by a suspicious guard who asked her to remove her matted fur bonnet. She did so and he let her pass. Filth, she said, was her greatest disguise.

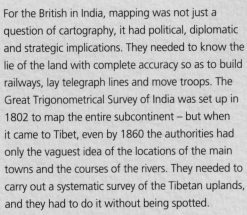

PACE MAKER *Nain Singh surveyed the Tibetan uplands on foot and under cover. The Royal Geographical Society in London later gave him a medal for his work.*

Secret surveyors

Tibet's ban on foreigners presented Britain's map-makers in India with a problem: how to do the cartographical fieldwork without attracting the attention of the Tibetan authorities. The solution that they found was ambitious and ingenious, and the data that was gathered surpassed all expectations.

For the British in India, mapping was not just a question of cartography, it had political, diplomatic and strategic implications. They needed to know the lie of the land with complete accuracy so as to build railways, lay telegraph lines and move troops. The Great Trigonometrical Survey of India was set up in 1802 to map the entire subcontinent – but when it came to Tibet, even by 1860 the authorities had only the vaguest idea of the locations of the main towns and the courses of the rivers. They needed to carry out a systematic survey of the Tibetan uplands, and they had to do it without being spotted.

Their solution to this problem constituted an extraordinary feat of geographical espionage. British officers recruited men from the Tibetan region and spent two years training them in surveying in the northern Indian city of Dehra Dun. They were given their specially adapted equipment: hand-held Buddhist prayer wheels fitted with brass tubes that contained notes, maps and sketches, and later a compass; a small sextant that could be hidden in the base of a trunk; and a thermometer concealed within a walking stick, to ascertain altitude by taking the temperature at which water boiled. They were taught to walk with a regularly spaced stride of exactly 33 inches, and to count their strides on a Buddhist rosary containing 100 beads rather than the 108 of Buddhist

tradition. They were also trained in their disguises, usually adopting the role of travelling merchants.

The British termed these walking spies 'pundits', from the Sanskrit for 'wise man'. One of the first to venture into Tibet was Nain Singh, codenamed 'Number One', who reached Lhasa in 1865 and determined its exact position. He

> *They were taught to take strides of exactly 33 inches.*

returned 18 months later, having also surveyed the sacred Lake Manasarowar, the supposed source of the Ganges, Indus and Brahmaputra rivers. He had covered 2,000km (1,250 miles). Over the next 35 years, the map was filled in by a team of more than 20 pundits. Many suffered great hardships; some were even murdered. But the information that they brought back was astonishingly accurate. In 1899 the last of the secret expeditions came to a close, after a pundit named Rinzu Namgyal circumnavigated Mount Kanchenjunga. The first modern map of Tibet was published in 1906.

The nameless pharaoh

In the 3,000-year-long history of ancient Egypt, there is one
pharaoh whose reign was considered so blasphemous that his successors
excised his name from the historical record. Archaeologists and historians
have now reconstructed the story of Akhenaten and his radical new religion.

In the temple of Karnak there is a stone
tablet, carved during the reign of the
pharaoh Tutankhamun. It describes
the state of the land under Akhenaten,
Tutankhamun's father, but it does not name
him: 'The temples of the gods and goddesses
had fallen into ruin,' reads the inscription.
'Their shrines had fallen into decay and
been overgrown with weeds … The land
was in distress, the gods were turning away
from it … If one prayed to a god in order to
ask a favour, he would not come at all.'

Elsewhere, on the walls of the temple
of Pharaoh Seti I at Abydos, is inscribed
the great king-list containing the names
of 76 successive rulers of ancient Egypt.
This list was compiled a generation after
Tutankhamun, yet both he and his father
are missing from the roll-call. By now the
mention of Akhenaten was anathema.
His successors had his name chiselled
out of inscriptions and did their best to
obliterate Akhenaten's own monuments.
If he was referred to at all, it was as 'that
criminal'. But what crime had Akhenaten
committed? What sin was so terrible that
his rule, the very fact of his existence, had
to be obliterated?

Akhenaten was the son of Amenhotep III,
whose 37-year reign was a golden age for
Egypt. The nation was at peace under his
rule, and international trade flourished as
gold flowed into the royal coffers from
mines in the south of the country. Yet
beneath the surface of opulence and luxury,
there was religious and political tension.
The people of Egypt worshipped many
gods, among them Amun, divine patron of
Thebes, the city where the ruling dynasty
was headquartered. Over time, Amun
had become linked with Re, the Sun-god.
The rise of Amun-Re had brought about
a corresponding surge in the power of the
Theban priesthood – to the point where
the earthly representatives of Amun-Re
threatened to challenge the pharaoh's own
authority. A power struggle was looming.

A NEW RELIGION
When Amenhotep III died in the middle
of the 14th century BC, the new pharaoh,
his son, was crowned like his predecessors
at Amun-Re's great temple of Karnak
outside Thebes. He was not yet known as
Akhenaten; at this time he took the regnal
name Amenhotep IV to emphasise the

THE HERETIC KING *The serene face of Akhenaten, carved naturalistically in stone. This is one of the few representations of the king to survive the destruction of his legacy after his death. He looks here like a saint or mystic, a man certain of his own spiritual insight.*

continuity between his father and himself. That link was underlined when he took as his principal wife the beautiful Nefertiti, a daughter of his father's chief minister.

But within five years of his accession, the pharaoh changed course, repudiating the past. He imposed a kind of cultural revolution that shook Egyptian society and led ultimately to his own eclipse. At the core of the project was a radical revision of Egypt's entire cosmogony. The pharaoh switched his religious allegiance – and with him the nation's – from the worship of

Egypt's multifarious gods to the sole cult of the *aten*, or Sun-disk, previously a minor aspect of the Sun-god Re. Amenhotep declared, in effect, that there was no pantheon of gods, there was just one God, and his name was Aten.

To proclaim his new idea, the pharaoh changed his regnal name to Akhenaten, 'servant of the aten'. And this symbolic gesture was just the start. He resolved to move his capital from priest-ridden Thebes to a new city, to be built on virgin soil 320km (200 miles) to the north. There,

But that soon changed, and before long workmen were being despatched with chisels to remove the name of Amun – and sometimes also references to 'gods' in the plural – from temple walls across the nation. From now on, only Aten was to be worshipped, and his earthly representative was not to be the established priesthood but the pharaoh himself, for 'there is none that knows thee save thy son Akhenaten; thou hast made him wise in thy plans and thy power'. Akhenaten himself is credited with writing the great 'Hymn to the Aten', often compared with Psalm 104 in the Bible, which praises the Sun as the creator of all things: 'Oh, sole God, than whom there is no other!' says the hymn, 'You created the world according to your desire, while you were alone. All men, cattle and wild beasts, whatever is on earth, going upon feet, and what is on high, flying with wings.'

A NEW KIND OF ART

The religious transformation of Egypt went in parallel with an upheaval in the world of official art. In place of the stiff formality of Egyptian tradition, Akhenaten introduced a new naturalism, instructing his sculptors to represent what they saw. Unlike the formalised rigid god-kings who had preceded him, Akhenaten was portrayed at home with his beautiful wife Nefertiti, playing affectionately with the couple's six daughters. The supreme ruler allowed his artists to depict his pot belly, curving haunches and oddly androgynous figure.

It may seem to modern minds that there is something humble or even democratic in that – but Akhenaten remained the autocrat, utterly aloof from his people. His single-minded pursuit of the cult of the Aten

on the east bank of the Nile at the site known today as el-Amarna, he created Akhetaten, 'horizon of the aten', a garden city of palaces and villas laid out on a grid beneath a natural amphitheatre of cliffs.

The temples that Akhenaten built in his new capital are an architectural and theological departure from the old ways. They were not dark, secretive places where priests alone had access to the gods. Instead, they were unroofed compounds in which worshippers could venerate the Sun's life-giving rays in the open air. To drive home the message, images showed the aten in the form of the solar disk issuing beams of light, each ending in a hand grasping the *ankh* – the cross with a looped top that is the Egyptian symbol for life.

In the first years of his revolution, Akhenaten seems to have been prepared to tolerate the persistence of other gods.

meant closing down the temples of Egypt's other gods. Almost overnight, the Egyptian people found themselves robbed of the patterns of worship that had comforted them for thousands of years. There was, of course, some political gain to be made from this. The power of the priesthood was shattered as their role was abolished, their temples shut and their rich revenues diverted to the king's treasury.

But Akhenaten, ensconced in his new capital, seems to have lost touch with the land he ruled. The archaeological record shows he neglected his empire: a cache of diplomatic papers found at el-Amarna contains letters from the rulers of tributary states in Palestine and Syria seeking Egyptian help to fight off their enemies, notably the rising Hittite state (in what is now Turkey). But no help was sent: the pharaoh's obsession with his creed distracted him from the business of government.

> *He was perhaps the first person to believe that God is one.*

The last years of Akhenaten's reign are shrouded in mystery. Nefertiti disappeared from the historical record in the 12th year of his rule, apparently having died, and her place as Great Royal Wife was taken by her own daughter. Five years later Akhenaten himself was dead, to be succeeded briefly by Smenkhare, a shadowy figure, possibly his younger brother. Just months later he, too, was no more. The throne passed to Tutankhamun, then aged just eight or nine.

It was during Tutankhamun's reign that the task of undoing Akhenaten's revolution

began – the new ruler was too young to prevent the political backlash against his father. The royal city of Akhetaten was abandoned to the desert sands, and the cult of Amun and the other gods was restored. At some point it seems likely that Akhenaten's mummified remains were removed from their first royal tomb in Akhetaten. There is a strong likelihood that a mummy found in an anonymous tomb in 1907 may be his. The tomb contained bricks inscribed with his forbidden name; it is close to the grave of Tutankhamun, and modern DNA evidence suggests that the one is the father of the other.

THE KING IN DECLINE

In several strange ways, Akhenaten's story anticipates later events in world history. He was the first ruler – perhaps the first person – to entertain the idea that God is one. In that conviction, he prefigures the rise of the three great monotheistic religions: Judaism, Christianity and Islam. His struggles with the religious hierarchy of his time, and his attempt to disenfranchise the priesthood, are oddly reminiscent of Henry VIII's rejection of the Roman Catholic Church and subsequent dissolution of the monasteries in England.

Another aspect of Akhenaten's rule that still resonates is his attempt to impose a new order, an entirely new mindset, on his people. This makes him look like some kind of ancient Oliver Cromwell. And there is something chillingly contemporary and totalitarian about the posthumous attempt to erase Akhenaten entirely from history. It puts one in mind of Stalin's treatment of defeated enemies such as Trotsky (*see* page 264), and it recalls George Orwell's bleak 20th-century dictum: 'He who controls the present, controls the past; he who controls the past, controls the future.'

What killed Tutankhamun?

The world was amazed when Tutankhamun's almost intact tomb was discovered in 1922. Recent DNA tests on the pharaoh's mummified body have cast new light on his likely ancestry and may well explain his untimely death.

DOOMED PRINCE
Without regal finery, Tutankhamun, son of Akhenaten, looks like the small, rather delicate boy he was.

Thanks to the wonders found in his tomb, Tutankhamun is today the best known of all the pharaohs. Yet in his own time he was something of a cipher, a boy-king who died while still in his teens and whose government was largely in the hands of his ministers. Tutankhamun was the last in the bloodline of the 18th Dynasty pharaohs, who had established Egypt's New Kingdom and raised the nation to imperial glory.

Following the Egyptian custom of securing the dynastic line by enthroning sister-queens, Tutankhamun took for his wife the daughter of Akhenaten by a different mother. The royal couple were not blessed with children; two mummified foetuses found in Tutankhamun's tomb are thought be their offspring, miscarried or stillborn.

Important changes were underway as Tutankhamun began his reign. His immediate predecessor was Smenkhare, Tutankhamun's uncle or possibly elder brother, who occupied the throne for just a matter of months after the death of Akhenaten. During Smenkhare's brief reign the decision had been taken to abandon Akhenaten's new city at Akhetaten and move the capital to Memphis in northern Egypt. It was there that Tutankhamun was crowned.

Since he was too young to rule – nine years old at most – the real power lay in the hand of the chief court officials: Ay, who had been Akhenaten's father-in-law and master of the horses; and Horemheb, the commander of the army. These two men took the decision to reverse the changes that Akhenaten had introduced, and so save Egypt. It was they who decreed, as early as the second year of the reign, that the young pharaoh's regnal title was to be changed from Tutankhaten ('living image of Aten') to Tutankhamun ('living image of Amun'). The switch signalled the restoration of Amun to his position as chief of the gods, as he had been under earlier New Kingdom pharaohs.

THE REVOLUTION UNDONE

The main evidence for this counter-reformation, which saw Akhenaten's life's works reversed, is a tablet detailing the restoration of the old order. The text records how royal patronage was once more lavished on the temples of the traditional gods and on the priests who served them: the pharaoh, it stated, 'has increased their property in gold, silver and bronze and copper without limit ... All the property of the temples has been doubled, tripled, quadrupled in silver, gold, lapis lazuli and turquoise.' At the same time, Tutankhamun's ministers set out to re-affirm the authority of the Egyptian empire, sending military expeditions to Syria and Nubia to quell border unrest.

Then, just as Tutankhamun was reaching an age to take over the reins of power, he died. The haste with which his tomb was prepared suggests his demise was unexpected; many of the grave

AT REST *Tutankhamun's mummy is now in a climatised glass case in his own tomb. His story, in the end, was as tragic as his life was short.*

goods that adorned it came out of storage rather than being specially prepared, as was usually the case for a pharaoh. Soon afterwards the non-royal Ay was established on the throne, having married Tutankhamun's widow as a way of strengthening his claim to rule.

MURDER OR SICKNESS?

The timing of the death was sufficiently suspect to have led at least one Egyptologist to claim that the young ruler was murdered in order to clear Ay's path to the throne. A small sliver of bone detected in the mummy's cranial cavity was taken as evidence of a head wound. Meanwhile, a letter from the widow, found in Hittite archives, heightened such suspicions. In it, she asked the Hittite ruler to send her a son to marry, presumably to strengthen her own position on the throne after Tutankhamun's death. A prince was duly despatched to Egypt, only to be killed on the border before he could reach the capital.

But the latest research suggests that there was no foul play. Forensic evidence has shown that the bone fragment was probably dislodged during post-mortem examinations. And tests on the mummy have identified signs of chronic illness that could have undermined the young ruler's health, leaving him with a weakened immune system. A 2010 study, for example, showed that he suffered from recurrent bouts of malaria.

Intriguingly, the same study also cast new light on Tutankhamun's parentage. DNA testing confirmed that his father was indeed Akhenaten but also indicated that his mother was not any of the elder pharaoh's known wives. Instead she was one of Akhenaten's five sisters, indicating that Tutankhamun was the product of an incestuous match. If so, this increases the likelihood that he suffered from congenital conditions, including a cleft palate and scoliosis (curvature of the spine). It is known that at the time of his death he was suffering complications from a broken leg. It seems that the pharaohs' obsession with protecting the royal line may have been self-defeating. The 18th Dynasty may well have died out as a result of efforts to keep the bloodline pure.

Priests out of sight

Under Elizabeth I and her successors England was home to
*a close-knit group of fugitives moving around a network of safehouses
equipped with purpose-built hiding places. The men were Catholic priests,
and the priest-holes were their best hope of avoiding torture and execution.*

On Easter Monday 1594, a Jesuit priest
named John Gerard was getting ready to
say an early-morning mass at Braddocks,
a private house near Saffron Walden in
Essex. Suddenly the preparations were
interrupted by the sound of galloping
hooves. Gerard and his congregation knew
at once what the sound meant: the priest-
hunters were upon them. With a speed
born of bitter experience – the house had
been raided twice before – the celebrants
stowed away the clerical vestments and
altar furniture in a specially prepared hide.
Gerard followed suit, taking refuge in a
priest-hole hollowed from the brickwork
of the house's chimneystack and accessed
through a trap door under a false hearth.

As the searchers spread out through
the house, Gerard remained cooped up in
a space just 1.6m (5ft 2in) wide and 1.7m
(5ft 6in) tall at its highest point. Its only
ornamentation was two brick steps serving
as a seat; the uppermost had a bowl
chiselled out at one end for a latrine. The
raiders had arrived so suddenly that there
was no time to stock the hide with food,
so all Gerard had to live on was a couple
of biscuits and a little quince jelly that the

lady of the house managed to hand him
as he took refuge.

The search continued for four days.
Guards were stationed in the rooms
overnight, and two of these men decided
one evening to light a fire in the grate
above the hide. A single layer of bricks was
all that concealed the wooden trap door,
and the heat soon warped the wood. Yet
even though the guards noticed the shifting
of the bricks and poked at the hearth with
a stick, they failed to detect the refuge
beneath. When the searchers eventually
gave up, Gerard emerged from his hiding
place 'like Lazarus, who was buried four
days … very wasted and weak with hunger
and lack of sleep'. Even so, his ordeal
failed to discourage him, and he continued
his underground mission for a further
12 years before eventually escaping to the
Continent, where he wrote a thrilling first-
person account of his life on the run.

KEEPING THE OLD FAITH
The reasons that Father Gerard and other
priests had to hide were bound up with
the religious politics of the Tudor age.
In 1559, the year after the Protestant

Elizabeth I came to the English throne, an Act of Uniformity was passed compelling obedience to the Church of England and outlawing any form of worship other than that spelled out in the Anglican Book of Common Prayer. Priests who rejected the new order either had to flee abroad or else go underground. In practice, this often meant taking employment in wealthy Catholic households in the guise of music masters or tutors to the family's children.

For a time the authorities showed tolerance in their dealings with 'recusants', as people who refused to give up their old Catholic faith were known. They had only to pay a weekly fine to avoid attending Church of England services, and were otherwise allowed to go about their business unmolested. But then, in 1568, Pope Pius V authorised the founding of a college at Douai in northern France that was specifically intended to train priests for work in England. In response, the attitude of English Protestants to the Catholics in their midst became harder, more hostile. This was not merely religious prejudice; there was a political aspect to it. England was increasingly at loggerheads with the great Catholic continental powers, notably Spain, and the half-hidden network of priests came to be seen as a Popish fifth column, an enemy within.

The first priests trained at Douai were smuggled into England in 1574. In all, some 300 entered the country over the next 12 years. The authorities replied with increasingly harsh countermeasures. From 1580 on, conversion to Roman Catholicism became high treason, and captured priests began to be tortured and executed. Five years later the mere presence in England of any priest ordained since 1559 merited death, and anyone sheltering such a person could be hanged.

In 1586 Margaret Clitherow, a butcher's wife from York, was charged with the offence. Refusing to enter a plea, she was sentenced to the *peine forte et dure*, pressed to death under a load of rocks.

In short, England became a highly dangerous place to be a Catholic, and especially a Catholic priest. In this climate of fear, secure hiding places for priests came to seem an urgent necessity. They needed to be both invisible and swiftly

A new breed of law enforcer, known as pursuivants, appeared in the land.

accessible. The first priest-holes were relatively unsophisticated affairs, typically consisting of a space just big enough to conceal a man hollowed out under a closet floor, with a disguised trap door serving as the entrance. Other, smaller spaces served to conceal the altars, candles, prayer books and other paraphernalia needed to perform the forbidden masses.

But these simple measures ceased to be enough when a new breed of law enforcer appeared in the land. Known as pursuivants, they were professional priest-hunters, and they soon grew wise to the simpler forms of hiding place. They used measuring rods to check the outside walls of buildings and compared the results against the internal plan to locate possible empty spaces. They also became skilled at spotting signs of recent occupancy inside houses. In response, families harbouring

UNDER THE BOARDS
A priest-hole at the top of a staircase, made by Nicholas Owen at Sawston Hall in Cambridgeshire. When closed, the crosspieces on the lid fit neatly into the sockets in the beams below: the planks look like the corner of an ordinary upstairs floor. The stone aperture in the foreground leads diagonally down to a secret chamber in the wall, where there is space enough to hold half a dozen people.

priests learned to turn mattresses, if they had time, so that the searchers would not be able to detect the telltale sign of residual body warmth in a hastily vacated bed.

THE CUNNING CARPENTER

The Armada scare of 1588, in which a Spanish fleet attempted to land an invasion force in England, turned up the heat on known Catholic families. In the wake of this episode, 31 priests and their protectors were hanged in a three-month period – more than at any other time. This escalation in the pursuit of Catholics lent new urgency to the demand for priest-holes – not just more of them, but more cunning designs, constructed to house and protect a network of priests who were forever on the move between safehouses. A man with the necessary skills to build them was soon found. His name was Nicholas Owen; he was a carpenter and a Jesuit, born in Oxford to a recusant household.

For 18 years Owen travelled around England as an attendant to Father Henry Garnet, one of the most prominent of the Jesuits who spearheaded the Catholic mission to England. Working in difficult conditions, always alone and usually by night, Owen installed dozens of ingenious hiding places in houses throughout the country. Many of his best hidey-holes were located around multi-flued chimneystacks where it was difficult for pursuivants to detect them. 'With incomparable skill,' wrote one Catholic contemporary, 'he knew how to conduct priests to a place of safety along subterranean passages, to hide them between walls and bury them in impenetrable recesses, and to entangle them in labyrinths and a thousand windings. But what was much more difficult of accomplishment, he so disguised the entrances to these as to make them most unlike what they really were.'

WATCHING AND WAITING

Sometimes an invisible hiding place was not enough. Searches could last for days or even weeks – especially when the pursuivants had reliable information that their quarry was on the premises – and all the hunters had to do was wait in order to starve the priests from their holes. But Owen had thought of this: at Hindlip Hall in Worcestershire he constructed a hole equipped with a feeding tube. It passed through a chink in the wall, so that 'caudles, broths and other warm drinks' could be supplied to the hiders within. In 1606 two men survived for five days in the hole thanks to Owen's device.

On that occasion, Owen himself was hiding in another priest-hole of his own construction inside the same house. He and a companion lasted for three days, until hunger drove them out, into the custody of the waiting pursuivants. Owen was taken to the Tower of London for questioning, but resolutely refused to reveal either the locations of the hides he had built or the names of the many priests he had helped conceal. He died under torture. In 1970 he was canonised by Pope Paul VI as one of the 40 martyrs of the English Church.

After the death of Elizabeth I in 1603 England's Catholics hoped for better treatment from the new king, James I. Those expectations were quickly dashed, though, and the disillusionment of one foolhardy group of recusants found expression in the Gunpowder Plot of 1605. Its failure led to a fresh round of

> *Owen refused to reveal the location of the hides that he had built.*

persecutions in which the priest-hole network was once again pressed into service. Yet by that time, the tide was on the turn. While the 1580s had seen more than 100 executions of recusants, the number dwindled to 30 in the first decade of the 17th century, just three in the 1620s and none at all in the 1630s – despite the fact that the number of Catholic priests operating in England had more than doubled to about 800.

But the growing tolerance of religious dissent did not do away with the need for hiding places – though their occupants changed. During the English Civil War, the old priest-holes sheltered Royalists on the run. Supporters of King Charles I took refuge in hides that, a generation before, had concealed those deemed to be enemies of the Crown.

Beneath the golden hill

An astonishing treasure trove was discovered in Afghanistan in 1978 – just before the Soviet invasion of the country. Then, as the nation collapsed into civil war, the golden artefacts went missing. But they were not lost, merely hidden, their secret in the safe-keeping of five silent 'keyholders'.

In the local Uzbek language, the site of the dig was known by the promising name of Tillia Tepe, 'Golden Hill'. It was a small hill outside the oasis village of Sheberghan in northern Afghanistan, about 50km (30 miles) south of the Soviet border. A Russian archaeological team was at work here, excavating the mound. The leader of the dig was a Russian of Greek extraction by the name of Viktor Sarianidi, an expert in Bronze Age sites. He and his diggers had already found traces of a fortified building of that era, which he thought looked like the remains of a temple. Then one of the workmen noticed something sparkling in the loose earth: a small disc of gold.

Sarianidi's team dug deeper. It soon became obvious that the gold they had found had nothing to do with the Bronze Age structure that the team had set out to explore. It had been placed in a grave dug many centuries later, when the temple was already in ruins. Further investigation quickly revealed the bones of a man – and he was not alone in death: he was surrounded by five females. All six seemed to have been interred at the same time, raising the possibility that the women

had been wives and servants, sacrificed to accompany a male chieftain into the afterlife. One thing that was certain was that they had been people of wealth and status, for their mass grave disgorged over 20,000 objects, mostly made of gold and adorned with decorations of turquoise and lapis lazuli. The great majority were personal adornments – earrings, necklaces, belts, chains, clasps, buckles, even a pair of shoe soles of pure gold. There were also some coins, and these permitted the archaeologists to date the find to the first century of the Christian era.

THE NOMAD WARRIORS

So who were these wealthy people? What did the golden ornaments say about them? The cache came from a dark period of Afghan history. Once part of the great Persian Empire, then conquered by Alexander the Great, the northern part of the country had become known to Alexander's Greek-speaking successors as Bactria, and had survived briefly as an independent kingdom. By the time of the burials, though, it was under attack from the east, pressed by nomadic peoples from

Forgotten riches, abandoned wealth

The Tillia Tepe trove is just one of many spectacular hoards of buried treasure found around the world. There have even been finds elsewhere in Afghanistan. In the 1960s and 1970s archaeologists unearthed magnificently decorated plates, statues, coins and jewellery from Ai Khanum, the site of a Greek city founded in the wake of Alexander the Great's conquests and abandoned a couple of centuries later when it fell to nomadic invaders. Thirty years earlier a team at Bagram, a town near Kabul where the Kushan emperors had their summer capital, excavated two sealed rooms containing ivory carvings, painted goblets, bronze statuettes and plaster medallions. Experts still argue over whether the objects were royal possessions or the stock of a merchant specialising in luxury goods; either way, they suggest the prosperity of the region at a period close to that of the Tillia Tepe burials.

Other treasures were left as votive offerings. One extraordinary assemblage was found at Flag Fen, near the English city of Peterborough, where an array of jewellery and weapons, some deliberately broken, was unearthed close to a sacred island. England has proved rich in buried treasures; some of the most spectacular finds date from the dark age following the withdrawal of Roman legions in the 5th century AD. One such was the Hoxne Hoard, discovered by a metal detector enthusiast outside the Suffolk village of that name in 1992. The trove, made up of almost 15,000 gold, silver and bronze coins and roughly 200 pieces of silver tableware and golden jewellery, was valued at the time at £1.75 million. It is now in the British Museum in London.

the Chinese borderlands driven westwards by the Huns. The Romans came to know these warriors as Scythians, the Chinese called them Yuezhi, and in time they would found an empire of their own, the Kushan realm, that would rule Afghanistan and much of northern India for around 200 years. The graves, then, were seemingly those of a Scythian prince and his retinue, strangers in a strange land.

The nomads had no writing with which to record their history, so it was all the more exciting to find such direct evidence of their wealth. It demonstrated the affluence of the northern Afghan lands at a time when the nascent Silk Road, stretching from China to the fringes of the Roman Empire, was bringing trade and prosperity to the lands around the Oxus River. The discovery was obviously of crucial importance to an understanding of Afghanistan's heritage. As winter closed

in, preventing further digging, Sarianidi arranged for the hoard to be transferred to the National Museum, located a few kilometres outside the capital, Kabul.

UNDER LOCK AND KEY

Sarianidi had hoped to return the following year to check if there were other graves to be explored, but history intervened. In 1979 the Soviet Union invaded Afghanistan, the inaugural event of a time of war and upheaval during which archaeological work was out of the question. For the next decade the treasures he had unearthed remained on display in the museum, though few people visited them while war raged outside. In 1989 the museum's curators came to the conclusion that the building could no longer provide a safe haven. A committee determined that many of its greatest treasures, among them the Tillia Tepe artefacts, should be dispersed to safe places known only to a handful of officials. Five individuals were designated *tahilwidar*, or keyholders, with special responsibility for protecting the treasure from looters and thieves. The keys that they held, or rather had tucked away in some hiding place, fitted locks on the chests in which it had been packed away. The chests were then stashed in a vault.

The decision to lock away the golden hoard proved a wise one. In the years that followed, the Soviet-backed regime collapsed, plunging the nation into civil strife. As chaos and anarchy descended on Afghanistan, the National Museum was

> *None of the keyholders broke under pressure; the hoard was secure.*

first robbed and then used as a military outpost, targeted by rocket attacks. One missile strike caused major damage, then a fire brought the roof down. Many of the collections that had been left inside the museum were destroyed.

Fresh dangers arose after 1996 when the Taliban took control of Kabul. One contingent in the leadership, considering representations of the human form to be idolatrous, sent out teams to destroy representational works of art. Others, despising Afghanistan's pre-Islamic heritage, sought to get their hands on the lost treasure for more practical reasons: they hoped to dispose of it for cash. The museum's staff were browbeaten to reveal its location, and some were threatened with violence when they failed to do so.

But none of the *tahilwidar* broke ranks under pressure, and the hoard remained securely hidden.

A SECOND UNEARTHING

After the Taliban government was toppled in late 2001, a degree of normality returned to the capital. By that time, though, most people thought that the Tillia Tepe treasure was gone for good. Rumours had long since spread that it had been looted, sold on the black market or melted down. The wall of silence that had protected the hoard was broken only the following year, when the new government revealed that the treasure had been hidden for years in a bank vault located in the grounds of the Presidential Palace in Kabul.

A preliminary investigation showed the vault was intact and the crates still sealed. It took a further two years to locate the keyholders and to assemble a body of experts endowed with the necessary resources to examine all the 20,000 objects and check that nothing was missing or replaced. Finally, in 2004, the vault was formally opened in the presence of 74-year-old Viktor Sarianidi himself, and the crates were unlocked or forced open. When a full inventory was taken, the collection was found to be entirely intact.

After its rediscovery, the Tillia Tepe hoard went on tour around the world. It was put on display in Paris, then in Turin, Amsterdam, various cities in the USA, Ottawa, Bonn and London. The collection was returned at last to its original home in the National Museum in Kabul. Since then, Afghanistan has been plunged into a new period of conflict and upheaval. The treasures of Golden Hill may have further travels ahead of them yet.

Erasing Trotsky

The camera has always lied, and it has never been so untruthful as in Russia during the 1930s. Under Stalin, photographs were routinely doctored so as to cut out political leaders who had fallen from grace. It was not enough to assassinate enemies: they had to be purged from the historical record too.

The men and women of the Bolshevik party, both before and after it came to power in 1917, were always very fond of group photographs. This was one of the peculiar foibles of the Russian revolutionary movement. There are numerous pre-revolutionary pictures of Vladimir Lenin, the rising Marxist thinker, posing for a formal snapshot with his inner circle – most of them serious, bearded young men in heavy suits. And there are many official images showing Lenin in power, seated at a conference table with his ministers ranged either side of him, or as the focal point of a crowd of supporters. A photographer was nearly always on hand at party congresses and official gatherings, at the unveiling of a statue or the signing of an important document, to record the moment for posterity.

CHANGING THE PAST

But posterity turned out to be rather different from what any revolutionary may have imagined. After Lenin died, the power struggle within the Bolshevik party ended in victory for Stalin. To consolidate his position, Stalin felt the need to discredit –

and in the fullness of time to physically eliminate – almost all the of 'old guard', the people who had been Lenin's closest comrades. They were now portrayed as revisionists, opportunists, anti-Leninist political deviants. The historical record – letters, documents and photographs – contained little to support this view, so the historical record had to be changed.

In the 1930s enemies of Stalin who had once been friends of Lenin were excised from official histories. Since the men and women of the old guard were picked off one or two at a time, over a period of years, there are many old photographs that exist in multiple published versions: first the original, then a version cropped so that one disgraced individual falls out of the frame, then with some second or third or fourth person airbrushed out. There are photographs that started out as group shots of Bolshevik comrades, but as a result of the rewriting of the past, ended up as solo portraits of Lenin or Stalin.

The principal victim of this process of erasure from the historical record was Leon Trotsky – founder and leader of the Red Army, theorist and historian of

ALTERED IMAGES *The original photograph (above) was taken in Moscow on May Day in 1920, during the Russian Civil War. Lenin speaks from the tribune, while Trotsky, halfway down the steps, surveys the crowd. After Trotsky was forced into exile in 1929, every photograph that hinted at his former importance was airbrushed. In the doctored photograph (right) he has been removed from the dais, and so from the presence of Lenin. The altered photograph was later re-created as an epic oil painting in which the rather passive and inattentive onlookers seen here are transformed into a spellbound audience, carrying red banners.*

the revolution, and Stalin's main rival for the leadership. In 1929 Trotsky was expelled from the party and the USSR (and was later murdered in exile by a Stalinist agent). Thereafter, his key role in the revolutionary movement was reduced to zero. If his name was mentioned at all, it was with furious disgust, because in Stalin's revised version of history, Trotsky had only ever been a traitor to the revolutionary cause. Trotskyism was, in the USSR of the 1930s, the worst of political crimes, and to be accused of it was as good as a death sentence.

> ## *Faces were blotted out with paint, or cut out with scissors.*

The manipulation of photography was key to this new propaganda project: a wholesale falsification of the recent past. The actual work was carried out by retouchers and graphic designers working in newspaper offices and publishing houses throughout the country. Some of the people charged with altering photographs were naturally less skilled than others – and so sometimes the new reality they created was not especially realistic. There are photographs where some *persona non grata* has been replaced by a ghostly grey smudge; others where the marks of the scalpel are clearly visible. In group portraits it was sometimes necessary to splice two or more copies of a photograph together, so as to close up an obvious gap in the ranks. The best falsifiers of photographs knew how to replace an excised human figure with a pot plant or a

column, or – as in the case of the famously altered picture of Lenin and Trotsky on May Day 1920 (*see* page 265) – they convincingly painted in a solid background where the offending individual once stood.

CENSORING MEMORY

The changing truth about the past created a problem for ordinary Soviet citizens. What were people to do if, say, they had bought a book of speeches by a party leader who was subsequently purged? Or if they had on their shelves an album containing a picture of a once-respected commissar later denounced as a Trotskyite wrecker or a British spy? In Stalin's Russia, political heresy was retrospective, and so to own a printed work by an 'enemy of the people', or even the image of an enemy inside the pages of a book, was evidence of treason against the Soviet state. To throw the offending book away was not a safe option: if you were spotted, then that very act might look like an attempt to cover up a guilty secret. And if the volume also contained the words or the face of Stalin, then to destroy or dispose of it was politically unthinkable.

So masses of ordinary citizens followed the government's example as best they could, and went through books scratching or inking out the names of people who had been denounced or purged. Faces were blotted out with black paint, or cut out with scissors and razor blades. Anyone undertaking this work had to be careful not to deface the features of a true Stalinist or – much worse – of Stalin himself. In effect, every citizen became his or her own censor. Monitoring and modifying one's own thoughts and one's own memories became an individual political duty. It was soul-destroying – and it was meant to be. Some people even felt constrained to cut husbands and fathers and brothers out of family snapshots after the secret police had come to take their loved ones away.

As the members of Lenin's entourage were demonised one by one, Stalin's own relationship with the genius of the revolution was exaggerated and glorified, as if he alone were to fill the gaps in the ranks of the old Bolsheviks. Stalin was not close to Lenin in the years before the revolution, he played a very minor role in the revolution itself, and in power Lenin came to view Stalin with deep suspicion. Yet once Stalin had gained complete control of the party and the state, he was able to set about creating the false myth that he had always been Lenin's best disciple and most trusted colleague, that he was by Lenin's side in exile and throughout the glorious events of October 1917.

> *The rescripting of the past went far beyond the medium of photography.*

Once again, the manipulation of photographs was vital. It was not now a case of deleting individuals but of adding Stalin to events in which he never took part. There is a well-known photograph showing Stalin sitting next to Lenin on a bench in 1922 or 1923. It looks like a picture of the author of the Revolution anointing his chosen successor, but any forensic study of the printed image suggests that this event did not happen in this way. Rather, a photograph of a seated Stalin has been pasted onto a picture of Lenin posing alone on a bench. The dishonest montage of Stalin and Lenin together was endlessly reproduced, then transmuted into paintings, book illustrations and monumental sculptures. All this reinforced the lie of an emotional and ideological bond between the two.

THE MOVING IMAGE

The rescripting of the past went beyond Stalin personally, and also beyond the medium of photography. It extended, for example, to cinema and to the key event of the Russian Revolution: the storming of the Winter Palace in Petrograd. In 1927, for the tenth anniversary of the revolution, the great Soviet filmmaker Sergei Eisenstein staged the event in the mythologised form that had already become accepted as historical fact inside the USSR. He had hundreds of extras race across Palace Square and swarm into the tsar's residence, tearing down the golden imperial eagles on the gates as they went.

No such thing happened in reality. There was no mass attack on the tsar's residence; the October Revolution was a targeted military coup that was hardly noticed on the night it occurred. Yet Eisenstein's staged shot was often shown in Soviet documentaries as if it were real documentary footage, because it implied that the Bolshevik takeover was a popular uprising. In the absence of a genuine film record, the same sequence also frequently cropped up in Western documentaries with no explanation – as if it had been filmed on the day of the Bolshevik victory. This was a kind of proof of the cynical dictum (attributed to Hitler's propaganda chief Josef Goebbels) that a lie repeated often enough becomes a truth. Stalin, or his ghost, would be delighted at what his propaganda machine had achieved.

Visual truth in the digital age

With digital photography, altering photographs has become commonplace. In most cases, the practice is cosmetic, but you can never know if a photograph is a real representation of a person or a true record of an event.

It is not unusual for individuals or vested interests to attempt to influence people's political views by creating false and misleading images of events. The utterly convincing result that can be achieved with photomanipulation software makes the practice all the more insidious: no photograph from any era is trustworthy any more, because there is always a possibility that it has been doctored.

At the same time it has become hard to sustain the deceit of a doctored image indefinitely, because someone somewhere is bound to be familiar with the unaltered version, and can make it known via the internet. Consequently, political photomanipulation is now most effective when used as a guerrilla weapon, to sway opinion temporarily but decisively ahead of an election, say; whereas in the past, when photographs were altered for political purposes, the intention was to change the historical record forever.

In the US presidential race of 2004, for example, a photograph of Democratic candidate John Kerry, as a young man in the early 1970s, was digitally spliced with a picture of the actress Jane Fonda from the same era, to make it appear that they shared a platform at the same anti-Vietnam War rally. The resulting composite was widely published, and until it was exposed it helped to reinforce the impression among some conservative American voters that Kerry's patriotic credentials were as questionable as those of 'Hanoi Jane'.

The tables were turned four years later, during the next presidential election, when an unknown Democrat photoshopped the head of Republican vice-presidential candidate Sarah Palin onto the body of a woman wearing a stars-and-stripes bikini and toting a rifle. This somewhat misogynistic image circulated widely on the internet, and it succeeded in fostering the impression that Palin was vulgar, lacking in seriousness, and politically irresponsible in her attitude to gun control.

A DIFFERENT COMPLEXION

Body image is an area where photomanipulation can make the world of difference, and tinkering with the visual truth is now often done for reasons of commerce or personal vanity. It is entirely normal for famous personalities to insist that their pictures be 'touched up' before publication, so as to show them in a light that is literally impossibly glamorous. And there have been instances where cosmetics companies have implied that their products have the power to, say, remove wrinkles, when in fact the effect was enhanced by a skilled digital artist. In 2011, for example, the Advertising Standards Agency in the UK required L'Oréal to withdraw make-up ads featuring the face of actress Julia Roberts because the 'aura of perfect skin' mentioned in the accompanying text had been achieved in part through what the firm called 'digital post-production techniques'.

The appearance of skin is easy to alter, and sometimes the change involves more than mere exaggeration. In 1989 a US listings magazine grafted the head of the black TV star Oprah Winfrey onto an archive photograph of the white actress Ann-Margret posing in a cocktail dress. Naturally, the skin tone of Ann-Margret had to be altered too. The intention seems to have been to make Winfrey look more attractive – but neither celebrity knew of the magazine's deception, and both were outraged when it came to light.

A more troubling case involving skin colour occurred in 1994, when *Time* magazine ran a police mugshot of the actor O.J. Simpson, who had just been arrested on suspicion of murder. The image had been altered to make his face look darker. The photographer later said that he only wanted to make the image 'more artful, more compelling', but *Time* was accused of racist intent for seeming to emphasise that Simpson was black. The digital manipulation of racial characteristics is fraught even when done with good intentions. In 2000 Wisconsin University added a black student to a crowd of white football fans on the cover of its in-house magazine. The aim was to illustrate diversity, and the university afterwards claimed it had searched without success for a photograph that reflected the true racial mix of its student body. But the published image was still a lie.

Before

After

LOOKING GOOD *One of the key modern uses of photomanipulation is to alter and, ostensibly, improve the appearance of celebrities. In this instance, George Clooney's grey hair has been darkened, his skin tone evened, and the skin around his eyes smoothed out, with a view to making him look younger than his years. Oddly, one effect of this is to drain the face of character. The eye is naturally drawn to the older-looking, more real George as he appears in the original, untouched image.*

Cities below the earth

One of the world's strangest landscapes is to be found in Cappadocia, Turkey: towering pinnacles of rock that look unearthly but are quite natural. Rooms and caves have been carved out of these towers, but they are not the only rock dwellings here. In the 1960s it was found that mysterious 'underground cities' had been hewn out of the soft volcanic earth.

Cappadocia's towers are known as 'fairy chimneys' – tall outcrops rising to 40m (130ft), many of them topped with large round boulders of basalt. The rock is so soft that it can be easily excavated, so for thousands of years the people of the region have been gouging out homes, churches, storerooms and staircases – a kind of architectural order imposed on the random forms that nature has provided. Who scooped these living spaces from the fairy chimneys? And what other marvels of town planning does the landscape conceal?

ANCIENT CROSSROADS

Cappadocia sits in the middle of the vast Anatolian plain, at the point where trade routes linking Asia to Europe intersect. The Hittites flourished here from about 1800 BC, and built a powerful empire that threatened even the Egyptians. Later this was the land of the Phrygians – famed in Greek mythology for the vast wealth of King Midas. The plain was criss-crossed by invaders as well as traders: Persians, Alexander's Greeks, then Romans, Byzantines, Arabs and Ottoman Turks.

The weird, labyrinthine landscape of central Cappadocia provided a refuge against these waves of intruders, and the fairy chimneys could serve as defensible hideouts. Early Christians retreated here to escape three centuries of Roman persecution, turning Cappadocia into an important Christian hub and making it the setting for some of the first Christian monasteries. In the fourth century AD St Basil, a founding figure of the Eastern Orthodox Church, was bishop of Caesarea Mazaca (now Kayseri) in Cappadocia. This was at the time when Christianity was becoming the state religion of the Roman Empire, so many of the fairy chimneys in the towns and valleys became churches with elaborately painted interiors dating from the later Byzantine era. Conflict came again to Cappadocia in the 12th century, as the Seljuks then the Ottoman Turks challenged the Byzantines for supremacy across the region.

Throughout this turbulent history, the people of central Cappadocia were not just gouging out the fairy chimneys, they were secretly digging into the thick layer of tufa – compacted volcanic ash – beneath

HUMAN BURROW *The underground complexes in Cappadocia are far more than glorified caves. The chambers carved from the rock are architecturally sophisticated, and astonishingly extensive.*

the surface. Most of this subterreanean architecture is in areas outside the main clusters of pinnacles around Göreme, such as Derinkuyu and Kaymakli to the south, and Özkonak to the north.

No one knows quite when these excavations started, perhaps in the times of the Hittites or the Phrygians. They may have begun as underground storerooms: the temperature beneath the ground remains constant at about 17°C (60°F), while the climate on the surface veers

between bitter winters and intensely hot summers. Over the centuries, further rooms and interlinking passageways were probably added piecemeal; it has been estimated that a single worker could dig out a space about 1.5m² (16 sq ft) in a day. Derinkuyu has the largest network of rooms and passages discovered so far, with some 200 rooms on about eight levels, dropping to 85m (280ft) below the surface. (The levels are difficult to count, as they are not strictly superimposed like the floors of a building.) There are stables for livestock, storerooms, kitchens, wine or oil presses, chapels and a large room with a barrel-vaulted ceiling that may have served as a religious school or a meeting room. The larger rooms are supported by rock-cut columns – essential for structural integrity. Fresh water came from a well that doubled as the main ventilation shaft, and there were numerous other smaller ventilation shafts leading to the surface.

At some point these artificial caves became underground hideouts, as witnessed today by their elaborate defence mechanisms. At strategic points along the interconnecting corridors there are huge round stones with a central hole, like millstones. Some of these are 1.5m (5ft) high and weigh half a tonne. In an attack, they could be rolled across the passageways from the inside and wedged into position, providing an impenetrable barrier, like a fire door or an airlock. The attackers, crammed into the low, narrow corridors, were then vulnerable to spears that the defenders could jab through holes in the walls, or boiling oil that could be poured through vents in the ceiling. Similar features have been found at the two other large underground cities, Özkonak and Kaymaklı. Özkonak also has communication tubes, enabling inhabitants to speak to each other between the levels.

SUBTERRANEAN SHELTERS

Estimates vary as to how many people could live in the underground cities. For Derinkuyu, a figure of 50,000 is frequently cited, but this looks far too high; 2,000 seems practicable, perhaps 4,000 in an emergency – and only for a short period. Conditions would have been difficult at the best of times in these dark, cool spaces, and so they were probably only ever used as temporary boltholes. Unlike many of the surface dwellings and chapels of Cappadocia, the rooms are rudimentary, and even the chapels lack the murals or sculptural adornment that might be expected if they had been used for long-term habitation.

The underground cities of Cappadocia are rumoured to be linked by passages several kilometres long, but none has so far come to light. The hidden entrances and ventilation shafts, coupled with the impenetrable interiors, may have provided sufficient escape routes when the warrenlike complex was under siege. But the cities' strongest defence may simply have been concealment. They seem to have been totally secret: there is virtually no written record of them from any time throughout their long history.

FORGOTTEN CITIES

During the Seljuk and Ottoman conquests, the Christians of Cappadocia evacuated the towns, or else converted to Islam. Their underground refuges were abandoned and forgotten. It was only in 1963 that a homeowner in Derinkuyu, in the course of some renovation, happened on the maze of rooms and passages beneath his house. This came as a complete surprise both to him and to historians of the region.

No one knows how many underground cities lie beneath the crust of Cappadocia. In all, around 40 with at least two levels were found, but 50 years on none has been fully excavated. Among the last excavations was a huge underground medieval caravanserai at Gaziemir. It served as an inn and depot for camel caravans, and is a vivid reminder of the ancient trade route that passed through Cappadocia, even before people began to hew towns from the living rock.

Going underground

Tunnels are invisible roads, secret routes from A to B. They provide channels for smuggling, for escape or rescue, for clandestine warfare. The right tunnel can save a life, or even change the course of history.

Rumours of secret tunnels are far more common than their reality. Castles, prisons, government institutions, international borders, celebrity homes: many are said to have secret connecting tunnels and passages, to serve some furtive purpose. There are countless stories, for instance, of secret passages or 'ley tunnels' connecting medieval castles in Britain to some other place – such as an abbey, or another house or an inn.

But some of history's most famous tunnels were real. Marie Antoinette used a secret passage to escape a mob that had invaded the Palace of Versailles in October 1789. Parading the severed head of a royal guard on a pike, they went in search of her, but she used a hidden door and passage that connected her bedroom to the king's apartment, where she found refuge among his entourage.

Cave systems and tunnels have been used by smugglers for centuries, and still are to this day. A warren of perhaps 1,000 tunnels, some 800m (2,600ft) long, has been created beneath the border close to the Egyptian town of Rafah. Through these, weapons and supplies, even livestock, are smuggled into Gaza – a lifeline for the Palestinians, and a security headache for the Israeli forces trying to control the border. Tunnels of similar length have been found beneath the border between California and Mexico. One, discovered in 2006, connected a warehouse near Tijuana airport to a warehouse in San Diego, and still contained 2 tonnes of undelivered marijuana.

Tunnels – often laboriously dug in secret with improvised tools – provide a classic means of escape, famously used by British and other POWs during the Second World War. One of the most ambitious prison escapes of all time took place in April 2011, when some 500 Taliban prisoners used a 320m (1,050ft) tunnel that had been dug beneath the walls of the Sarposa high-security prison in Kandahar, Afghanistan. The tunnel emerged inside a house, from where the prisoners melted into the city.

Tunnels have also been used to attack the enemy. During the First World War, miners from both sides on the Western Front tunnelled under enemy lines to plant massive bombs, which were often detonated at the start of a surface offensive. During the Vietnam War, the Viet Cong created the Cu Chi tunnels, a vast network totalling 250km (155 miles) in length that stretched from Saigon to the Cambodian border. Even carpet-bombing by US forces failed to eradicate them entirely.

DUG FOR VICTORY *A soldier in a tunnel used by communist forces in the Vietnam War. They were not merely rat-runs: some had hospitals, kitchens and weapons stores.*

The maiden of Tonnerre

Diplomat, spy, cavalry officer, swordsman, Le Chevalier d'Éon *pursued a high-profile career at the heart of France's Ancien Régime. Then, at the age of 48, he suddenly announced that he was a woman. For the rest of his long life, 'La Chevalière' lived as a lady, and revelled in his strange fame.*

Even if he had not switched genders at the peak of his public career, the exploits of Charles d'Éon de Beaumont would still be remarkable. His was a life full of enough scandal, celebrity, high politics, adventure and danger, personal triumph and tragedy to satisfy any biographer.

THE KING'S SECRET

D'Éon was born in the Burgundian town of Tonnerre in 1728. There was aristocratic ancestry on his mother's side, and later he claimed that he was born a girl, then was dressed as a boy so that his parents could claim an inheritance that could be passed only to a male heir. But this story was pure invention, part of his own myth. Charles d'Éon de Beaumont was – whatever else he later claimed – undoubtedly a boy. He shone at school, showing unusual gifts in languages and feats of memory. In 1743, at the age of 14, he went to Paris to continue his education, eventually graduating in law. He found good employment at the fiscal offices of the government, and also became a royal censor of books.

In 1756 he was recruited into Louis XV's private secret service, Le Secret du Roi (The King's Secret). This was the real beginning of his good fortune. D'Éon was sent to St Petersburg on a mission to dissuade Empress Elizabeth of Russia from pursuing an alliance with Britain, France's enemy. It is not clear precisely how he went about the task, but his own telling of it is extraordinary because it has him using the fact that he was actually a woman (or rather claiming to be one) as a means of achieving his diplomatic goal.

According to d'Éon, the empress was forbidden by protocol to meet male French diplomats in private. So he changed out of his male disguise and adopted his true female aspect. Using the name Lia de Beaumont he presented himself at court, where he performed the role of *lectrice,* or private reader, to the empress – thereby gaining the crucial access to her presence. There is, however, no record of a Lia de Beaumont at the court of Empress Elizabeth, and so this cannot be the means by which d'Éon carried out his mission. But somehow the empress was persuaded

EN GARDE *D'Éon taking part in a fencing competition. He has been made to look rather more feminine in the picture than he was in real life.*

to shun Britain's advances and enter an alliance with France and Austria. D'Éon returned to Paris in triumph.

He was soon sent back to Russia to serve on the staff of the new French embassy, but in 1761 he pleaded to be allowed to participate in the ongoing Seven Years War. He was granted a commission as captain in a regiment of dragoons, an appointment that evidently delighted him as he wore his elegant uniform on every possible occasion for the next 20 years. A consummate swordsman, d'Éon took part in a series of campaigns and distinguished himself at the Battle of Villinghausen in Germany.

By then the war was drawing to a close. In 1762 d'Éon was sent to London to assist in the peace negotiations that culminated in the Treaty of Paris, signed the following year. For his role in these talks he was made a *chevalier*, or knight. Afterwards he returned to London, where he served as minister plenipotentiary, a kind of temporary ambassador.

The Chevalier d'Éon was now at the height of his career, networking with British aristocracy and leading a glamorous and fashionable life of balls and dinners. He was also still operating as an agent of Le Secret du Roi, commissioned to collect information for an old pet project of Louis XV: the invasion of England.

But then d'Éon's career foundered. He deeply resented the appointment of Comte de Guerchy as the new French ambassador to Britain. This spelled the end of his time as plenipotentiary, and he convinced himself that he had been passed over. Even before de Guerchy arrived in London, d'Éon had fallen out with him, primarily over money. D'Éon had been spending lavishly on the new embassy, using de Guerchy's funds.

The disagreement rapidly degenerated into a scandalous public row. De Guerchy tried to have d'Éon removed from London; d'Éon refused to go. Louis XV requested his extradition, but the British government declared that it had no legal power to oblige. De Guerchy hired scandalmongering writers to discredit d'Éon, who responded by accusing De Guerchy of plotting to abduct or poison him. To the great embarrassment of the French authorities, the matter went to court. The English jury found against de Guerchy, who was recalled to France in disgrace and died soon after.

THE PRIVATE LETTERS

All this erupted in the rumbustious social whirl of late 18th-century England, where malicious social gossip was fuelled by pamphleteers and vicious caricaturists who had little fear of censure and little respect for the truth. D'Éon was also a master of this game. In the midst of the quarrel, he published a book called *Lettres, mémoires, et négotiations particulières* ('Private letters, memoirs and negotiations'), which made public various letters and documents that supported his case against de Guerchy. In so doing he broke all diplomatic codes. The French court was horrified. D'Éon's actions showed that he was willing to go public, and he was in possession of highly

compromising letters from Louis XV about the proposed invasion of England. So his book was a subtle kind of blackmail, a shot across the bows of his superiors in France. Louis XV took the hint and bought his silence: d'Éon was granted a handsome annual pension of 12,000 livres.

At this point d'Éon could easily have faded into a comfortable and enjoyable retirement. But the phase of his greatest celebrity was only just about to begin. In around 1770, stories began to circulate that he was a woman. This ignited gossip in London's coffee houses, where wagers were placed on his true gender. D'Éon threatened to duel with anyone who laid a bet, but refused to dignify the rumours by resolving the question one way or the other.

TO FRANCE AND BACK

D'Éon's life took a complicated turn when Louis XV died in 1774. Louis XVI agreed to maintain d'Éon's pension, knowing its purpose. But he was also determined to repatriate the compromising material that was in d'Éon's possession, and also d'Éon himself. In 1775 *Le Secret du Roi* dispatched an agent, Pierre de Beaumarchais, to negotiate a deal. Discussions lasted 14 months, at the end of which a contract was drawn up. D'Éon would hand over the royal documents and return to France, and he would continue to receive his pension. He also agreed to go and live in his home town of Tonnerre, and to dress as the woman that the French authorities now believed him to be. D'Éon had officially – but falsely – confirmed to Beaumarchais that he was indeed female.

In 1777, after 14 years of political exile, d'Éon came home. He was still attired in his dragoon's uniform, but in Versailles he was provided with the services of Marie Antoinette's dressmaker, who made him some clothes to take with him to Tonnerre. He remained there for seven years, running his family estate. And in all that time he never put on men's clothes.

In 1779 the story of d'Éon's life was published under the title *La vie militaire, politique et privée de Mademoiselle d'Éon* ('The Military, Political and Private Life of Miss d'Éon'). The name of the author was given as La Fontelle, but d'Éon was, at the very least, a willing primary source. It was here, in this work, that the falsehoods concerning d'Éon's birth and his cross-dressing diplomacy in Russia were first told – later to be embroidered and embellished by other authors. In 1785 d'Éon received permission to return to London, ostensibly to settle his debts – and he seized the opportunity to abscond. When the French Revolution erupted in

> *To earn his keep, he toured as a female fencing master.*

1789, he lost his pension, and with it the obligation to dress as a woman. But he did not take this option: he remained in England, and in women's clothes.

To earn his keep, d'Éon began to exploit his celebrity by touring as a female fencing master. In 1796, at the age of 68, he was badly wounded in Southampton, which put an end to his late career as an entertainer. Those that saw d'Éon at this time observed that he looked very much like a man dressed as a woman – with large hands, hairy arms, the shadow of a beard and a deep voice. Contemporary portraits bear this out, but d'Éon was determined to maintain this front

to the end. Imprisoned for debt in 1804, he secured his release with an advance for his autobiography, which he planned to call *La Pucelle de Tonnerre* ('The Maiden of Tonnerre'), echoing his more celebrated cross-dressing compatriot Joan of Arc, the Maid of Orléans. The book was never written, and he lived out his days in poverty. Paralysed after a fall, d'Éon died in London on May 21, 1810, at the age of 81. With the post-mortem, the truth came out.

THEORIES AND HOMAGES

Charles d'Éon de Beaumont has remained an object of fascination ever since, the subject of countless biographies, films, a Japanese anime TV series, and academic gender studies. The cross-dressing itself is not so unusual – what is strange in d'Eon's case is that he was perfectly happy to live entirely as a man for the first half of his life, and utterly determined to live as a woman for the second half. What happened?

There are some outlandish theories. One biographer, writing in the 1830s, concocted a tale whereby d'Éon was the secret lover of Queen Charlotte, wife of George III, and had fathered a son, the future George IV. When surprised in the queen's apartments by the king, d'Éon managed to convince him that he was a woman, and then had to keep up the pretence for the rest of his life. According to the theory, it was the posthumous revelation of d'Éon's true sex that precipitated King George's madness.

The story is untrue. Barely less credible is the idea that d'Éon adopted woman's guise to discourage his enemies in France – the king and his agents, or the family of de Guerchy – from trying to assassinate him. But d'Éon must surely have had some inner motive, some psychological reason, for altering his identity so radically? If he did, he chose never to speak of it.

The Wikileaks affair

In 2010 thousands upon thousands of classified US files were put on the internet for all to see. The documents included diplomatic cables and despatches from the wars in Iraq and Afghanistan. Together they were the biggest data breach in history. But what else were they: a journalistic coup? A victory for freedom of information? Or an act of cyber-terrorism?

The footage made news around the world. It was an operational video shot from inside a US Apache attack helicopter as it patrolled Baghdad. The on-board camera showed the crew's view of the ground, and the soundtrack recorded their conversation as they circled above a dusty suburb. Down below on the street stood a relaxed cluster of about a dozen men. One of them was carrying some kind of tube, which a crew member from his high vantage point identified as a rocket launcher. The helicopter's gunner, perceiving a threat, fired a burst of shells at the men. Some went down in a cloud of dust raised by the bullets, others tore across the street for cover. A van happened by, and its driver stopped, got out and helped one of the wounded into the van. The helicopter now fired on the vehicle, though children could be seen seated in the back.

This film was published in April 2010 on the Wikileaks website. It was headlined 'Collateral Murder', a reference to the military euphemism 'collateral damage', meaning unplanned or unfortunate civilian casualties. Millions watched this film on their home computers and were shocked by the seemingly casual way in which the soldiers had taken the decision to open fire. As it turned out, the men were not insurgents at all. The object taken to be a rocket launcher was in fact a camera's long lens, and the man carrying it was an Iraqi photographer with the Reuters news agency. As for the van driver who stopped to help the wounded, he was a father taking his children to school. The children survived, but he was killed.

THE ECOLOGY OF NEWS

The film was clearly damaging to the US military and its mission in Iraq. The American government was outraged that it had been made public – and that it had patently been stolen. 'Collateral Murder' was a single item in a huge cache of material that originated inside the US military communications network. Its leak and subsequent release was an act of protest, a way of objecting to the conduct of the war in Iraq. But it was also a brilliant news scoop for Wikileaks, which until this point was not widely

known, but now captured the attention of the world. Here was an info-organisation with no offices or physical distribution network, no columnists or commentators, no advertisers or payment structure, just vast amounts of raw data, freely accessible, stored on humming servers in some anonymous basement. People began to say that Wikileaks had 'changed the ecology of news', and it was true: there was a new species of beast in the media jungle.

INFORMATION ACTIVISM

Wikileaks had its roots not in the world of news-gathering, but in computer hacking. Julian Assange, who later became the public face of Wikileaks, learned his trade as a member of a hackers' circle in Melbourne, where he operated under the cyber-pseudonym Mendax. When the Australian authorities caught up with him he was put on trial for breaching commercial and military computer networks. He was convicted, and narrowly avoided a prison sentence.

From the start Assange saw himself as an 'ethical hacker', an 'information activist'. He took the view that secrecy in government was incompatible with democracy; it followed that the best way to hold the authorities to account was to enforce transparency by laying bare the workings of government, forcing officials – politicians, generals, diplomats – to justify the things that they said and did behind closed doors.

In 2006 Assange was instrumental in setting up Wikileaks.org. Other founders are believed to have included politically engaged hackers and programmers,

Chinese dissidents and mathematicians, and campaigning journalists. The website was intended to function as a kind of virtual dead-letter drop. Whistleblowers inside governments and corrupt corporations could upload private or secret documents that exposed wrong-doing, and Wikileaks' cryptographic expertise ensured that no digital trail led back from the site to the source of the leak. Moreover, the fact that the site had no national allegiance or presence meant that, when it published leaked documents, it was usually outside the jurisdiction of any court injunction and beyond any government's judicial gagging apparatus. The ethereal nature of the internet meant that Wikileaks had a much freer hand than traditional news outlets, such as TV stations and newspapers, which have to obey the laws and court rulings of the land in which they operate.

SERVERS AND MIRRORS

All the same, the leaked files that Wikileaks now began to amass had to be kept on a physical computer somewhere in the world. Wikileaks' host server was sited in Sweden, which has one of the world's strongest laws protecting freedom of information: that small operational fact made the site all but untouchable by legal means. And if a court or a government agency tried to block Wikileaks, or if it was subject to a covert 'denial of service' attack intended to disable the site, then the same information was always a click away on myriad 'mirror sites'. Once a leak was out, there was no practical way that anybody could stop it spreading.

But technical know-how would have counted for little without newsworthy content. In the first two years of Wikileaks' existence, anonymous whistleblowers uploaded more than 1.2 million

documents; buried among them was some front-page dynamite. In 2008 the site published in full a manual for US army personnel working at Camp Delta, the detention centre for suspected terrorists at Guantanamo Bay. Human rights activists had been trying for years to get hold of a copy of that same document. In 2009 Wikileaks published 570,000 text messages sent by individuals caught up in the 2001 attacks on the World Trade Centre. Among them were some deeply personal goodbyes tapped out on phones by people who knew they were about to die.

THE WIKI MODEL

Such leaks were not printable news, but they were the rich raw material of news. Wikileaks, therefore, was not so much a news organisation as a virtual archive of secret documents, a citizen-led intelligence agency. Wikileaks' organisers thought at first that visitors to the site would not just read its material, they might also analyse it and contribute articles of their own – much as people do at Wikipedia, the online encyclopedia (this hopeful model is the sole source of the 'wiki' name: Wikileaks has never had any connection to Wikipedia).

In fact, the politically committed volunteer journalism that Wikileaks dreamed of never transpired: amateur analysts proved unwilling or unable to sift and synthesise the database. So Wikileaks chose to make alliances with established media set-ups – those same newspapers and TV stations that were wary of handling the leaked material at first hand, lest a court demand they disclose their source, or an aggrieved corporation slap an injunction or libel suit on them. If the media simply reported and analysed material that was freely available on the internet, they were relatively safe from legal attacks. Wikileaks, for its part, could use the traditional media to achieve maximum impact with its leaks.

Yet to begin with, despite its efforts and its immense cache of documents, Wikileaks was not much more than an irritant to governments with something to hide. All that changed at the start of 2010. Someone on the inside accessed SIPRNet, the US government network that is used to share classified information between the Defense Department and the State Department. That person copied huge amounts of classified material; a very similar cache of material found its way to Wikileaks.

The leak was staggering in its depth and scope. The Apache helicopter film was one tiny fragment of it – and Wikileaks made it public as a kind of taster, a sample of its new wares. Much more was released later that year. Among the new documents were thousands of diplomatic cables in which world leaders, among them US allies, were characterised in frank or critical terms. Their publication was deeply embarrassing to the American government. There were also nearly half a million operational logs from the front line of the Afghanistan and Iraq wars. This, the largest leak of classified documents in history, amounted to a kind of day-by-day chronicle of those conflicts. Newspapers spent weeks filleting them for stories; historians will be poring over them for decades to come.

THE END OF SECRECY

In the pre-digital age, it would have taken years to copy so many documents, fleets of trucks to transfer them, and great warehouses to store them. But the technology that made it possible to share classified information between government departments also made it easy for that huge amount of information to be taken –

invisibly, instantaneously and irrevocably. It was as if an information dam had broken, a great torrent released, flooding the global village with classified data.

The US government was furious, and demanded the return of its papers, but that was impossible. The leak could no more be taken back than spilled ink can be extracted from clear water. The Wikileaks affair proved that no document or archive today is entirely secure. As many as half a million people had clearance for SIPRNet; it took only one disgruntled or idealistic person, equipped with a stack of writeable CDs, to compromise its security utterly.

> *No document or archive today is entirely secure.*

It is a fact that information has become highly porous and endlessly reproducible. All kinds of commercial and government organisations hold information about customers and citizens – their financial affairs, shopping habits, family status, legal and medical history. The agencies that hold such data do not always make a good job of keeping it private. Sometimes it is leaked by accident; sometimes it is purposefully passed on without the knowledge of the individuals concerned. Wikileaks and sites like it claimed that they were aiming to redress the balance, to make sure that information flows both ways, because that is only fair and just. The digital revolution has given them the power and the tools to make it happen. And that may mean that the age of secrecy is over for ever.

Index

Carlisle 131
Castro, Fidel 52, 91, 174–6
Catholic -s 36, 47, 60, 75–6, 92, 105, 222, 253, 256–9
Cavanagh, Kit (*aka* 'Kit Walsh') 129–32
Cavell, Edith 11
Cecil, William 84
Chamberlain, Owen 235
Chandler, Paul and Rachel 182
Chaplin, Charlie 214, 216
Charles I 259
Charles II 31–2, 104
Charles III 35
Charles V 135
Charlotte, Queen 277
Charmouth 106–7
Cheka, the 60
Chenhalls, Alfred 16
Chevalier, Haakon 237
Chicago 98, 111, 167–8, 188–91
Chile 177, 195
Cholmondeley, Charles 73–6
Christianity 42, 60, 122, 222, 247, 253, 270
Church
    Catholic 36, 60, 222, 253
    Christian 186
    of England 82, 257
    Orthodox 270
Churchill, Winston 16, 53, 68–73, 139–42, 155
CIA 24, 52, 143, 161, 178–9
Cigrand, Emeline 189
Cincinnati 111–12
Civil War
    American 38, 108, 112, 131–2
    English 104, 129, 259
    Russian 265
    Spanish 114, 119, 176
Clemenceau, Georges 69
Cleopatra 216
Clouston, Thomas 162
Coffin, Levi 111
Colombia 166
Communist -s 40, 50, 60, 70–1, 78, 81, 88–9, 91, 100, 122, 150, 152, 170, 177, 212–13, 235, 241–3, 273
Confucius 90
Congo 174–6
Connally, John 52–3
Conner, Julia 189
Constantinople, *see also* Byzantium *and* Istanbul, 42, 184–7
Copperhead, Operation 16
Córdoba 62
Corsica 31

Cortes, Manuel 114–19
Crimean War 133
Crockatt, Norman 124–5
Cromwell, Daisy 24
Cromwell, Oliver 24, 31, 104, 253
Cromwell, Richard 31
Cu Chi tunnels 273
Cuba 52, 174–9
Cumberland, Duke of 132
Curzon Line 69
Czechoslovakia 70, 242

D
Dadaev, Felix 14–15
Dalai Lama 248
Damascus 245–7
Danger, Eustache 32
Dangerous Drugs Act of 1920 164
David-Néel, Alexandra 248
D-Day landings 17, 77
Dead Sea 245
Dee, Dr John 67, 82–6
Defence of the Realm Act 164
Defoe, Daniel 132
Dehra Dun 249
Delaware 109–11
Delmarva Peninsula 109
Denmark 47, 49
Derinkuyu 271–2
Diana, Princess 52, 55
Dijon 30
Dix, Otto 203
Dominican Republic 174
Douai 257
Doughty, Charles 247
Douglass, Frederick 112
Dresden 207, 224
Dudley, Robert 84
Dumas, Alexandre 33
Durova, Nadezhda 128–9, 132
Dzerzhinsky, Felix 208

E
Eastern Orthodox Church 210, 270
Edinburgh 65, 133
Edward VI 82
Egypt 186, 203, 223, 244–5, 250–5, 270, 273
Einstein, Albert 233
Eisenhower, Dwight 16, 143
Eisenstein, Sergei 267
el-Amarna 252–3
Elizabeth I 82, 84, 86, 92, 215, 218, 256, 259
Elizabeth, Empress of Russia 274
Engels, Friedrich 25
England, Church of 82, 257
English Civil War 104, 129, 259

Enigma machine 93–5
Enkhbayar, Nambaryn 243
Erasmus 82
Erfurt 78
Euclid 84

F
Fabius, Laurent 147
Falcius, John Damian de 65
Falcone, Giovanni 172
Faust, Johann 67
FBI 24, 52, 172, 236
Federal Bureau of Narcotics 164
Feynman, Richard 235–7
Fez 245
Finland 49, 51
First World War 13, 16, 24, 38–41, 44, 59, 113, 124–7, 138–9, 163, 273
Flag Fen 262
Flanders 139
Fleming, Ian 72–3, 127
Florence 187, 198, 207
Florida 111, 166
Fonda, Jane 268
Ford, Henry 41
Forres, Nathan Bedford 38
Fortitude, Operation 77
Foster, William 141
France 16, 21, 24, 26–7, 31–2, 34, 41, 47–8, 60, 65, 77, 89, 106–7, 113, 119, 127–8, 135, 139, 141, 144–7, 187, 198–9, 215, 245–6, 257, 274–7
Francis II 222
Franco, General Francisco 114
François I 199
Franco-Prussian War 26
Fraser, Ronald 118
Fraser-Smith, Charles 127
Freemasonry 23, 38, 41, 222
French Polynesia 144
French Revolution 27, 30, 34–5, 222, 277
Freud, Sigmund 202, 214, 217
Friedrich Wilhelm IV 25–6
Friedrichsdorf 13
Frobisher, Martin 84
FSB, *see also* KGB *and* NKVD, 24

G
Gabet, Joseph 248
Galante, Carmine 'The Cigar' 172
Garnet, Father Henry 258
Garrett, Thomas 111
Gautier, Théophile 199–202
Gaza 273
Gaziemir 272
Gelovani, Mikheil 15